THE
WORKS

Of the REVEREND

WILLIAM LAW, M.A.,

Sometime Fellow of *Emmanuel*
College, *Cambridge*.

In Nine Volumes.

Volume I.

Three LETTERS to the
Bishop of *Bangor*.

Wipf and Stock Publishers
150 West Broadway • Eugene OR 97401
2001

Volume I - Three Letters to the Bishop of Bangor

By Law, William

ISBN: 1-57910-615-3

Reprinted by *Wipf and Stock Publishers*
150 West Broadway • Eugene OR 97401

Previously published by G. Moreton, Setley, 1892.

Prefatory Memoir.

THE 'Life' of the Rev. *William Law* has been fully, even diffusively, set forth in his Biography written by Canon *Overton* and published by *Longmans* in the year 1881 : and to that work—of which the more interesting particulars are drawn from the late Mr. *Walton's** Collections—such readers of *Law's* Works who desire to obtain some general idea of their Writer's life, are referred.

Unfortunately, Canon *Overton's* Work, excellent and painstaking as is its compilation, conveys to the earnest reader only a very vague and unsatisfactory impression of *William Law* himself : being composed chiefly of well-selected extracts from Law's publications with criticisms thereon and numerous explanations and conjectures in well-meant but misplaced, elucidations of motives and actions. In fact, Canon *Overton* has performed a kind of literary autopsy upon *William Law :* quite in the manner of biographical writing of the day ; unimpeachable, indeed, in respect of 'scholarly' execution, although occasionally lapsing into ill-chosen expressions as when he describes his subject as a 'grand *specimen* of Humanity,' instead of example ; as if poor *Law* were some Museum specimen to be gazed at and remarked upon, with due pedantry accordingly. This too, in the absence of any authentic portrait of *William Law*, represses the curiosity of the expectant reader who, abandoning the biography, consoles himself with the remark made by Miss *Hester Gibbon*—when requested to write a 'Life' of *William Law*—that his Life was in his Works.

William Law was born at *King's Cliffe* a considerable Village in *Northamptonshire* so long ago as the year 1686, in the Reign of *James* the Second. His father was a 'Grocer and Chandler' in the Village, residing in a house of his own ; but, Canon *Overton*

---

* CHRISTOPHER WALTON, a 'Diamond Jeweller,' of *Ludgate* Street, *London*, and apparently a man of considerable literary ability—of the diamond-jewelling kind—who had a most enthusiastic veneration for WILLIAM LAW. He printed in the year 1856 a ' Cyclopædia of Pure Christian Theology and 'Theosophic Science in Elucidation of the Sublime Genius and Theosophian 'Mission of WILLIAM LAW,' containing nearly 700 pages of the smallest and closest printing, which is perhaps the most laborious, bombastic and generally unreadable compilation ever printed—excepting the Biographical footnotes relating to *Law* commencing at page 334. No wonder the Printers' names are humorously and fictitiously given as ' *Reed* and *Pardon*, Printers, ' *London*.'

tells us 'his social standing was different from that of an ordinary 'Village tradesman of the present day.' From various evidence it appears that the *Laws* were not of humble origin in respect of 'Gentility'; and mention is made by *Walton* of a Tradesman's token, dated 1659, which bore their ' Coat of Arms '—an evidence of 'Gentility' of more account at that time of ' Heraldic Visita-'tions' than it would be at the present. It may be remembered that *Law's* great Contemporary Bishop *Butler*, was the son of a Linen-Draper; and other instances might be recalled—*Shakespeare* for example—of what has been accomplished by members of that class.

William Law was the fourth son of a family of eight sons and three daughters. His early disposition appears to have been noticed by his father, who alone of all his sons, sent *William* to the University ; and he entered as a Sizar of *Emmanuel* College, *Cambridge*, in the year 1705. He proceeded to the Arts Degrees in the usual course; and was elected to a Fellowship of his College and ordained in the year 1711—no doubt therefore, well fulfilling his father's expectations of him. His political principles (never mere 'Views' with him), obliged him to decline the Oath of Allegiance to *George* the First in the year 1716; which deprived him of his College Fellowship and of all prospect of advancement in the Church. In a note which he wrote to his eldest brother on that occasion he says : ' My prospect indeed is 'melancholy enough. . . . The benefits of my education seem ' partly at an end, but that same education had been more miser-'ably lost, if I had not learnt to fear something worse than mis-' fortunes.' In this great, though providential disappointment to his hopes and those of his family respecting him, his father did not live to share, having died two years previously.

It is said that on leaving *Cambridge*, *William Law* came to *London :* and there is some tradition that he officiated as Curate at S. *Mary's* Church in the *Strand*. Various vague reports are current respecting him at that period ; but little is known of him until he published his first letter to Dr. *Hoadley*, the latitudinarian Bishop of *Bangor*, followed by his other letters on that Controversy. The Bangorian discussion produced a copious amount of theological literature which was no doubt of intense interest at the time, but which has become rather tedious lumber reading.

The following ' Rules for my Future Conduct ' drawn up by *William Law**—it is said, when he was at *Cambridge*—are worthy of being reproduced with his Works :—

---

* *Walton's* ' Cyclopædia,' Footnotes, pp. 345-6.

Rev. William Law.

TO fix it deep in my Mind, that I have one business upon my hands —to seek for eternal happiness, by doing the Will of God.
 II. To examine everything that relates to me in this view, as it serves or obstructs this only end of Life.
 III. To think nothing great or desirable, because the World thinks it so ; but to form all my judgments of things from the infallible Word of God, and direct my Life according to it.
 IV. To avoid all concerns with the World, or the ways of it, but where Religion and Charity oblige me to act.
 V. To remember frequently, and impress it upon my Mind deeply, that no condition of this Life is for enjoyment, but for trial ; and that every power, ability, or advantage we have, are all so many Talents to be accounted for, to the Judge of all the World.
 VI. That the Greatness of Human Nature consists in nothing else but in imitating the Divine Nature. That therefore, all the Greatness of this World, which is not in good actions, is perfectly beside the point.
 VII. To remember, often and seriously, how much of Time is inevitably thrown away, from which I can expect nothing but the charge of Guilt ; and how little there may be to come, on which an Eternity depends.
 VIII. To avoid all excess in eating and drinking.
 IX. To spend as little time as I possibly can, among such persons as can receive no benefit from me, nor I from them.
 X. To be always fearful of letting my time slip away without some fruit.
 XI. To avoid all idleness.
 XII. To call to mind the Presence of God, whenever I find myself under any Temptation to sin, and to have immediate recourse to Prayer.
 XIII. To think humbly of myself ; and with great Charity of all others.
 XIV. To forbear from all evil speaking.
 XV. To think often of the Life of Christ, and to propose it as a pattern to myself.
 XVI. To pray, privately, thrice a day, besides my morning and evening Prayer.
 XVII. To keep from———* as much as I can without offence.
 XVIII. To spend some time in giving an account of the day, previous to Evening Prayer : how have I spent this day ? what Sin have I committed ? what Temptations have I withstood ? have I performed all my Duty ?

It was about the year 1727 that *William Law* having achieved a good reputation by his Controversial writings, *Christian Perfection*, *&c.*, became Tutor in the *Gibbon* family, residing at *Putney*, in particular to the father of the Historian *Gibbon* whom he accompanied to *Emmanuel* College ; and on his pupil's departure thence upon his travels, *Law* returned to *Putney* where he continued to reside for the next twelve years in the capacity of Spiritual Director with the *Gibbon* family, by whom he was much esteemed. It was during his residence at *Putney* that he produced his fame-piece, but not perhaps his master-piece, the *Serious Call*, by which he is now most generally known. It appears to have been at *Putney* also, that he became acquainted with the writings of *Jacob Behmen* the German Mystic, for whom

---

* Left blank by *Walton*.

and his Commentators, he acquired a great veneration which deepened with him until his death.

On leaving *Putney*, *Law* returned to *King's Cliffe* to reside; where shortly afterwards Mrs. *Hutcheson*, a Widow lady, and Miss *Hester Gibbon*, who were each possessed of ample means and of strict piety, joined him and devoted themselves and the greater part of their joint income* to the relief of the Poor in a most benevolent, but it would seem, indiscriminate manner. Their Charity becoming notorious, attracted to them all the Vagrants from the whole country round, demoralizing the Village of *King's Cliffe*; and exciting the rebuke of the then Incumbent administered to them from his pulpit.

Some interesting particulars of the daily life of *William Law's* household at *King's Cliffe* were collected many years ago by Mr. *Walton*, and are abridged, as follows:

MR. LAW rose early each morning, probably about five o'clock, spending some time in devotion; after which he breakfasted, generally on a cup of chocolate in his bedroom, and then commenced study.... Mr. *Law* kept four cows, the produce of which, beyond what was required for his household, he gave to the poor, distributing the milk every morning with his own hands.... At nine o'clock a bell was rung for family devotion, of which the Collects and Psalms for the day formed a portion. From... the performance of this duty Mr. *Law* retired in silence to his chamber, where he passed the morning in study; not unfrequently, indeed, interrupted by the message of some poor mendicant for aid, which never failed to secure his immediate attention... he inquired into the particular needs of his suppliants, and caused relief to be administered in the shape either of money, apparel, or food. ... He manifested displeasure if room was not found on the kitchen fire for a vessel for the poor; and sometimes he has been known to quit his studies in order to taste the broth which had been made for them.... In the winter season, he occasionally added ale and wine to these charitable provisions. ... Amongst the articles of clothing which he provided for the indigent were shirts made of strong coarse linen; and, that he might not give away what he himself could not thankfully receive, he always wore them himself first... after which they were washed and distributed.... Instances of hypocrisy are narrated of mendicants, who have been known to change their better clothing, sheltered by the projecting buttresses of the neighbouring church, for rags, and, thus disguised, repair again for relief to the well-known window. Though suspicions at times crossed his mind, Mr. *Law* would give his supplicants the benefit of a doubt, the result of all which was that *King's Cliffe* became the resort of the idle and worthless, and obtained a character for Pauperism which the place did not deserve; and so much annoyance did it cause to the inhabitants that the Rector... endeavoured to put an end to

---

* Mrs. HUTCHESON's income is said by *Walton* to have been £2,000, and Miss GIBBON's between five and seven hundred pounds yearly. It also appears that WILLIAM LAW gave the profits of only the *first* editions of his Works to the Bookseller, so that there would be a considerable income from that source.

the alleged mistaken benevolence of Mr. *Law* and his companions by openly preaching against them from the Pulpit. . . . At noon in winter, and at one in summer, dinner was laid upon the table, of which Mr. *Law* partook very moderately, allowing himself one glass of wine. . . . Immediately after dinner they reassembled (for devotional exercises). That duty performed, Mr. *Law* once more retired to his study and remained there a few hours, again rejoining the ladies at the tea-table. Of this refreshment he did not ordinarily partake, but supplied its place with a raisin or two from his pocket, generally standing and indulging in cheerful conversation. After tea exercises of piety were resumed, and varied by the servants in turn reading a chapter from the Bible. . . . Mr. *Law* and his companions, Mrs. *Hutcheson* and Miss *Gibbon*, were constant in their attendance at Church whenever Divine Service was performed. After the morning service on *Wednesdays* and *Fridays*, it was their custom to ride out for an airing, Mr. *Law* and Miss *Gibbon* being on horseback, and Mrs. *Hutcheson*, with the Honourables the Misses *Hatton*, their neighbours (who usually dined with them every alternate Friday) . . . in the carriage. . . . As regards the regular occupations of the ladies,* apart from the time dedicated to outward offices of charity among their Neighbours, or spent in private devotion, it would appear that they consisted in storing their minds with the instructions of Wisdom, and the impressions of Eternity, by transcribing daily portions out of the writings of the ancient . . . divines as in the way of school exercises. . . . As no authentic portrait of Mr. *Law* is in existence . . . we give a sketch of his personal appearance, as nearly as can be gathered from the testimony left upon record, assisted by our knowledge of his character.† . . . In stature . . . rather over than under the middle size, his frame not corpulent, but stoutly built. . . . The general form of his countenance was round ; and he possessed a blunt, felicitous expression of utterance. . . . He had well-proportioned features . . . a cheerful, open expression. . . . His face was ruddy, his eyes grey, clear, vivacious. . . . His general manner was lively and unaffected, and, though his walk and conversation among his friends was that of a Sage . . . he was accustomed to see company, and was a man of free conversation. . . . A sister of the . . . *Wesleys* describes him as the very picture of the Law itself for severity and gravity. . . . Perhaps the gravity of his looks and demeanour was a little

---

* Mrs. HUTCHESON and Miss HESTER GIBBON, each of whom survived WILLIAM LAW ; and are buried at the foot of his grave in *King's Cliffe* Churchyard. Canon *Overton*, in his ' Biography of *Law*,' rather ungallantly and frivolously records a foolish tradition 'that during ' *Law's* lifetime the ladies dressed in the severely simple style recom-'mended in the *Serious Call*, but that after his death the feminine 'love of finery broke out,' and ' Miss *Gibbon* appeared resplendent in yellow 'stockings :' as if Miss *Gibbon's* stockings had been an apparent and prominent rather than an obscured and withdrawn portion of her apparel ; for which supposition there is no evidence, although Dr. *Byrom* reports on hearsay that ' she was said to be a very good lady, though some people thought ' she was mad.'

† Mr. WALTON here adds the following note (p. 502), which will be read with a shudder : ' If our endeavours to obtain possession of his Skull should be ' crowned with success, we shall then, perhaps, be enabled to offer a more just ' and complete delineation of his exterior . . . ; his hardy, economic physical 'training and classically tutored mind rendering it probable that nature in ' him was regular and true'—and very unlike what it was in poor Mr. WALTON !

heightened by the soberness of his dress, which was usually a clerical hat with the loops let down, black coat, and grey wig.

Of the many who applied to *William Law* for spiritual advice and guidance, and who for a time implicitly followed his directions, the most notable was *John Wesley*: of whom *Law* subsequently wrote, 'I was at one time a sort of Oracle with Mr. '*Wesley*.' The occasion of their estrangement was because in *Wesley's* opinion, *William Law's* teaching did not sufficiently dwell upon the Saving Merits of the Atonement; and the instantaneous kind of Salvation comprehended in the Divine words 'Believe; and thou shalt be saved.' This Doctrine *Wesley* in a lengthy but rather weak and petulant, note charged *Law* with neglecting to teach him; and asks him ' How will you justify it 'to our common Lord that you never gave me this advice'—of instantaneous Salvation—'Why did I scarcely ever hear you 'name the name of Christ, never so as to ground anything on 'faith in His blood?'; and concludes with some personal reflections upon *William Law's* morose disposition, which he thinks cannot be the result of a living faith, &c., and which certainly might have been spared. To this *Law* sent a most admirable and charitable reply, sweeping away *Wesley's* insinuations like so many cobwebs; in which he says ' A holy man you say taught 'you this " Believe and thou shalt be saved." I am to sup-'pose that till you met with this holy man you had not been 'taught this Doctrine. Did you not above two years ago give a 'new translation of *Thomas à Kempis*. Will you call *Thomas* to 'account and to answer it to God, as you do me for not teaching 'you that doctrine? Or will you say that you took upon you to 'restore the true sense of that Divine Writer, and instruct others 'how they might profit by reading him, before you had so much 'as a literal knowledge of the most plain, open, and repeated 'doctrine in his book. You cannot but remember what value I 'always expressed of *à Kempis*, and how much I recommended 'it to your meditations. You have had a great many conver-'sations with me, and I dare say you never was with me half an 'hour without my being large upon that very doctrine which you 'make me totally silent and ignorant of . . . . I am to suppose 'that you had been meditating upon an Author that of all others 'leads us the most directly to a real living Faith in *Jesus Christ*: 'after you had judged yourself such a master of his sentiments 'and doctrines as to be able to publish them . . . . after you had 'done this you had only the faith of a *Judas*.' And concluding: 'Your last paragraph, concerning my sour, rough behaviour, I 'leave in its full force. Whatever you can say of me of that

'kind, *without hurting yourself*, will be always well received by
'me.'

William Law's veneration for *Jacob Behmen* and belief in his
System of Philosophy; and what has been termed, his own
'mysticism,' has by many been misunderstood and misrepre-
sented. His latest Biographer, Canon *Overton*, places too much
stress upon a quotation from a letter written by *William Law* to
a friend; in which, probably in an unguarded moment of strong
enthusiasm, he says 'All pretences and endeavours to hinder the
'opening of this Mystery revealed' in *Jacob Behmen* 'and its
'bearing down all before it, will be as vain as so many attempts
'to prevent or retard the coming of the last day'—and this
statement made in the privacy of correspondence—Canon *Overton*
describes as a 'Prophecy' unfulfilled. It is therefore, only fair
to *William Law's* memory to quote the following extract from a
letter written by him five years later—and within two years of
his death, to a friend : 'Next to the Scriptures, my only book is
'the illuminated *Behmen. And him I only follow so far as he
'helps to open in me that which God had opened in him, concerning
'the death and the life of the fallen and redeemed man.* The
'whole Kingdom of Grace and Nature was opened in him; and
'the whole Kingdom of Grace and Nature lies hid in myself.
'And, therefore, in reading of him, I am always at home and
'kept close to the Kingdom of God that is within me.'

Another of the charges brought against *Law* is, that he was
a 'declared Universalist.' The final Restitution of all things,
was a subject upon which he spoke and wrote most guardedly;
in one instance as follows :—'Put away all needless curiosity in
'Divine matters; and look upon everything to be so but that
'which helps you to die to yourself, that the Spirit and Life of
'Christ may be found in you.'

William Law retired to *King's Cliffe* when he was fifty-one
years of age, and he resided there until his death, twenty-two
years later. It appears that at Eastertide in the year 1761,
when occupying himself as usual about the annual audit of the
Schools, which he had founded and endowed in his native place,
he caught cold, producing inflammation of the kidneys; which,
after a few days' acute suffering, ended his life here. His death
occurred between seven and eight o'clock in the morning of
Thursday, 9th April, 1761. 'When near expiring,' it is reported,
'he sang a hymn with a strong and very clear voice;' and Miss
Gibbon, who was present, wrote :—'This death-bed instead of
'being a state of Affliction, was, providentially, a state of Divine
'Transport. As to THE TRUTH, all his behaviour bore full
'testimony to it, and the gracious words that proceeded out of

'his mouth were all love, all joy, and all Divine Transport . . .
'after taking leave of everybody in the most affecting manner,
'and declaring the opening of the Spirit of Love in the Soul to
'be all in all—he expired in Divine raptures.'

G. B. M.

Brockenhurst, Hants.
  19th October, 1892.

Three LETTERS to the Bishop of *Bangor*.

The TITLES of The CONTENTS of the NINE VOLUMES of the Rev. *William Law's* Works.

I. Three Letters to the Bishop of *Bangor*.

II. (*a*) Remarks upon a late Book entitled 'The 'Fable of the Bees.' (*b*) The Case of Reason, or Natural Religion fairly and fully stated. (*c*) The absolute Unlawfulness of Stage Entertainments fully demonstrated.

III. A Practical Treatise upon Christian Perfection.

IV. A Serious Call to a Devout and Holy Life.

V. (*a*) A Demonstration of the Gross and Fundamental Errors of a late Book, called 'A plain 'Account of the Sacrament of the Lord's 'Supper.' (*b*) The Grounds and Reason of Christian Regeneration.

VI. (*a*) An Earnest and Serious Answer to Dr. *Trapp's* Discourse of the Folly, Sin and Danger of being Righteous over-much. (*b*) An Appeal to all that Doubt or disbelieve the Truths of the Gospel.

VII. (*a*) The Spirit of Prayer : or the Soul rising out of the Vanity of Time into the Riches of Eternity. In Two Parts. (*b*) The Way to Divine Knowledge; being several Dialogues between *Humanus, Academicus, Rusticus* and *Theophilus*.

VIII. (*a*) The Spirit of Love. In Two Parts. (*b*) A Short but Sufficient Confutation of the Rev. Dr. *Warburton's* projected Defence of Christianity.

IX. (*a*) Of Justification by Faith and Works. (*b*) An Humble, Earnest, and Affectionate Address to the Clergy. (*c*) A Collection of Letters on the most Interesting and Important Subjects.

THE Bishop of BANGOR's LATE SERMON,

AND HIS

LETTER to Dr. SNAPE in Defence of it,

ANSWERED.

And the Dangerous Nature of some Doctrines in his *Preservative*,

Set forth in a

Letter to his Lordship.

By *WILLIAM LAW*, M. A.

LONDON:
Printed for W. INNYS and J. RICHARDSON, in *Pater-noster-Row.* 1753.

The First Letter to the Bishop of *Bangor*.

My Lord,

THAT your Lordship may be prepared to receive what I here presume to lay before you, with the greater Candor, I sincerely profess, that it does not proceed from any Prejudice; but from certain Reasons, upon which I find myself invincibly obliged to differ from your Lordship in Opinion.

To prevent all Suspicion of my designing anything injurious to your Lordship's Character in this Address, I have prefixed, what otherwise I should have chosen to conceal, my Name to it.

Your Lordship is represented as at the Head of a Cause, where every Adversary is sure to be reproached, either as a furious Jacobite, or Popish Bigot, or an Enemy to the Liberty of his Country, and the Protestant Cause. These hard Names are to be expected, my Lord, from a Set of Men who dishonour your Lordship with their Panegyrics upon your Performances; whose Praises defile the Character they would adorn.

When Dr. *Snape* represents your Lordship as no Friend to the good Orders, and necessary Institutions of the Church, you complain of the ill Arts of an Adversary, who sets you out in false Colours, perverts your Words on purpose to increase his own *Imaginary Triumphs*. But, my Lord, in this, Dr. *Snape* only thinks with those who would be counted your best Friends; and would no longer be your Friends, but that they conclude, you have declared against the Authority of the Church. Does your Lordship suppose, that the T———ds, the H———ks, the B———ts, would be at so much Expense of Time and Labour, to justify, commend and enlarge upon your Lordship's Notions, if they did not think you engaged in their Cause? There is not a Libertine, or Loose-Thinker in *England*, but he imagines you intend to dissolve the Church as a *Society*, and are ready to offer Incense to your Lordship for so meritorious a Design. It is not my Intention to reproach your Lordship with their Esteem, or to involve you in the Guilt of their Schemes; but to show, that an Adversary does not need any Malice to make him believe you no Friend to the Constitution of the Church, as a Regular Society, since your greatest Admirers every Day publish it by necessary Construction to the World in Print.

After a Word or two concerning a Passage in your Lordship's *Preservative*, I shall proceed to consider your Answer to Dr. *Snape*. In the 98th Page you have these Words: *But when you are secure of your Integrity before God, — this will lead you (as it ought all of us) not to be afraid of the Terrors of Men, or the vain Words of Regular Uninterrupted Successions, Authoritative Benedictions, Excommunications, — Nullity, or Validity of God's Ordinances to the People upon Account of Niceties and Trifles, or any other the like Dreams.*

My Lord, thus much must be implied here: Be not afraid of the Terrors of Men, who would persuade you of the Danger of being in this, or that Communion, and fright you into particular Ways of Worshipping God, who would make you believe such Sacraments, and such Clergy, are necessary to recommend you to his Favour. For these, your Lordship affirms, we may contemn, if we be but secure of our Integrity.

So that if a Man be not a *Hypocrite*, it matters not what Religion he is of. This is a Proposition of an unfriendly Aspect to Christianity: But that it is entirely your Lordship's, is plain from what you declare, p. 90: *That every one may find it in his own Conduct to be true, that his Title to God's Favour cannot depend upon his actual being or continuing in any particular Method; but upon his real Sincerity in the Conduct of his Conscience.* Again, p. 91: *The Favour of God follows Sincerity, considered as such, and consequently equally follows every equal Degree of Sincerity.* So that I hope I have not wrested your Lordship's Meaning, by saying, that, according to these Notions, if a Man be not a Hypocrite, it matters not what Religion he is of. Not only sincere *Quakers, Ranters, Muggletonians,* and *Fifth Monarchy-Men,* are as much in the Favour of God, as any of the Apostles; but likewise sincere *Jews, Turks* and *Deists,* are upon as good a Bottom, and as secure of the Favour of God, as the sincerest Christian.

For your Lordship saith, it is *Sincerity,* as *such,* that procures the Favour of God. If it be Sincerity, as such, then it is *Sincerity* independent and exclusive of any particular Way of Worship. And if the *Favour of God equally follows* every equal *Degree of Sincerity,* then it is impossible there should be any

Difference, either as to Merit or Happiness, between a sincere *Martyr* and a sincere *Persecutor ;* and he that burns the Christian, if he be but in earnest, has the same Title to a Reward for it, as he that is burnt for believing in Christ.

Your Lordship saith, you can't help it, if People will charge you with* *Evil Intentions* and *Bad Views.* I intend no such Charge: But I wonder your Lordship should think it hard, that anyone should infer from these Places, that you *are against the Interest of the Church of* England.

For, my Lord, cannot the *Quakers, Muggletonians, Deists, Presbyterians,* assert you as much in their interest as we can? Have you said anything for us, or done anything for us in this *Preservative,* but what you have equally done for them? Your Lordship is ours, as you fill a *Bishopric;* but we are at a loss to discover from this Discourse what other Interest we have in your Lordship. For you openly expose our Communion, and give up all the advantages of it, by telling all sorts of People, if they are but sincere in their own Way, they are as much in God's Favour as anybody else. Is this supporting our Interest, my Lord?

Suppose a Friend of King *George* should declare it to all *Britons* whatever, that though they were divided into Five thousand different Parties, to set up different *Pretenders ;* yet if they were but sincere in their Designs, they would be as much in the Favour of God, as those who are most firmly attached to his *Majesty.* Does your Lordship think, such a one would be thought any great Friend to the Government? And, my Lord, is not this the Declaration you made as to the Church of *England?* Have you not told all Parties, that their Sincerity is enough? Have you said so much as one Word in Recommendation of our Communion: Or, if it was not for your Church-Character in the Title-Page of this Discourse, could anyone alive conceive what Communion you were of? Nay, a Reader, that was a Stranger, would imagine, that he who will allow no Difference between Communions, is himself of no Communion. Your Lordship, for aught I know, may act according to the strictest Sincerity, and may think it your Duty to undermine the Foundations of the Church. I am only surprised, that you should refuse to own the Reasonableness of such a Charge.

Your Lordship hath cancelled all our Obligations to any particular Communion, upon pretence of *Sincerity.*

I hope, my Lord, there is Mercy in store for all sorts of People, however erroneous in their Way of worshipping God; but cannot believe, that to be a sincere Christian, is to be no more in the Favour of God, than to be a sincere *Deist,* or a

---

* Answer, p. 46.

sincere *Destroyer* of Christians. It will be allowed, that Sincerity is a necessary Principle of true Religion ; and that without it, all the most specious Appearances of Virtue are nothing worth. But still, neither common Sense, nor plain Scripture, will suffer me to think, that when our Saviour was on Earth, they were as much in the Favour of God, who sincerely refused to be his Disciples, and sincerely called for his Crucifixion, as those who sincerely left all and followed him. If they were, my Lord, where is that Blessedness of Believing so often mentioned in the Scripture? Or, where is the Happiness of the Gospel Revelation, if they are as well, who refuse it sincerely, as those who embrace it with Integrity?

Our Saviour declared, that those who believed, should be saved; but those who believed not, should be damned. Will your Lordship say, that all Unbelievers were insincere; or, that though they were damned, they were yet in the same Favour with God, as those who were saved ?

The Apostle assures us, *that there is no other Name under Heaven given unto Men, whereby they can be saved, but* Jesus Christ. But your Lordship hath found out an Atonement, more universal than that of his Blood; and which will even make those blessed and happy, who count it an *unholy Thing*. For seeing it is *Sincerity, as such,* that alone recommends us to the Favour of God, they who sincerely persecute this Name, are in as good a Way, as those that sincerely worship it. Has God declared this to be the only Way to Salvation? How can your Lordship tell the World, that Sincerity will save them, be they in what Way they will? Is this all the Necessity of Christ's Satisfaction? Is this all the Advantage of the Gospel Covenant, that those who sincerely condemn it, are in as good a State without it, as those that embrace it?

My Lord, here is no Aggravation of your Meaning. If Sincerity, as such, be the only thing that recommends us to God, and every equal Degree of it procures an equal Degree of Favour; it is a Demonstration, that Sincerity *against* Christ is as pleasing to God, as Sincerity *for* him. My Lord, this is a Doctrine which no Words can enough decry. So I shall leave it, to consider what Opinion St. *Paul* had of this kind of Sincerity. He did not think, when he persecuted the Church, though he did it *ignorantly*, and in Unbelief, and out of Zeal towards God, that he was as much in the Favour of God, as when he suffered for Christ. *I am the least,* saith he, *of the Apostles, not fit to be called an Apostle; because I persecuted the Church of Christ.* The Apostle does not scruple to charge himself with Guilt, notwithstanding his Sincerity.

A little Knowledge of human Nature will teach us, that our Sincerity may be often charged with Guilt; not as if we were guilty because we are sincere; but because it may be our Fault that we are hearty and sincere in such or such ill-grounded Opinions. It may have been from some ill Conduct of our own, some Irregularities, or Abuse of our Faculties, that we conceive things as we do, and are fixed in such and such Tenets. And can we think so much owing to a *Sincerity* in Opinions, contracted by ill Habits and guilty Behaviour? There are several faulty Ways, by which People may cloud and prejudice their Understandings, and throw themselves into a very odd Way of thinking; for some Cause or other *God may send them a strong Delusion, that they should believe a Lie.* And will your Lordship say, that those who are thus sunk into Errors, it may be, through their own ill Conduct, or as a Judgment of God upon them, are as much in his Favour, as those that love and adhere to the Truth? This, my Lord, is a shocking Opinion, and has given Numbers of Christians great Offence, as contradicting common Sense and plain Scripture; as setting all Religion upon the Level, as to the Favour of God.

The next thing that, according to your Lordship, *we ought not to be concerned at, is, the vain Words of Regular and Uninterrupted Successions, as Niceties, Trifles, and Dreams.* Thus much surely is implied in these Words, that no kind of *Ordination* or *Mission* of the Clergy is of any Consequence or Moment to us. For if the Ordination need not be *Regular*, or derived from those who had Authority from Christ to Ordain, it is plain, that no one particular kind of Ordination can be of any more Value than another. For no Ordination whatever can have any worse Defects, than as being *Irregular*, and not derived by a Succession from Christ. So that if these Circumstances are to be looked on as *Trifles* and *Dreams*, all the Difference that can be supposed betwixt any Ordinations, comes under the same Notion of *Trifles* and *Dreams;* and consequently, are either Good alike, or Trifling alike. So that *Quakers, Independents, Presbyterians*, according to your Lordship, have as much Reason to think their Teachers as useful to them, and as True Ministers of Christ, as those of the Episcopal Communion have to think their Teachers. For if *Regularity* of Ordination and *Uninterrupted Succession* be mere Trifles, and nothing; then all the Difference betwixt us and other Teachers, must be nothing: for they can differ from us in no other respects. So that, my Lord, if Episcopal Ordination, derived from Christ, hath been contended for by the Church of *England*, your Lordship hath in this Point deserted her: And you not only give up Episcopal Ordination, by ridiculing a

Succession; but likewise by the same Argument exclude any *Ministers* on Earth from having Christ's Authority. For if there be not a Succession of Persons authorised from Christ to send others to act in his Name, then both Episcopal and Presbyterian Teachers are equally *Usurpers*, and as mere *Laymen* as any at all. For there can't be any other Difference between the Clergy and Laity; but as the one hath Authority derived from Christ, to perform Offices which the other hath not. But this Authority can be no otherwise had, than by an Uninterrupted Succession of Men from Christ, empowered to qualify others. For if the Succession be once broke, People must either go into the Ministry of their own Accord, or be sent by such as have no more Power to send others, than to go themselves. And, my Lord, can these be called Ministers of Christ, or received as his Ambassadors? Can they be thought to act in his Name, who have no Authority from him? If so, your Lordship's Servant might Ordain and Baptize to as much purpose as your Lordship: For it could only be objected to such Actions, that they had no Authority from Christ. And if there be no Succession of Ordainers from him, everyone is equally qualified to Ordain. My Lord, I should think it might be granted me, that the Administering of a Sacrament is an Action we have no Right to perform, considered either as Men, Gentlemen, or Scholars, or Members of a Civil Society. Who then can have any Authority to interpose, but he that has it from Christ? And how that can be had from him, without a Succession of Men from him, is not easily conceived. Should a private Person choose a Lord Chancellor, and declare his Authority good; would there be any thing but Absurdity, Impudence and Presumption in it? But why he cannot as well commission a Person to act, sign and seal in the King's Name, as in the Name of Christ, is unaccountable.

My Lord, it is a plain and obvious Truth, that no Man, or Number of Men, considered, as such, can any more make a Priest, or commission a Person to officiate in Christ's Name, *as such*, than he can enlarge the Means of Grace, or add a New Sacrament for the Conveyance of spiritual Advantages. The Ministers of Christ are as much positive *Ordinances*, as the Sacraments; and we might as well think, that Sacraments not instituted by him, might be Means of Grace, as those pass for his Ministers, who have no Authority from him.

Once more, all things are either in common in the Church of Christ, or they are not. If they are, then everyone may Preach, Baptize, Ordain, &c. If all things are not thus common, but the Administering of the Sacrament, and Ordination, &c., are Offices appropriated to particular Persons ; then I desire to know how, in this present Age, or any other since the Apostles, Christians can know their respective Duties, or what they may, or may not do, with respect to the several Acts of Church-Communion, if there be no *Uninterrupted Succession* of Authorised Persons from Christ : For until Authority from Christ appears, to make a Difference between them, we are all alike ; and anyone may officiate as well as another. To make a Jest therefore of the *Uninterrupted Succession,* is to make a Jest of Ordination ; to destroy the sacred Character, and make all Pretenders to it, as good as those that are sent by Christ.

If there be no *Uninterrupted Succession,* then there are no Authorised Ministers from Christ ; if no such Ministers, then no Christian Sacraments ; if no Christian Sacraments, then no Christian Covenant, whereof the Sacraments are the Stated and Visible Seals.

My Lord, this is all your own. Here are no Consequences palmed upon you ; but the first, plain, and obvious Sense of your Lordship's Words — and yet, after all, your Lordship asks Dr. *Snape, Why all these Outcries against you** ? Indeed, my Lord, you have only taken the main Supports of our Religion away : You have neither left us Priests, nor Sacraments, nor Church : Or, what is the same thing, you have made them all *Trifles* and *Dreams*. And what has your Lordship given us in the room of all these Advantages ? Why, only *Sincerity :* This is the great Universal Atonement for all. This is that, which, according to your Lordship, will help us to the Communion of Saints hereafter, though we are in Communion with anybody, or nobody here.

The next Things we are not to be afraid of, are, *The vain Words of Nullity and Validity of God's Ordinances, i.e.,* whether they are administered by a Clergyman or a Layman. This indeed I have shown was included in what you said about the Trifle of *Uninterrupted Succession*. But, for fear we should have overlooked it there, you have given it us in express Words in the next Line.

Your Lordship tells Dr. *Snape,* That *you know no Confusion,* Glorious *or* Inglorious, *that you have endeavoured to introduce* into the Church.†

My Lord, If I may presume to repeat your own Words, *Lay your Hand on your Heart, and ask yourself,* Whether the encouraging all manner of Divisions, be not endeavouring to introduce Confusion ? If there were in *England* Five thousand

---

* Answer, p. 40.   † Answer, p. 47.

different Sects, has not your Lordship persuaded them to be content with themselves; not to value what they are told by other Communions; That if they are but sincere, they need not have regard to anything else? Is not this to introduce Confusion? What is Confusion, but Difference and Division? And does not your Lordship plainly declare to the World, that there is no need of uniting? That there is no particular Way or Method, that can recommend us more to the Favour of God, than another? Has your Lordship so much as given the least Hint, that it is better to be in the Communion of the Church of *England*, than not? Have you not exposed her Sacraments and Clergy; and, as much as lay in you, broke down every thing in her, that distinguishes her from Fanatical Conventicles? What is there in her, as a Church, that you have left untouched? What have you left in her, that can any way invite others into her Communion? Are her Clergy authorised more than others? For fear that should be thought, you make a Regular Succession from Christ, a *Trifle*. Are her Sacraments more regularly administered? Lest that should recommend her, you slight the *Nullity or Validity of God's Ordinances*. Is there any Authority in her Laws, which enjoin Communion with her? Lest this should be believed, you tell us, that our being or continuing in any particular Method (or particular Communion) cannot recommend us more to the Favour of God than another.

I must observe to your Lordship, that these Opinions are very oddly put in a *Preservative from ill Principles;* or, *An Appeal to the Consciences and common Sense of the Laity*. Are they to be persuaded not to join with the Nonjurors, because no particular Priests, no particular Sacraments, no particular Communion, is anything but a Dream and Trifle; and such things as no way recommend us to the Favour of God more than others? Are the Nonjurors only thus to be answered? Is the Established Church only thus to be defended? Your Lordship indeed has not minced the Matter: But, I hope, the Church of *England* is to be supported upon better Principles, or not at all.

If I should tell a Person that put a Case of Conscience to me, that all Cases of Conscience are Trifles, and signify nothing; it would be plain, that I had given him a direct Answer: But if he had either Conscience, or common Sense, he would seek out a better Confessor.

Your Lordship tells Dr. *Snape*, that she saith and unsaith, to the *great Diversion of the Roman Catholics.** But if your Lord-

---

* Answer, p. 46.

ship would unsay some things you have said, it would be a greater Mortification to them, than all that ever you said or writ in your Life.

To deny the Necessity of any particular Communion, to expose the Validity of Sacraments, and rally upon the Uninterrupted Succession of Priests, and pull down every Pillar in the Church of Chrift, is an Errand on which *Rome* hath sent many Messengers. And the Papists are no more provoked with your Lordship for these Discourses, than they were angry at *William Penn*, a reputed Jesuit, for preaching up *Quakerism*. So long as they rejoice in our Divisions, or are glad to see the City of God made a mere *Babel*, they can no more be angry at your Lordship, than at your Advocates.

Dr. *Snape* says, you represent the Church of Christ as a Kingdom, in which Christ neither acts himself, nor hath invested anyone else with Authority to act for him. At this your Lordship cries, p. 22, *Lay your Hand upon your Heart, and ask, Is this a Christion, Human, Honest Representation of what your own Eyes read in my Sermon?*

My Lord, I have dealt as sincerely with my Heart as it is possible; and I must confess, I take the Doctor's Representation to be Christian and Honest. For though you sometimes contend against Absolute and Indispensable Authority; yet it is plain, that you strike at all Authority, and assert, as the Doctor saith, that Christ hath not invested anyone on Earth with an Authority to act for him.

Page 11. You expressly say, *That as to the Affairs of Conscience and eternal Salvation, Christ hath left no Visible Human Authority behind him.*

Now, my Lord, is not this saying, that he has left no Authority at all? For Christ came with no other Authority Himself but as to Conscience and Salvation, he erected a Kingdom which related to nothing but Conscience and Salvation: And therefore they who have no Authority as to Conscience and Salvation, have no Authority at all in his Kingdom. Conscience and Salvation are the only Affairs of that Kingdom.

Your Lordship denies, that anyone has Authority in these Affairs; and yet you take it ill to be charged with asserting, that Christ hath not invested anyone with Authority for him. How can anyone act for him, but in his Kingdom? How can they act in his Kingdom, if they have nothing to do with Conscience and Salvation, when his Kingdom is concerned with nothing else?

Again, Page 16, your Lordship saith, that no one of them (Christians) *any more than another, hath Authority either to make* new Laws for *Christ's Subjects*, or to impose a Sense upon the old ones; or to Judge, Censure, or Punish the Servants of another Master, in Matters purely relating to Conscience.

I can meet with no Divine, my Lord, either Juror or Non-Juror, High or Low, Churchman or Dissenter, that does not think your Lordship has plainly asserted in these Passages, what the Doctor has laid to your Charge, *that no one is invested with Authority from Christ to act for him.*

Your Lordship thinks this is sufficiently answered, by saying, you contend against an Absolute Authority. You do indeed sometimes join Absolute with that Authority you disclaim. But, my Lord, it is still true, that you have taken all Authority from the Church: For the Reasons you everywhere give against this Authority, conclude as strongly against any Degrees of Authority, as that which is truly Absolute.

First, You disown the Authority of any Christians over other Christians, because they are the *Servants of another Master*, p. 16. Now this concludes as strongly against *any* Authority, as that which is *Absolute:* For no one can have the least Authority over those that are entirely under another's Jurisdiction. A small Authority over another's Servant, is as inconsistent as the greatest.

Secondly, You reject this Authority, because of the Objects it is exercised upon, *i.e.* Matters purely relating to Conscience and Salvation. Here this Authority is rejected, because it relates to *Conscience* and *Salvation;* which does as well exclude every Degree of Authority, as that which is Absolute. For if Authority and Conscience cannot suit together, Conscience rejects Authority, *as such;* and not because there is this or that Degree of it. So that this Argument banishes all Authority.

Thirdly, Your Lordship denies any Church Authority, because Christ doth not *interpose to convey Infallibility, to assert the true Interpretation of His own Laws.** Now, this Reason concludes as full against *all Authority*, as that which is *Absolute*. For if Infallibility is necessary to found an Obedience upon in Christ's Kingdom, it is plain, that nobody in Christ's Kingdom hath any Right to any Obedience from others, nor consequently any Authority to command it; no Members, or Number of Members of it, being infallible.

Fourthly, Another Reason your Lordship gives against Church-Authority, is this; *That it is the taking Christ's Kingdom out of his Hands, and placing it in their own*, p. 14. Now this Reason proves as much against Authority in general, or *any Degrees* of

---

* Sermon, p. 15.

it, as that which is *Absolute.* For if the Authority of others is inconsistent with Christ's being King of his own Kingdom, then *every Degree* of Authority, so far as it extends, is an Invasion of so much of Christ's Authority, and usurping upon his Right.

The Reason likewise which your Lordship gives to prove the Apostles not Usurpers of Christ's Authority, plainly condemns every Degree of Authority which any Church can now pretend to. *They were no Usurpers, because he then interposed to convey Infallibility; and was in all that they ordained: So that the Authority was his in the strictest Sense.** So that where he does not interpose to convey Infallibility, there every *Degree* of Authority is a *Degree* of Usurpation; and consequently, the present Church having no Infallibility, has no Right to exercise the *least Degree* of Authority, without robbing Christ of his Prerogative.

Thus it plainly appears, that every Reason you have offered against Church-Authority, concludes with as much Strength against *all* Authority, as that which is *Absolute.* And therefore Dr. *Snape* has done you no Injury in charging you with the Denial of *All* Authority.

There happens, my Lord, to be *only* this Difference between your Sermon and the Defence of it, that That is so many Pages against Church-Authority, *as such*, and This is a Confutation of the *Pope's Infallibility.* It is very strange, that so *clear a Writer*, who has been so long inquiring into the Nature of *Government*, should not be able to make himself be understood upon it: That your Lordship should be only preaching againt the Pope; and yet *All the Lower House of Convocation* should unanimously conceive, that your Doctrine therein delivered, tended to *subvert all Government and Discipline in the Church of Christ.*

And, my Lord, it will appear from what follows, that your Lordship is even of the same Opinion yourself; and that you imagined, you had banished *all* Authority, *as such*, out of the Church, by those Arguments you had offered against an *Absolute Authority.* This is plain from the following Passage, where you ridicule *that* which Dr. *Snape* took to be an *Authority*, though not Absolute. When Dr. *Snape* said, That no Church-Authority was to be obeyed in anything contrary to the Revealed Will of God, your Lordship triumphs thus: *Glorious Absolute Authority indeed, in your own Account, to which Christ's Subjects owe no Obedience, till they have examined into his own Declarations; and then they obey not this Authority, but him.*†

---

* Answer, p. 38. † Answer, p. 27.

Here you make nothing of that Authority which is not *Absolute;* and yet you think it hard to be told, that you have taken away all *Church-Authority.* That which is Absolute, you expressly deny; and here you say, that which is not Absolute, is nothing at all. Where then is the *Authority* you have left? Or how is it that Christ has empowered anyone to act in his Name?

Your Lordship fights safe under the Protection of the Word *Absolute;* but your Aim is at all Church-Power. And your Lordship makes too hasty an Inference, that because it is not *Absolute,* it is none at all. If you ask, Where you have made this Inference, it is on occasion of the above-mentioned Triumph; where your Lordship makes it an insignificant Authority, which is only to be obeyed so long as it is not contrary to Scripture.

Your Lordship seems to think all is lost, as to Church-Power; because the Doctor does not claim an *Absolute one,* but allows it to be subject to Scripture : As if *all* Authority was *Absolute,* or else nothing at all. I shall therefore consider the Nature of this Church-Power, and show, that though it is not *Absolute,* yet it is a *Real Authority,* and is not such a mere Notion as your Lordship makes it.

An *Absolute Authority,* according to your Lordship, is what is to be always obeyed by every Individual that is subject to it, in all Circumstances. This is an Authority that we utterly deny to the Church. But, I presume, there may be an *Authority* inferior to this, which is nevertheless a *Real Authority,* and is to be esteemed as such, and that for these Reasons:

First, I hope it will be allowed me, that our Saviour came into the World with Authority. But it was not lawful for the *Jews* to receive him, if they thought his Appearance not agreeable to those Marks and Characters they had of him in their Scriptures. May not I here say, My Lord, *Glorious Authority of Christ indeed, to which the* Jews *owed no Obedience, till they had examined their Scriptures; and then they obey, not Him, but Them !*

Again; The Apostles were sent into the World with Authority : But yet, those who thought their Doctrines unworthy of God, and unsuitable to the Principles of Natural Religion, were obliged not to obey them. *Glorious Authority indeed of the Apostles, to whom Mankind owed no Obedience, till they had first examined their own Notions of God and Religion ; and then they obeyed, not the Apostles, but Them.*

I hope, my Lord, it may be allowed, that the Sacraments are Real Means of Grace : But it is certain they are only *conditionally* so, if those that partake of them are endowed with suitable Dispositions of Piety and Virtue. *Glorious Means of Grace of the Sacraments, which is only obtained by such pious Dispositions ; and then it is owing to the* Dispositions, and not the Sacraments. Now, my Lord, if there can be such a thing as instituted *Real Means* of Grace, which are only *conditionally applied,* I cannot see, why there may not be an instituted Real Authority in the Church, which is only to be *conditionally* obeyed.

Your Lordship has written a great many Elaborate Pages to prove the *English* Government Limited ; and that no Obedience is due to it, but whilst it preserves our Fundamentals ; and, I suppose, the People are to judge for themselves, whether these are safe, or not. *Glorious Authority of the* English *Government, which is to be obeyed no longer than the People think it their Interest to obey it !*

Will your Lordship say, There is *no Authority* in the *English* Government, because only a *conditional Obedience* is due to it, whilst we think it supports our Fundamentals ? Why then must the *Church-Authority* be reckoned nothing at all, because only a *Rational Conditional* Obedience is to be paid, whilst we think it not contrary to Scripture ? Is a Limited, Conditional Government in the State, such a Wise, Excellent, and Glorious Constitution ? And is the same Authority in the Church, such Absurdity, Nonsense, and nothing at all, as to any actual Power ?

If there be such a thing as Obedience upon Rational Motives, there must be such a thing as Authority that is not absolute, or that does not require a *Blind, Implicit* Obedience. Indeed, Rational Creatures can obey no other Authority ; they must have Reasons for what they do. And yet because the Church claims only this *Rational* Obedience, your Lordship explodes *such* Authority as none at all.

Yet it must be granted, that *no other* Obedience was due to the *Prophets,* or our *Saviour* and his *Apostles :* They were only to be obeyed by those who Thought their Doctrines *worthy* of God. So that if the Church has *no* Authority, because we must first consult the Scriptures before we obey it ; neither our Saviour, nor his Apostles, had *any Authority,* because the *Jews* were first to consult their Scriptures, and the *Heathens* their Reason, before they obeyed them. And yet this is all that is said against *Church-Authority ;* That because they are to judge of the *Lawfulness* of its Injunctions, therefore they owe it no Obedience : Which false Conclusion I hope is enough exposed.

If we think it unlawful to do anything that the Church requires of us, we must not obey its Authority. So, if we think it unlawful to submit to any Temporal Government, we are not to comply. But, I hope, it will not follow, that the Government has *no Authority*, because some think it unlawful to comply with it. If we are so unhappy as to judge wrong in any Matter of Duty, we must nevertheless act according to our Judgments; and the Guilt of Disobedience either in *Church* or *State*, is more or less, according as our Error is more or less voluntary, and occasioned by our own Mismanagement.

I believe I have shown, First, That all your Lordship's Arguments against *Church-Authority*, conclude with the same Force against *all* Degrees of Authority: Secondly, That though *Church-Authority* be not Absolute in a *certain Sense;* yet if our Saviour and his Apostles had any Authority, the Church may have a *Real Authority:* For neither he, nor his Apostles, had *such* an *Absolute* Authority, as excludes all *Consideration* and *Examination:* Which is your Notion of *Absolute* Authority.

Before I leave this Head, I must observe, that in this very Answer to Dr. *Snape*, where you would be thought to have exposed *this Absolute* Authority *alone*, you exclude *all* Authority along with it. You ask the Doctor,* *Is this the whole you can make of it, after all your boasted Zeal for* Mere Authority? You then say, *Why may not I be allowed to say, No Man on Earth hath an* Absolute Authority, *as well as you?* My Lord, there can be no understanding of this, unless *Mere Authority* and *Absolute Authority* be taken for the same thing by your Lordship.

But, my Lord, is not the smallest *Particle* of Matter, *Mere Matter?* And is it therefore the same as the *Whole Mass* of Matter? Is an Inch of Space, because it is *Mere Space*, the same as *Infinite* Space? How comes it, then, that *Mere* Authority is the same as *Absolute* Authority? My Lord, *Mere* Authority implies *only* Authority, as a *Mere* Man implies *only* a Man: But your Lordship makes no Difference between *this*, and Absolute Authority; and therefore hath left *no* Authority in the Church, unless there be Authority, that is not *Mere Authority*, i.e. Matter that is not *Mere Matter;* or Space that is not *Mere Space*.

When the Church enjoins Matters of Indifference, is she obeyed for any Reason, but for her *Mere* Authority? But your Lordship allows no Obedience to *Mere Authority;* and therefore no Obedience even in Indifferent Matters.

Thus do these Arguments of yours lay all waste in the Church: And I must not omit *one*, my Lord, which falls as

---

* Answer, p. 26.

heavy upon the *State*, and makes all *Civil Government* unlawful. Your words are these: As *the Church of Christ is the Kingdom of Christ, He himself is King; and in this it is implied, that He is the* sole *Law-giver to his* Subjects, *and Himself the* sole *Judge of their Behaviour in the Affairs of Conscience and Salvation.* If there be any *Truth* or Force in this Argument, it concludes with the same *Truth* and *Force* against all Authority in the *Kingdoms* of this World. In Scripture we are told, *the Most High ruleth in the Kingdom of Men* (Dan. iv. 17), *that the Lord is our Law-giver, the Lord is our King* (Isa. xxxiii. 22). Now, if because Christ is *King* of the Church, it must be in *this implied*, that he is *sole* Law-giver to his *Subjects;* it is plain to a Demonstration, that because *God* is *King* and *Law-giver* to the whole Earth, that therefore *He* is *sole Law-giver* to his *Subjects;* and consequently, that *all Civil Authority, all Human Laws,* are mere *Invasions* and *Usurpations* upon God's Authority, as *King* of the whole Earth.

Is nobody to have any Jurisdiction in *Christ's Kingdom, because* He is *King* of it? How then comes anyone to have *any* Authority in the *Kingdoms* of this World, when God has declared himself the *Law-giver,* and *King* of the whole World? Will your Lordship say, that Christ hath left us the *Scriptures,* as the *Statute-Laws* of his *Kingdom,* to prevent the Necessity of *After-Laws?* It may be answered, That God has given us *Reason* for our constant Guide; which, if it were as duly attended to, would as *certainly* answer the *Ends* of *Civil Life,* as the Observance of the Scriptures would make us good Christians.

But, my Lord, as human Nature, if left to itself, would neither answer the *Ends* of a *Spiritual* or *Civil* Society; so a *constant Visible* Government in both, is *equally* necessary: And, I believe, it appears to all unprejudiced Eyes, that in this Argument *at least,* your Lordship has declared both *equally Unlawful.*

Your Lordship saith,* *The Exclusion of the Papists from the Throne, was not upon the Account of their Religion.* Three Lines after you say, *I have contended indeed elsewhere, that it was their unhappy Religion which* alone *made them uncapable in themselves, of governing this Protestant Nation by the Laws of the Land.* My Lord, I can't reconcile these two Passages. *Popery alone,* you say, was their *Incapacity.* From which it may be inferred, they had *no other Incapacity.* Yet your Lordship saith, They were not excluded upon the Account of their *Religion.* A

---

* Answer, p. 25.

little after you say, *The Ground of their Exclusion was not their Religion, considered as such; but the Fatal, Natural, Certain Effects of it upon themselves to our Destruction.*

As for Instance, your Lordship may mean thus: If a *Man* of a *great Estate* dies, he loses his *Right* to his Estate; not upon the Account of *Death*, considered *as such;* but for the *Certain, Fatal, Natural Effect* of it upon himself. Or, suppose a Person be excluded for being an *Idiot;* it is not for his Idiocy, considered *as such;* but for the *Certain, Fatal, Natural Effect of it* upon himself to our Destruction.

My Lord, this is prodigious deep: I wish it be clear; or, that it be not too refined a Notion for common Use on this Subject. Likewise I do not conceive, my Lord, what you can call the *Fatal, Natural, Certain Effects* of any one's Religion. I am sure, among *Protestants* there are no *Natural, Certain Effects* of their Religion upon them; that their Practices don't *Fatally* follow their Principles: Neither is there any demonstrative Certainty, that a *Bishop* cannot be against *Episcopacy*.

If the *Papists* are so *unalterably sincere* in their Religion, that we can prove their *certain* Observation of it, it's pity but they had our Principles, and we had their Practice. I have not that good Opinion of the Papists, which your Lordship hath: I believe several of them sit as loose to their Religion, *as other Folks*.

Does you Lordship think, that all *Papists* are alike? That natural Temper, Ambition and Education, don't make as much Difference amongst them, as the *same things* do amongst us? Are all *Protestants* loose and libertine alike? Why should all *Papists* be the same Zealots? If not, my Lord, then these *Effects* you call *Fatal, Natural,* and *Certain*, may be not to be depended upon.

Your Lordship knows, that it was generally believed, that King *Charles* the Second was a *Papist*: But I never heard of any *Fatal, Natural, and Certain Effects of his Religion upon him.* All that one hears of it is, that he lived like a *Protestant*, and died like a *Papist*. I suppose your Lordship will allow, that several who were lately *Papists*, are now true *Protestants*. I desire therefore to know, what is become of the *Fatal, Certain, and Natural Effects of their Religion?*

My Lord, I beg of you to lay your Hand again upon your Heart, and ask, Whether this be strict Reasoning? Whether it is possible in the very Nature of the thing, *that such Fatal, Natural, and Certain Effects should follow such a Giddy, Whimsical, Uncertain* Thing, as *Human and Free Choice?* My Lord, is it neither possible for Papists to change or conceal their Religion for Interest, or leave it through a conscientious Conviction? If the former is impossible, then, according to your Lordship, it is the *safest Religion* in the World; because they are all sure of being *sincere*, and consequently, the First Favourites of God. If the latter is impossible, then a great many fine Sermons and Discourses have been written to as wise Purposes, as if they had been directed to the Wind.

I come now to your Lordship's Definition of *Prayer*, a *Calm and Undisturbed Address to God*. It seems very strange, that so great a Master of Words as your Lordship, should pick out Two so very exceptionable, that all your Lordship's Skill could not defend them, but by leaving their first and obvious Sense. Who would not take *Calm* and *Undisturbed* to be very like *Quiet* and *Unmoved*? Yet your Lordship dislikes those Expressions. But if these do not give us a true *Idea* of *Prayer*, you have made a very narrow Escape, and have given us a Definition of *Prayer* as near to a *wrong one* as possible.

Prayer chiefly consisteth of *Confession* and *Petition*. Now, to be *Calm*, and free from all *worldly Passions*, is a necessary Temper to the right Discharge of such Duties: But why our *Confession* must be so *Calm*, and free from all *Perturbation* of Spirit; why our *Petitions* may not have all that Fervour and Warmth, with which either *Nature* or *Grace* can supply them, is very surprising.

My Lord, we are advised to be *Dead to the World;* and I humbly suppose, no more is *implied* in it, than to keep our Affections from being too much engaged in it; and that a *Calm, Undisturbed*, i.e. *Dispassionate* Use of the World is very *consistent* with our being dead to it. If so, then this *Calm, Undisturbed Address to Heaven*, is a kind of *Prayer* that is very consistent with our being *dead to Heaven*.

We are forbid to *love* the World; and yet no greater *Abstraction* from it is required, than to use it *Calm and Undisturbed*. We are commanded to *set our Affections on Things above;* and yet, according to your Lordship, the *same Calm, Undisturbed Temper is enough*. According to this therefore we are to be *affected*, or rather *unaffected* alike, with *this* and the *next* World; since we are to be *Calm* and *Undisturbed* with respect to *both*.

The Reason your Lordship offers for this *Definition* of Prayer, is this; because you* *look upon Calmness and Undisturbedness to be the* Ornament and Defence of *human Understanding in all its Actions*. My Lord, this plainly supposes, there is no such thing as the *Right Use* of our *Passions :* For if we could ever use them

---

* Answer, p. 11.

to any Advantage, then it could not be the Ornament of our Nature to be *dispassionate alike* in *all* its Actions. It is as much the *Ornament* and *Defence* of our Nature, to be differently *affected* with Things according to their *respective* Differences, as it is to understand or conceive *different Things* according to their real Difference. It would be no *Ornament* or *Credit* to us, to conceive no Difference betwixt a *Mountain* and a *Mole-Hill:* And our Rational Nature is as much disgraced, when we are no more *affected* with *great* Things than with *small.* It is the Essential *Ornament* of our Nature, to be as sensibly *affected* in a different Manner with the different Degrees of Goodness of Things, as it is to perceive exactly the different *Natures* or Relations of Things. *Passion* is no more a Crime, *as such*, than the *Understanding* is, *as such.* It is nothing but mistaking the *Value* of Objects, that makes it criminal. An *Infinite Good* cannot be too *passionately* desired, nor a *Real Evil* too *vehemently* abhorred. *Mere Philosophy*, my Lord, would teach us, that the Dignity of *Human Nature* is best declared by a *Pungent Uneasiness* for the *Misery* of Sin, and a *passionate warm Application* to Heaven for Assistance.

Let us now consult the Scripture. St. *Paul* describes a *godly Sorrow* something different from your Lordship's *Calm and Undisturbed Temper*, in these Words: *When ye sorrowed after a godly sort, what* Carefulness *it wrought in you!* Yea, what Indignation, *yea, what* Fear, *yea, what* Zeal, *yea, what* Revenge! (2 Cor. vii. 11). My Lord, I suppose *these* are not so many Words for *Calm* and *Undisturbed.* Yet, as different as they are, the Apostle makes them the *Qualities* of a *godly Sorrow.* And all this, at the Expense of that *Calmness* which your Lordship terms the *Ornament* of human Nature. Dr. *Snape* pleads for the *Fervency* and *Ardour* of our Devotions, from our *Saviour's praying more earnestly* before his *Passion.*

Your Lordship replies, that *this* can give no Directions as to our *daily Prayers;* because it was what our *Saviour* himself knew nothing of, but this once. The Author of the Epistle to the *Hebrews* knew nothing of this way of Reasoning. For, as an Argument for *daily Patience*, he bids us look to *Jesus*, who endured the *Cross*, because he died for us, leaving us an *Example.*

Our Saviour, my Lord, *suffered* and *died* but *once;* yet is it made a Reason for our *daily Patience*, and proposed as an Example for us to imitate.

If therefore, my Lord, his Passion, so *extraordinary* in itself, and as much above the Power of human Nature to bear, as the *Intenseness* of his Devotions *exceeded* our Capacities for Prayer, be yet proposed as an *Example* to us in the *ordinary* Calamities of Life; how comes it, that *his Devotion* at that time should have no manner of Use or Direction in it as to our Devotions, especially in our *Distress*? How comes it, that his Suffering should have so much of Example in it, so much to be imitated; but the Manner of his *Devotion then* have nothing of Instruction, nothing that need be imitated by us? All the Reason that is offered, is the *Singularity* and *Extraordinariness* of it, when the same may be said of his *Passion*; yet that is allowed to be an *Example*.

Your Lordship is pleased, for the Information of your *Unwary Readers*, to reason thus upon the Place: *If this be the Example of our Saviour*, to assure us of his *Will about the Temper* necessary *to* Prayer, *it will follow that our Blessed Lord Himself never truly prayed before this time: And yet again, if he prayed more earnestly, it will follow, that he had prayed before; and consequently, that this Temper in which He now was, was not* necessary *to* Prayer.

My Lord, one would think this Elaborate Proof was against something asserted. Here you have indeed a thorough Conquest; but it is over *nobody*. For did anyone ever assert, that such *Extraordinary Earnestness* was *necessary* to Prayer? Does Dr. *Snape*, or any Divines, allow of no Prayers, except we sweat *Drops of Blood*? Will your Lordship say, that the *Necessity* of this Temper is implied in the Quotation of this Text, as a Direction for Prayer? I answer, just as much as we are all obliged to die upon the *Cross*, because his *Sufferings* there are proposed to us as an *Example*.

The plain Truth of the Matter, my Lord, I take to be this: Our *Saviour's Sufferings* on the Cross were such as no Mortal can undergo; yet they are justly proposed an an *Example* to us to bear with Patience such Sufferings as are within the Compass of human Nature. His earnest Devotion before this Passion, far *exceeded* any *Fervours* which the Devoutest of Mankind can attain to: Yet it is justly proposed to us as an *Example*, to excite us to be as fervent as we can; and may be justly alleged in our Defence, when our *warm* and *passionate* Addresses to God in our Calamities, are condemned as *superstitious Folly*. My Lord, must nothing be an *Example*, but what we can exactly come up to? How then can the *Life* of our *Saviour*, which was entirely free from *Sin*, be an Example to us? How could it be said in the Scripture, *Be ye holy, for I am holy*? Can anyone be *Holy* as *God is*?

My Lord, one might properly urge the *Practice* of the Primitive Christians, who parted with *all* they had for the Support of their

Indigent Brethren, as an Argument for Charity, without designing to oblige People to part with all they have. And *he* that should, in answer to such an Argument, tell the World, that *Charity* is only a *calm, undisturbed Good Will to all Mankind*, would just as much set forth the *true Doctrine of Charity*, as he that defines Prayer to be a *calm and undisturbed Address to Heaven*, for no other Reason, but because no *certain* Degrees of Fervour or Affection are necessarily required to constitute Devotion. My Lord, has *Charity* nothing to do with the *Distribution of Alms*, because no certain Allowance is fixed? Why then must *Prayer* have nothing to do with *Heat* and *Fervency*, because no fixed Degrees of it are necessary?

Therefore, my Lord, as I would define *Charity* to be a pious Distribution of so much of our Goods to the Poor, as is suitable to our Circumstances; so I would define *Prayer*, an *Address* to *Heaven, enlivened with such Degrees* of Fervour *and* Intenseness, *as our* Natural Temper, *influenced* with a true Sense *of God, could beget in us*.

Your Lordship says, you only desire to strike at the Root of *superstitious Folly*, and *establish* Prayer *in its room;* and this is to be effected by making our Addresses *calm and undisturbed:* By which we are to understand, a *Freedom* from *Heat and Passion*, as your Lordship explains it, by an Application to yourself.

If therefore anyone should happen to be so *disturbed* at his Sins, as to offer a *broken* and *contrite Heart* to God, instead of one *calm* and *undisturbed;* or, like holy *David*, his Soul should be athirst for God, or pant after him, as the *Hart panteth after the Water-brooks*, this would not be *Prayer*, but *superstitious Folly*.

My Lord, *Calmness* of *Temper*, as it signifies a Power over our *Passions*, is a *happy Circumstance* of a *Rational Nature*, but no farther: When the Object is well chosen, there is no Danger in the Pursuit.

The Calmness your Lordship hath described, is fit for a *Philosopher* in his *Study*, who is solving *Mathematical* Problems. But if he should come abroad into the World, thus entirely empty of all Passion, he would live to as much Purpose, as if he had left his Understanding behind him.

What a fine Subject, my Lord, would such a one make, who, when he heard of *Plots, Invasions*, and *Rebellions*, would continue as *calm* and *undisturbed*, as when he was *comparing Lines and Figures?* Such a calm Subject would scarce be taken for any Great Loyalist.

Your Lordship, in other Places, hath recommended an *open*

and *undisguised Zeal*,* and told us such things as ought to *alarm the coldest Heart*.† Sure, my Lord, this is somewhat more than *Calm* and *Undisturbed:* And will your Lordship, who hath expressed so much Concern for this *Ornament and Defence of human Understanding*, persuade us to part with the least Degree of it upon any Account? I am, my Lord, (with all Respect that is due to your Lordship's Station and Character),

Your most Humble and

Obedient Servant,

William Law.

---

* Sermon, *Nov.* 5, p. 5.   † Sermon, p. 14.

A SECOND
LETTER
TO THE
Bishop of *BANGOR*;

WHEREIN

His Lordship's NOTIONS

OF

Benediction, Absolution, and *Church-Communion,*

Are proved to be Destructive of every Institution of the *Christian Religion.*

To which is added, A

POSTSCRIPT,

In answer to the OBJECTIONS that have been made against his former Letter.

By *WILLIAM LAW*, M. A.

LONDON:
Printed for J. RICHARDSON, in Pater-noster-Row.
1762.

The Second Letter to the Bishop of *Bangor*.

My Lord,

A Just Concern for Truth, and the First Principles of the Christian Religion, was the only Motive that engaged me in the Examination of your Lordship's Doctrines, in a former Letter to your Lordship. And the same Motive, I hope, will be thought a sufficient Apology for my presuming to give your Lordship the Trouble of a Second Letter.

Amongst the Vain Contemptible Things, whereof your Lordship would create an Abhorrence in the Laity, are, the *Trifles* and *Niceties of Authoritative Benedictions, Absolutions, Excommunications.** Again, you say, that *to expect the Grace of God from any Hands, but his own, is to affront him*——.† And *that all depends upon God and ourselves; That Human Benedictions, Human Absolutions, Human Excommunications, have nothing to do with the Favour of God.*‡

It is evident from these Maxims (for your Lordship asserts them as such) that whatever Institutions are observed in any Christian Society, upon this Supposition, that thereby Grace is conferred through *Human Hands*, or by the Ministry of the Clergy, such Institutions ought to be condemned, and are condemned by your Lordship, as *trifling, useless, and affronting to God.*

There is an *Institution*, my Lord, in the *yet* Established Church of *England*, which we call *Confirmation* : It is founded upon the express Words of Scripture, Primitive Observance, and the Universal Practice of all succeeding Ages in the Church. The Design of this Institution is, that it should be a Means of conferring Grace, by the Prayer and Imposition of the *Bishop's Hands* on those who have been already Baptized. But yet against all this Authority, both Divine and Human, and the

---

* *Preservative*, p. 98.   † P. 89.   ‡ P. 101.

express Order of our own Church, your Lordship teaches the Laity, *that all Human Benedictions are useless Niceties ; and that to expect God's Grace from any Hands but his own, is to affront him.*

If so, my Lord, what shall we say in Defence of the Apostles? We read (*Acts* 8. 14) that when *Philip* the Deacon had baptized the *Samaritans*, the Apostles sent *Peter* and *John* to them, who having prayed, and *laid their Hands on them, they received the Holy Ghost, who before was fallen upon none of them ; only they were baptized in the Name of the Lord Jesus.*

My Lord, several things are here out of Question ; *First*, That something else, even in the Apostolical Times, was necessary, besides Baptism, in order to qualify Persons to become complete Members of the Body, or Partakers of the Grace of Christ. They had been baptized, yet did not receive the Holy Ghost, till the Apostles' Hands were laid upon them. *Secondly*, That God's Graces are not only conferred by means of *Human Hands*, but of some particular Hands, and not others. *Thirdly*, That this Office was so strictly appropriated to the Apostles, or Chief Governors of the Church, that it could not be performed by inspired Men, though empowered to work Miracles, who were of an inferior Order ; as *Philip* the Deacon. *Fourthly*, That the Power of the Apostles for the Performance of this Ordinance, was entirely owing to their superior Degree in the Ministry, and not to any extraordinary Gifts they were endowed with : For then *Philip* might have performed it ; who was not wanting in those Gifts, being himself an Evangelist, and Worker of Miracles: Which is a Demonstration, that his Incapacity arose from his inferior Degree in the Ministry.

And now, my Lord, are all *human Benedictions Niceties and Trifles?* Are the Means of God's Grace in his *own Hands alone?* Is it wicked, and *affronting to God*, to suppose the contrary? How then comes *Peter* and *John* to confer the Holy Ghost by the Imposition of their Hands? How comes it, that they appropriate this Office to themselves? Is the Dispensation of God's Grace in his *own Hands alone?* And yet can it be dispensed to us by the Ministry of some Persons, and not by that of others?

Were the Apostles so wicked as to distinguish themselves by a Pretence to vain Powers, which God had reserved to himself; And which your Lordship supposes, from the Title of your *Preservative*, that it is inconsistent with *common Sense*, to imagine that God could or would have communicated to Men?

Had any of your Lordship's well-instructed Laity lived in the Apostles' Days, with what Indignation must they have rejected this senseless chimerical *Claim* of the Apostles? They must have said, Why do you, *Peter* or *John*, pretend to this *Blasphemous Power*? *Whilst we believe the Gospel, we cannot expect the Grace of God from any Hands but his own.* You give us the *Holy Ghost!* You confer the Grace of God! Is it not impious to think, that *he should make our Improvement* in Grace depend upon your Ministry; or hang our Salvation on any *particular* Order of Clergymen? We know, that God is Just, and Good, and True, *and that all* depends upon Him and ourselves, and that *human Benedictions* are *Trifles.* Therefore whether you *Peter*, or you *Philip*, or both, or neither of you lay *your* Hands upon us, we are neither better nor worse; but just in the *same State of Grace* as we were before.

This Representation has not one Syllable in it, but what is founded in your Lordship's Doctrine, and perfectly agreeable to it.

The late most Pious and Learned Bishop *Beveridge* has these remarkable Words upon *Confirmation:* 'How any Bishops in 'our Age dare neglect so considerable a Part of their Office, I 'know not; but fear they will have no good Account to give of 'it, *when they come to stand before God's Tribunal.*'*

But we may justly, and therefore I hope, with Decency, ask your Lordship, how you dare perform this Part of your Office? For you have condemned it as *Trifling* and *Wicked;* as *Trifling*, because it is an *human Benediction;* as *Wicked*, because it supposes Grace conferred by the *Hands of the Bishop.* If therefore any baptized Persons should come to your Lordship for Confirmation, if you are *sincere* in what you have delivered, your Lordship ought, I humbly conceive, to make them this Declaration:

'My Friends, for the sake of *Decency* and *Order*, I have taken 'upon me the Episcopal Character; and, according to Custom, 'which has long prevailed against common Sense, am now to 'lay my Hands upon you: But I beseech you, as you have any 'Regard to the Truth of the Gospel, or to the Honour of God, 'not to imagine there is anything in this Action, more than an 'useless empty Ceremony: For if you expect to have any 'Spiritual Advantage from *human Benedictions*, or to receive 'Grace from the Imposition of a Bishop's Hands, you affront 'God, and in effect, renounce Christianity.'

Pray, my Lord, consider that Passage in the Scripture, where the Apostle speaks of *Leaving the Principles of the Doctrine of Christ, and going on unto Perfection ; not laying again the Foun-*

---

* First Volume of Sermons.

dation of *Repentance from dead Works, of Faith towards God, of the Doctrine of Baptisms, and of Laying on of Hands, and of the Resurrection of the Dead, and of eternal Judgment* (Heb. vi. 1, 2).

My Lord, here it is undeniably plain, that this Laying on of Hands (which is with us called *Confirmation*) is so fundamental a Part of Christ's Religion, that it is called one of the first Principles of the Doctrine of Christ; and is placed amongst such primary Truths, as the Resurrection of the Dead, and of Eternal Judgment.

St. *Cyprian* speaking of this Apostolical Imposition of Hands, says, *The same is now practised with us; they who have been baptized in the Church, are brought to the Presidents of the Church, that by our Prayer and Imposition of Hands, they may receive the Holy Ghost, and be consummated with the Lord's Seal.*

And must we yet believe, that all *human Benedictions* are Dreams, and the Imposition of human Hands trifling and useless; and that to expect God's Graces from them, is to affront him; though the Scriptures expressly teach us, that God confers his Grace by means of certain *particular human Hands*, and not of others; though they tell us, this *human Benediction*, this Laying on of Hands, is one of the first Principles of the Religion of Christ, and as much a Foundation-Doctrine, as the Resurrection of the Dead, and Eternal Judgment; and though every Age since that of the Apostles, has strictly observed it as such, and the Authority of our own Church still requires the Observance of it?

I come now, my Lord, to another sacred and Divine Institution of Christ's Church, which stands exposed and condemned by your Lordship's Doctrine; and that is, the *Ordination* of the Christian Clergy; where, by means of a human Benediction, and the Imposition of the Bishop's Hands, the Holy Ghost is supposed to be conferred on Persons towards consecrating them for the Work of the Ministry.

We find it constantly taught by the Scriptures, that all Ecclesiastical Authority, and the Graces whereby the Clergy are qualified and enabled to exercise their Functions to the Benefit of the Church, are the Gifts and Graces of the Holy Spirit. Thus the Apostle exhorts the Elders *to take heed unto the Flock, over which the Holy Ghost had made them Overseers* (Eph. iv. 7). But how, my Lord, had the Holy Ghost made them Overseers, but by the laying on of the Apostles' Hands? They were not immediately called by the Holy Ghost; but being consecrated by *such human Hands* as had been authorised to that Purpose, they were as truly called by him, and sanctified with Grace for that Employment, as if they had received an immediate or miraculous Commission. So again, St. *Paul* puts *Timothy* in mind *to stir up the Gift of God that was in him, by laying on of his Hands* (2 Tim. ii. 6).

And now, my Lord, if *human Benedictions* be such idle *Dreams* and *Trifles;* if it be *affronting to God*, to expect his Graces from them, or through *human Hands ;* do we not plainly want new Scriptures? Must we not give up the Apostles as furious High-Church Prelates, who aspired to presumptuous Claims, and talked of conferring the Graces of God by their own Hands? Was not this Doctrine as strange and unaccountable then, as at present? Was it not as inconsistent with the Attributes and Sovereignty of God at that Time, to have his Graces pass through other Hands than his own, as in any succeeding Age? Nay, my Lord, where shall we find any Fathers or Councils, in the primitive Church, but who owned and asserted these Powers? They that were so ready to part with their Lives, rather than do the least Dishonour to God, or the Christian Name, yet were all guilty of *this horrid Blasphemy*, in imagining that they were to bless in God's Name; and that by the Benediction and laying on of the Bishop's Hands, the Graces of the Holy Ghost could be conferred on any Persons.

Agreeable to the Sense of Scripture and Antiquity, our Church uses this Form of Ordination : *The Bishop laying his Hands on the Person's Head, saith, Receive the Holy Ghost, for the Office and Work of a Priest in the Church of God, committed unto thee, by the Imposition of our Hands.* From this Form, it is plain, *First,* That our Church holds, that the Reception of the Holy Ghost is necessary to constitute a Person a Christian Priest. *Secondly,* That the Holy Ghost is conferred through *human Hands. Thirdly,* That it is by the Hands of a Bishop that the Holy Ghost is conferred.

If, therefore, your Lordship is right in your Doctrine, the Church of *England* is evidently most corrupt: For if it be dishonourable and affronting to God, to expect his Grace from any human Hands, it must of Necessity be dishonourable and affronting to him, for a Bishop to pretend to confer it by his Hands. And can that Church be any ways defended, that has established such an Iniquity by Law, and made the Form of it so necessary? How can your Lordship answer it to your Laity, for taking the Character or Power of a Bishop from such a Form of Words? You tell them it is affronting to God, to expect his Grace from *human Hands ;* yet, to qualify yourself for a Bishopric, you let human Hands be laid on you, after a Manner which directly supposes you thereby receive the Holy Ghost ! Is it wicked in them to expect it from *human Hands?* And is it less so in your Lordship, to pretend to receive it from human Hands? He that believes it is affronting to God, to expect his Grace from human Hands, must likewise believe, that our Form of Ordination, which promises the Holy Ghost by the *Bishop's Hands*, must be also affronting to God. Certainly he cannot be said to be very jealous of the Honour of God, who will submit himself to be made a Bishop by a Form of Words derogatory, upon his own Principles, to God's Honour.

Suppose your Lordship were to have been consecrated to the Office of a Bishop by these Words; *Take thou Power to sustain all Things in Being, given thee by my Hands.* I suppose your Lordship would think it entirely unlawful to submit to the Form of such an Ordination. But, my Lord, *Receive thou the Holy Ghost, &c.*, is as impious a Form, according to your Lordship's Doctrine, and equally injurious to the eternal Power and Godhead, as the other. For if the Grace of God can only be had from *his own* Hands, would it not be as innocent in the Bishop to say, *Receive thou Power to sustain all Things in Being*, as to say, *Receive the Holy Ghost, by the Imposition of my Hands?* And would not a Compliance with either Form be equally unlawful? According to your Doctrine, in each of them God's Prerogative is equally invaded, and therefore the Guilt must be the same.

It may also well be wondered, how your Lordship can accept of a Character, which is, or ought to be, chiefly distinguished by the Exercise of that Power which you disclaim, as in the Offices of *Confirmation* and *Ordination.* For, my Lord, where can be the Sincerity of saying, *Receive the Holy Ghost by the Imposition of our Hands*, when you declare it affronting to God, to expect it from any Hands but his own? Suppose your Lordship had been preaching to the Laity against owning any Authority in the Virgin *Mary*, and yet should acquiesce in the Conditions of being made a Bishop in her Name, and by recognising her Power; could such a Submission be consistent with Sincerity? Here you forbid the Laity to expect God's Grace from any Hands but his; yet not only accept of an Office, upon Supposition of the contrary Doctrine; but oblige yourself according to the Sense of the Church wherein you are ordained a Bishop, to act frequently in direct Opposition to your own Principles.

So that, I think, it is undeniably plain, that you have at once, my Lord, by these Doctrines condemned the Scriptures, the Apostles, their martyred Successors, the Church of *England*, and your own Conduct; and have thereby given us some Reason (though I wish there were no Occasion to mention it) to suspect, whether you, who allow of no other Church, but what is founded in Sincerity, are yourself really a Member of any Church.

I shall now proceed to say something upon the Consecration of the Lord's Supper, which is as much exposed as a *Trifle*, by your Lordship's Doctrine, as the other Institutions. St. *Paul* says, *The Cup of Blessing which we bless, is it not the Communion of the Blood of Christ?* My Lord, is not this Cup still to be blessed? Must there not therefore be such a Thing as a *human Benediction?* And are human Benedictions to be all despised, though by them the Bread and Wine become Means of Grace, and are made the spiritual Nourishment of our Souls? Can anyone bless this Cup? If not, then there is a Difference between human Benedictions: Some are authorised by God, and their Blessing is effectual; whilst others only are vain and presumptuous. If the Prayer over the Elements, and the Consecration, be only a Trifle and a Dream, and it be offensive to God to expect they are converted into Means of Grace by a human Benediction; why then did St. *Paul* pretend to bless them? Why did he make it the Privilege of the Church? Or, why do we keep up the same Solemnity? But if it be to be blessed only by God's Ministers, then how can your Lordship answer it to God, for ridiculing and abusing human Benedictions, and telling the World that a particular Order of the Clergy are not of any Necessity, nor can be of any Advantage to them? For if the Sacrament can only be blessed by God's Ministers, then such Ministers are as necessary as the Sacraments themselves.

St. *Paul* says, the Cup must be blessed; If you say, anyone may bless it, then, though you contemn the Benedictions of the Clergy, you allow of them by everybody else: If every Body cannot bless it, then you must confess; that the Benedictions of some Persons are effectual, where others are not.

My Lord, the great Sin against the Holy Ghost, was the Denial of his Operation in the Ministry of our Saviour. And how near does your Lordship come to it, in denying the Operation of that same Spirit, in the Ministers whom Christ hath sent? They are employed in the same Work that he was. He left his Authority with them, and promised that the Holy Spirit should remain with them to the End of the World; that whatsoever they should bind on Earth, should be bound in Heaven; and whatsoever they should loose on Earth, should be loosed in Heaven; and that whosoever despises them, despises him, and him that sent him. And yet your Lordship tells us, we need not to trouble our Heads about any particular Sort of Clergy, that all is to be transacted betwixt God and ourselves; that human Benedictions are insignificant Trifles.

But pray what Proof has your Lordship for all this? Have you any Scripture for it? Has God anywhere declared that no Men on Earth have any Authority to bless in his Name? Has he anywhere said, that it is a wicked, presumptuous Thing, for anyone to pretend to it? Has he anywhere told us that it is inconsistent with his Honour to bestow his Graces by *human Hands*? Has he anywhere told us that he has no Ministers, no Ambassadors on Earth; but that all his Gifts and Graces are to be received immediately from his own Hands? Have you any Antiquity, Fathers, or Councils, on your Side? No; the whole Tenor of Scripture, the whole Current of Tradition is against you: Your novel Doctrine has only this to recommend it to the Libertines of the Age, who universally give into it, that it never was the Opinion of any Church, or Churchman. It is your Lordship's proper Assertion, *That we offend God in expecting his Graces from any Hands but his own.*

Now it is strange, that God should be offended with his own Methods, or that your Lordship should find us out a Way of pleasing him, more suitable to his Nature and Attributes, than what he has taught us in the Scriptures. I call them his own Methods; for what else is the whole *Jewish* Dispensation, but a Method of God's Providence, where his Blessings and Judgments were dispensed by *human Hands*? What is the Christian Religion but a Method of Salvation, where the chief Means of Grace are offered and dispensed by human Hands? Let me here recommend to your Lordship, the excellent Words of a very learned and judicious Prelate on this Occasion.

'This will have no Weight with any reasonable Man, against
'the Censures of the Church, or any other Ordinance of the
'Gospel, that they make the Intervention of other Men necessary
'to our Salvation; since it has always been God's ordinary
'Method, to dispense his Blessings and Judgments by the Hands
'of Men.'*

Your Lordship exclaims against your Adversaries as such romantic strange sort of Men, for talking of Benedictions and Absolutions, and of the Necessity of receiving God's Ordinances from proper Hands: Yet, my Lord, here is an excellent Bishop, against whose *Learning, Judgment,* and *Protestantism,* there can be no Objection; who says, if a Person has but the *Use of his Reason,* he will have nothing to object to any Ordinances of the Gospel, which make the Intervention of other Men necessary

---

* *Dr.* Potter's *Church Government,* p. 336.

towards the Conveyance of them, since that has always been God's ordinary Method. The Bishop does not say, it is necessary a Man should be a *great Divine* to acknowledge it; so he be but a *reasonable Man*, he will allow it. Yet your Lordship is so far from being this *reasonable Man*, that you think your Adversaries void both of Reason and common Sense, for teaching it. You expressly exclude *all* Persons from having any Thing to do with our Salvation, and say, it wholly depends upon God and ourselves.

You tell us, that *authoritative Benediction is another of the Terms of Art used by your Protestant Adversaries; in which they claim a Right, in one regular Succession, of blessing the People.** An ingenious Author, my Lord, (in the Opinion of many, if not of most of your Friends) calls the *Consecration* of the Elements *Conjuration*:† Your Lordship calls the *Sacerdotal Benediction* a *Term of Art;* too plain an Intimation, though in more remote and somewhat softer Terms, that in the Sense of a *certain Father* of the Church, her Clergy are little better than so many Jugglers.

Your Lordship says, *If they only meant hereby to declare upon what Terms God will give his Blessings* to Christians, *or to express their own hearty Wishes for them, this might be understood.* So it might, my Lord, very easily; and I suppose every Body understands that they may do this, whether they be Clergy or Laity, Men or Women: For I presume anyone may declare what he takes to be the Terms of the Gospel, and wish that others may faithfully observe them. But I humbly presume, my Lord, that the good Bishop above-mentioned meant something more than this, when he spake of *Ordinances which make the Intervention of other Men* necessary *to our Salvation, and of God's dispensing his Blessings* in virtue of them through their Hands.

There is a superstitious Custom (in your Lordship's Account it must be so) yet remaining in most Places, of sending for a Clergyman to minister to sick Persons in imminent Danger of Death: Even those who have abused the Clergy all their Lives long, are glad to beg their Assistance when they apprehend themselves upon the Confines of another World. There is no Reason, my Lord, to dislike this *Practice*, but as it supposes a Difference between the *Sacerdotal Prayers* and *Benedictions*, and those of a Nurse.

We read, my Lord, that God would not heal *Abimelech*, though he knew the Integrity of his Heart, till *Abraham* had prayed for

---

* Page 91.   † *Rites of the Christian Church.*

him: *He is a Prophet*, said God, *he shall pray for thee, and thou shalt live* (Gen. xx. 7).

Pray, my Lord, was not God just, and good, and true, in the Days of *Abraham*, as he is now? Yet you see, *Abimelech's Integrity* was not available itself. He was to be pardoned by the Prayer of *Abraham*, and his Prayer was effectual; and so represented, because it was the Prayer of a *Prophet*.

Suppose, my Lord, that *Abimelech* had said with your Lordship, *That it is affronting to God, that we should expect his Graces from any Hands* but his own; *that all is to be transacted between God and ourselves;* and so had rejected the Prayer of *Abraham*, as a mere Essay of *Prophet-Craft;* he had then acted with as much Prudence and Piety as your Lordship's Laity would do, if you could persuade them to despise *Benedictions* and *Absolutions*, to regard no *particular sort of Clergy;* but entirely depend upon God and themselves, without any other Assistance whatever.

We read also, *that* Joshua *was full of the Spirit of Wisdom, for* Moses *had laid his Hands upon him* (Deut. xxxiv. 9). Was it not as absurd, my Lord, in the Days of *Joshua*, for *human Hands* to *bless*, as it is now? Did there not then lie the same Objection against *Moses*, that there does now against the Christian Clergy? Had *Moses* any more *natural Power* to give the Spirit of Wisdom, &c., by his Hands, than the Clergy have to confer Grace by theirs? They are both equally weak and insufficient for these Purposes of themselves, and equally powerful when it pleases God to make them so.

Again, when *Eliphaz* and his Friends had displeased God, they were not to be reconciled to God by their own Repentance, or transact that Matter only between God and themselves; but they were referred to apply to *Job*. *My Servant* Job *shall pray for you, for him will I accept* (Job xlii. 8). Might not *Eliphaz* here have said, shall I so far affront God, as to think I cannot be blessed without the Prayers of *Job?* Shall I be so weak or senseless, as to imagine, my own Supplications and Repentance will not save me; or that I need apply to any one but God alone, to qualify me for the Reception of his Grace?

Again, *The Lord spake unto Moses, saying, speak unto Aaron and his sons, saying, on this wise shall ye bless the children of Israel, saying unto them,* The Lord bless and keep thee, &c., *and I will bless them* (Numb. vi. 22).

Again, *The Priests of the Sons of Levi shall come near; for them hath the Lord thy God chosen to minister unto him, and to bless in the Name of the Lord* (Deut. xxi. 5).

Now, my Lord, this is what we mean by the authoritative

Administrations of the Christian Clergy; whether they be by way of Benediction, or of any other kind. We take them to be Persons whom God has chosen to minister unto him, and to bless in his Name. We imagine that our Saviour was a greater *Priest and Mediator* than *Aaron*, or any of God's former Ministers. We are assured that Christ sent his Apostles, as his Father had sent him, and that therefore they were his true Successors: And since they did commission others to succeed them in their Office, by the Imposition of Hands, as *Moses* commissioned *Joshua* to succeed him; the Clergy who have succeeded the Apostles, have as divine a Call and Commission to their Work, as those who were called by our Saviour; and are as truly his Successors, as the Apostles themselves were.

From the Places of Scripture above-mentioned, it is evident, and indeed from the whole Tenor of Sacred Writ, that it may consist with the Goodness and Justness of God to depute Men to act in his Name, and be ministerial towards the Salvation of others; and to lay a Necessity upon his Creatures of qualifying themselves for his Favour, and receiving his Graces by the Hands and Intervention of mere Men.

But, my Lord, if there be now any Set of Men upon Earth that are more peculiarly God's Ministers than others, and through whose Administrations, Prayers, and Benedictions, God will accept of returning Sinners, and receive them to Grace; you have done all you can to prejudice People against them: You have taught the Laity that all is to be transacted between God and themselves, and that they need not value any particular Sort of Clergy in the World.

I leave it to the Great Judge and Searcher of Hearts, to judge from what Principles, or upon what Motives your Lordship has been induced to teach these Things; but must declare, that, for my own Part, if I had the greatest Hatred to Christianity, I should think it could not be more expressed than by teaching what your Lordship has publicly taught. If I could rejoice in the Misery and Ruin of Sinners, I should think it sufficient Matter of Triumph, to drive them from the Ministers of God, and to put them upon inventing new Schemes of saving themselves instead of submitting to the ordinary Methods of Salvation appointed by God.

It will not follow from anything I have said, that the Laity have lost their Christian Liberty, or that no Body can be saved but whom the Clergy please to save; that they have the arbitrary Disposal of Happiness to Mankind. Was *Abimelech's* Happiness in the Disposition of *Abraham*, because he was to be received by Means of *Abraham's* Intercession? Or could *Job* damn *Eliphaz*, because he was to mediate for him, and procure his Reconciliation to God?

Neither, my Lord, do the *Christian Clergy* pretend to this despotic Empire over their Flocks. They do not assume to themselves a Power to damn the Innocent, or to save the Guilty; but they assert a sober and just Right to reconcile Men to God, and to act in his Name, in restoring them to his Favour. They received their Commission from those whom Christ sent with full Authority to send others, and with a Promise that he would be with them to the End of the World. From this they conclude, that they have his Authority, and that in consequence of it, their Administrations are necessary, and effectual to the Salvation of Mankind; and that none can despise them, but who despise him that sent them; and are as surely out of the Covenant of Grace, when they leave such his Pastors, as when they openly despise, or omit to receive his Sacraments.

And what is there in this Doctrine, my Lord, to terrify the *Consciences* of the *Laity?* What is there here to bring the profane Scandal of *Priestcraft* upon the *Clergy?* Could it be any Ground of *Abimelech's* hating *Abraham*, because that *Abraham* was to reconcile him to God? Could *Eliphaz* justly have any Prejudice against *Job*, because God would hear *Job's* Intercession for him? Why then, my Lord, must the Christian Priesthood be so horrid and hateful an Institution, because the Design of it is to restore Men to the Grace and Favour of God? Why must we be abused and insulted for being sent upon the Errand of Salvation, and made Ministers of eternal Happiness to our Brethren? There is a Woe due to us if we preach not the Gospel, or neglect those ministerial Offices that Christ hath entrusted to us. We are to watch for their Souls, as those who are to give an Account. Why then must we be treated as arrogant Priests, or *popishly* affected, for pretending to have any Thing to do in the Discharge of our *Ministry* with the Salvation of Men? Why must we be reproached with *blasphemous Claims*, and *absurd senseless Powers*, for assuming to bless in God's Name, or thinking our Administrations more effectual than the Office of a common *Layman?*

But farther, To what Purpose does your Lordship except against these Powers in the *Clergy*, from their *common Frailties* and *Infirmities* with the rest of Mankind? Were not *Abraham* and *Job*, and the *Jewish* Priests, Men of like Passions with us? Did not our Saviour command the *Jews* to apply to their Priests, notwithstanding their personal Faults, because they sat in *Moses'* Chair? Did not the Apostles assure their Followers that they were Men of like Passions with them? But did they therefore disclaim their Mission, or Apostolical Authority? Did they teach, that their natural Infirmities made them less the Ministers of God, or less necessary to the Salvation of Men? Their personal Defects did not make them depart from the Claim of those Powers they were invested with, or desert their Ministry, but, indeed, gave St. *Paul* Occasion to say, *We have this Treasure in earthen Vessels,* (*i.e.*, this Authority committed to mere Men) *that the excellency of it may be of God, and not of Men.* The Apostle happens to differ very much from your Lordship: He says, such weak Instruments were made use of that the Glory might redound to God. Your Lordship says, to suppose Instruments to be of any Benefit to us, is to lessen the Sovereignty of God, and, in Consequence, his Glory.

Your Lordship imagines you have sufficiently destroyed the *sacerdotal Powers*, by showing, that the Clergy are only Men, and subject to the common Frailties of Mankind. My Lord, we own the Charge, and do not claim any *sacerdotal Powers* from our personal Abilities, or to acquire any Glory to ourselves. But, weak as we are, we are God's Ministers, and if we are either afraid or ashamed of our Duty, we must perish in the Guilt. But is a Prophet therefore proud, because he insists upon the Authority of his Mission? Cannot a Mortal be God's Messenger, and employed in his Affairs, but he must be insolent and assuming, for having the Resolution to own it? If we are to be reproved for pretending to be God's Ministers, because we are but Men, the Reproach will fall upon Providence; since it has pleased God, chiefly to transact his Affairs with Mankind by the Ministry of their Brethren.

Your Lordship has not one Word from Scripture against these sacerdotal Powers; no Proof that Christ has not sent Men to be effectual Administrators of his Graces: You only assert, that there can be no such Ministers, because they are mere Men.

Now, my Lord, I must beg Leave to say, that if the natural Weakness of Men makes them incapable of being the Instruments of conveying Grace to their Brethren; if the Clergy cannot be of any Use or Necessity to their Flocks, for this Reason; then it undeniably follows, that there can be no *positive Institutions* in the Christian Religion that can procure any spiritual Advantages to the Members of it; then the Sacraments can be no longer any Means of Grace. For, I hope, no one thinks that Bread and Wine have any natural Force or Efficacy to convey Grace to the Soul. The Water in Baptism has the common Qualities of Water, and is destitute of any intrinsic Power to cleanse the Soul, or purify from Sin. But your Lordship will not say, because it has only the common Nature of Water, that therefore it cannot be a Means of Grace. Why then may not the Clergy, though they have the common Nature of Men, be constituted by God, to convey his Graces, and to be ministerial to the Salvation of their Brethren? Can God consecrate inanimate Things to spiritual Purposes, and make them the Means of eternal Happiness? And is Man the only Creature that he cannot make subservient to his Designs? The only *Being*, who is too weak for an Omnipotent God to render effectual towards attaining the Ends of his Grace?

Is it just and reasonable, to reject and despise the *Ministry* and *Benedictions* of Men, because they are Men like ourselves? And is it not as reasonable, to despise the Sprinkling of Water, a Creature below us, a senseless and inanimate Creature?

Your Lordship therefore, must either find us some other Reason for rejecting the Necessity of *human Administrations*, than because they are *human;* or else give up the Sacraments, and *all* positive Institutions along with them.

Surely, your Lordship must have a mighty Opinion of *Naaman* the *Syrian*, who, when the Prophet bid him go wash in *Jordan* seven times, to the end he might be clean from his Leprosy, very *wisely* remonstrated, *Are not* Abana *and* Pharpar, *Rivers of* Damascus, *better than all the Waters of* Israel?

This, my Lord, discovered *Naaman's* great Liberty of Mind; and it is much, this has not been produced before, as an Argument of his being a *Free-Thinker*. He took the Water of *Jordan* to be *only Water;* as your Lordship justly observes a Clergyman to be *only* a Man: And if you had been with him, you could have informed him, that the washing *seven Times* was a mere *Nicety* and *Trifle* of the Prophet; and that since it is God alone who can work *miraculous Cures*, we ought not to think, that they depend upon any external Means, or any stated Number of repeating them.

This, my Lord, is the true Scope and Spirit of your Argument: If the *Syrian* was right in despising the Water of *Jordan*, because it was only *Water;* your Lordship might be right in despising any particular Order of Clergy, because they are but Men. Your Lordship is certainly as right, or as wrong, as he was.

And now, my Lord, let the common Sense of Mankind here judge, whether, if the Clergy are to be esteemed as having no Authority, because they are but Men; it does not plainly follow, that everything else, every Institution that has not some *natural* Force and Power to produce the Effects designed by it, is not also to be rejected as equally trifling and ineffectual.

The Sum of the Matter is this: It appears from many express Facts, and indeed, from the whole Series of God's Providence, that it is not only consistent with his Attributes, but also agreeable to his ordinary Methods of dealing with Mankind, that he should substitute Men to act in his Name, and be *authoritatively* employed in conferring his Graces and Favours upon Mankind. It appears, that your Lordship's Argument against the authoritative Administrations of the Christian Clergy, does not only contradict those Facts, and condemn the ordinary Method of God's Dispensations; but likewise proves the Sacraments, and every positive Institution of Christianity, to be ineffectual, and as mere *Dreams* and *Trifles*, as the several *Offices and Orders* of the Clergy.

This, I hope, will be esteemed a sufficient Confutation of your Lordship's Doctrine, by all who have any true Regard or Zeal for the Christian Religion; and only expect to be saved by the Methods of divine Grace proposed in the Gospel.

I shall now in a word or two set forth the Sacredness of the Ecclesiastical Character, as it is founded in the New Testament; with a particular regard to the Power of conferring Grace, and the Efficacy of human Benedictions.

It appears therein that all sacerdotal Power is derived from the Holy Ghost. Our Saviour himself took not that Ministry upon him, till he had this Consecration: And during the time of his Ministry, he was under the Guidance and Direction of the Holy Ghost. Through the Holy Spirit he gave Commandment to the Apostles whom he had chosen. When he ordained them to the Work of the Ministry, it was with these Words, *Receive the Holy Ghost.* Those whom the Apostles ordained to the same Function, it was by the same Authority: They laid their Hands upon the Elders, exhorting them to take care of the Flock of Christ, over which the Holy Ghost had made them Overseers.

Hereby they plainly declared, that however this Office was to descend from Man to Man through *human Hands*, that it was the Holy Ghost which consecrated them to that Employment, and gave them Authority to execute it.

From this it is also manifest, that the Priesthood is a Grace of the Holy Ghost: That it is not a Function founded on the Natural or Civil Rights of Mankind, but is derived from the special Authority of the Holy Ghost; and is as truly a positive Institution as the Sacraments. So that they who have no Authority to alter the Old Sacraments, and substitute New ones, have no Power to alter the Old Order of the Clergy, or introduce any other Order of them.

For why can we not change the Sacraments? Is it not because they are only Sacraments, and operate as they are instituted by the Holy Ghost? Because they are useless ineffectual Rites without this Authority? And does not the same Reason hold as well for the Order of the Clergy? Does not the same Scripture tell us, they are equally instituted by the Holy Ghost, and oblige only by virtue of his Authority? How absurd is it therefore to pretend to abolish, or depart from the settled Order of the Clergy, to make new Orders, or think any God's Ministers, unless we had his Authority, and could make new Sacraments, or a new Religion?

My Lord, how comes it, That we cannot alter the Scriptures? Is it not, because they are Divinely inspired, and dictated by the Holy Ghost? And since it is express Scripture, That the *Priesthood* is instituted and authorised by the same Holy Spirit, Why is not the Holy Ghost as much to be regarded in one Institution, as in another? Why may we not as well make a Gospel, and say, it was writ by the Holy Ghost, as make a new Order of Clergy, and call them his? Or esteem them as having any relation to him?

From this it likewise appears, That there is an absolute Necessity of a strict Succession of authorised Ordainers from the Apostolical Times, in order to constitute a *Christian Priest*. For since a Commission from the Holy Ghost is necessary for the exercise of this Office; no one now can receive it, but from those who have derived their Authority in a true Succession, from the Apostles. We could not, my Lord, call our present Bibles *the Word of God*, unless we knew the Copies from which they are taken were taken from other true ones, till we come to the Originals themselves. No more could we call any true Ministers, or authorised by the Holy Ghost, who have not received their Commission by an uninterrupted Succession of lawful Ordainers.

What an excellent Divine would he be, who should tell the World, it was not necessary that the several Copies and Manuscripts through which the Scriptures have been transmitted through different Ages and Languages, should be all true ones, and none of them forged? That *this was a Thing subject to so great Uncertainty, that God could not hang our Salvation on such Niceties?* Suppose, for Proof of this, he should appeal to the Scriptures; and ask, where any mention is made of ascertaining the Truth of all the Copies? Would not this be a Way of Arguing very Theological? The Application is very easy.

Your Lordship has not one Word to prove the uninterrupted Succession of the Clergy a *Trifle* or *Dream;* but that it is subject to so great Uncertainty, and is never mentioned in the Scriptures. As to the Uncertainty of it, it is equally as uncertain, as whether the Scriptures be *Genuine*. There is just the same sufficient Historical Evidence for the Certainty of one as the other. As to its not being mentioned in the Scripture, the Doctrine upon which it is founded, plainly made it unnecessary to mention it. Is it needful for the Scriptures to tell us, that if we take our Bible from any false Copy, that it is not the Word of God? Why then need they tell us, that if we are ordained by usurping false Pretenders to Ordination, nor deriving their Authority to that end from the Apostles, that we are no Priests? Does not the thing itself speak as plain in one Case as in the other? The Scriptures are only of use to us, as they are the Word of God: We cannot have this Word of God, which was written so many Years ago, unless we receive it from authentic Copies and Manuscripts.

The Clergy have their Commission from the Holy Ghost: The Power of conferring this Commission of the Holy Ghost, was left with the Apostles: Therefore the present Clergy cannot have the same Commission, or Call, but from an Order of Men, who have successively conveyed this Power from the Apostles to the present time. So that, my Lord, I shall beg leave to lay it down, as a plain, undeniable, Christian Truth, that the Order of the Clergy is an Order of as necessary Obligation as the Sacraments; and as unalterable as the Holy Scriptures; the same Holy Ghost being as truly the Author and Founder of the Priesthood, as the Institutor of the Sacraments, or the Inspirer of those Divine Oracles. And when your Lordship shall offer any fresh Arguments to prove that no particular sort of Clergy is necessary; that the Benedictions and Administrations of the present Clergy of our most excellent Church, are trifling Niceties; if I cannot show that the same Arguments will conclude against the Authority of the Sacraments and the Scriptures, I faithfully promise your Lordship to become a Convert to your Doctrine.

What your Lordship charges upon your Adversaries, as an absurd Doctrine, in pretending the Necessity of one regular, successive, and particular Order of the Clergy, is a true Christian Doctrine; and as certain from Scripture, as that we are to keep to the Institution of particular Sacraments; or not to alter those particular Scriptures, which now compose the Canon of the old and new Testament.

By authoritative Benediction, we do not mean any natural or intrinsic Authority of our own: But a Commission from God, to be effectual Administrators of his Ordinances, and to bless in his

Name. Thus, a Person who is sent from God, to foretell things, of which he had before no Knowledge or Notion; or to denounce Judgments, which he has no natural Power to execute; may truly be said to be an *authoritative Prophet;* because he has the Authority of God for what he does. Thus, when the Bishop is said to confer Grace in Confirmation, this is properly an *authoritative Benediction;* because he is then as truly doing what God has commissioned him to do, as when a Prophet declares upon what Errand he is sent.

It is in this Sense, my Lord, that the People are said to be *authoritatively* blessed by the regular Clergy; because they are *God's Clergy*, and act by his Commission; because by their Hands the People receive the Graces and Benefits of God's Ordinances; which they have no more Reason to expect from other Ministers of their own Election, or if the Word may be used in an abusive Sense, of their own *Consecration*, than to receive Grace from Sacraments of their own Appointment. The Scriptures teach us, That the Holy Ghost has instituted an Order of Clergy: We say, a Priesthood, so authorised, can no more be changed by us, than we can change the Scriptures, or make new Sacraments; because they are all founded on the same Authority, without any Power of a Dispensation delegated to us in one Case more than another. If therefore we have a Mind to continue in the Covenant of Christ, and receive the Grace and Benefit of his Ordinances, we must receive them through such Hands as he has authorised for that Purpose, to the end we may be qualified to partake of the Blessings of them. For as a *true* Priest cannot benefit us by administering a *false* Sacrament; so a *true* Sacrament is nothing, when it is administered by a *false uncommissioned Minister*. Besides this Benediction which attends the Ordinances of God, when they are thus performed by authorised Hands, there is a Benediction of Prayer, which we may justly think very effectual, when pronounced or dispensed by the same Hands.

Thus when the Bishop or Priest intercedes for the Congregation, or pronounces the Apostolical Benediction upon them, we do not consider this barely as an Act of Charity and Humanity, of one Christian praying for another; but as the Work of a Person who is commissioned by God to *bless in his Name,* and be effectually ministerial in the Conveyance of his Graces; or as the Prayer of one who is left with us in Christ's stead, to carry on his great Design of saving us; and whose Benedictions are ever ratified in Heaven, but when we render ourselves in one Respect or other incapable of them.

Now, my Lord, they are these *sacerdotal Prayers*, these authorised Sacraments, these commissioned Pastors, whom the Holy Ghost has made Overseers of the Flock of Christ, that your Lordship encourages the Laity to despise. You bid them *contemn the vain Words of Validity or Invalidity of God's Ordinances;* to *heed no particular sort of Clergy, or the pretended Necessity of their Administrations.*

Your Lordship sets up in this Controversy for an Advocate for the Laity, against the *arrogant Pretences,* and *false Claims* of the Clergy. My Lord, we are no more contending for ourselves in this Doctrine, than when we insist upon any Article in the Creed. Neither is it any more our particular Cause, when we assert our Mission, than when we assert the Necessity of the Sacraments.

Who is to receive the Benefit of that Commission which we assert, but they? Who is to suffer, if we pretend a false one, but ourselves? Sad Injury, indeed, offered to the Laity! that we should affect to be thought Ministers of God for their Sakes! If we really are so, they are to receive the Benefit; if not, we are to bear the Punishment.

But your Lordship comes too late in this glorious Undertaking, to receive the Reputation of it; the Work has been already, in the Opinion of most People, better done to your Lordship's Hands. The famous Author of *The Rites of the Christian Church,* has carried this *Christian Liberty* to as great Heights as your Lordship. And though you have not one Notion, I can recollect, that has given Offence to the World, but what seems taken from that pernicious Book; yet your Lordship is not so just as ever once to cite or mention the Author; who, if your Lordship's Doctrine be true, deserves to have a Statue erected to his Honour, and receive every Mark of Esteem which is due to the greatest Reformer of Religion.

Did not mine own Eyes assure me that he has cast no Contempt upon the Church, no Reproach upon the Evangelical Institutions, or the Sacred Function, but what has been seconded by your Lordship, I would never have placed your Lordship in the same View with so scandalous a Declaimer against the Ordinances of Christ. Whether I am right, or not, in this Charge, I freely leave to the Judgment of those to determine, who are acquainted with both your Works. Yet this Author, my Lord, has been treated by the greatest and best Part of the Nation, as a Free-thinking Infidel. But for what, my Lord? Not that he has declared against the Scriptures; not that he has rejected Revelation; (we are not, blessed be God, still so far corrupted with the Principles of Infidelity) but because he has reproached every particular Church, as such, and denied all

Obligation to Communion; because he has exposed Benedictions, Absolutions, and Excommunications; denied the Divine Right of the Clergy, and ridiculed the pretended Sacredness and Necessity of their Administrations, as mere Niceties and Trifles, though commonly in more distant, I was going to say more decent Ways: In a Word, because he made all Churches, all Priests, all Sacraments, however administered, equally valid, and denied any particular Method necessary to Salvation. Yet after all this profane Declamation, he allows, my Lord, that *Religious Offices may be appropriated to particular Men, called* Clergy, *for Order sake only; and not on the Account of any peculiar Spiritual Advantages, Powers, or Privileges, which those who are set apart for them, have from Heaven.**

Agreeable to this, your Lordship owns, that you are not against the *Order*, or *Decency*, or *Subordination belonging to Christian Societies*.†

But, pray, my Lord, do you mean any more by this, than the above-mentioned Author? Is it for any Thing, but the Sake of a little external *Order* or *Conveniency*? Is there any Christian Law that obliges to observe this kind of Order? Is there any real essential Difference between Persons ranked into this Order? Is it a Sin for any Body, especially the Civil Magistrate, to leave this Order, and make what other Orders he prefers to it? This your Lordship cannot resolve in the Affirmative; for then you must allow, that some Communions are safer than others, and that some Clergy have more Authority than others.

Will your Lordship say, that no *particular* Order can be necessary; yet some Order necessary, which may be different in different Communions? This cannot hold good upon your Lordship's Principles; for since Christ has left no Law about any Order, no Members of any particular Communion need submit to that Order; since it is confessed by your Lordship, That in Religion no Laws, but those of Christ, are of any Obligation. So that though you do not disclaim all external Order and Decency yourself, yet you have taught other People to do it if they please, and as much as they please.

Suppose, my Lord, some Layman, upon a Pretence of your Lordship's Absence, or any other, should go into the Diocese of *Bangor*, and there pretend to ordain Clergymen; could your Lordship quote one Text of Scripture against him? Could you allege any Law of Christ, or his Apostles, that he had broken? Could you prove him guilty of any Sin? No, my Lord, you would not do that; because this would be acknowledging such a

---

* Page 131.   † *Answer to Dr.* Snape, p. 48.

Thing as a *Sinful Ordination*; and if there be Sinful Ordinations, then there must be some Law concerning Ordinations: For *Sin is the Transgression of the Law*: And if there be a Law concerning Ordinations, then we must keep to the Clergy *lawfully* ordained; and must confess, after all your Lordship has said, or can say, that still some Communions are safer than others.

If you should reprove such a one, as an *Englishman*, for acting in Opposition to the *English* Laws of *Decency* and *Order*; he would answer, That he has nothing to do with such *Trifles*; That Christ was sole Lawgiver in his Kingdom; That he was content to have his Kingdom as *orderly* and *decent* as Christ had left it; and since he had instituted no Laws in that Matter, it was presuming, for others to take upon them to add any Thing by way of *Order* or *Decency*, by Laws of their own: That as he had as much Authority from Christ to ordain Clergy as your Lordship, he would not depart from his Christian Liberty.

If he should remonstrate to your Lordship in these, or Words to the like Effect, he would only reduce your Lordship's own Doctrine to Practice. This, my Lord, is part of that Confusion the learned Dr. *Snape* has charged you with being the Author of, in the Church of God: And all Persons, my Lord, whom you have taught not to regard any particular Sort of Clergy, must know (if they have the common Sense to which you appeal) that then no Clergy are at all necessary; and that it is as lawful for any Man to be his own Priest, as to solicit his own Cause. For to say that no particular Sort of Clergy are necessary, and yet that in general the Clergy are necessary, is the same as to say, that Truth is necessary to be believed; yet the Belief of no particular Truth is necessary.

The next Thing to be considered, my Lord, is your Doctrine concerning Absolutions. You begin thus: *The same you will find a sufficient Reply to their presumptuous Claim to an authoritative Absolution. An infallible Absolution cannot belong to fallible Man. But no Absolution can be authoritative, which is not infallible. Therefore no authoritative Absolution can belong to any Man living.**

I must observe here, your Lordship does not reject this *Absolution*, because the Claim of it is not founded in Scripture; but by an Argument drawn from the Nature of the Thing: Because you imagine such Absolution requires Infallibility for the Execution of it; therefore it cannot belong to Men. Should this be true, it would prove, that if our Saviour had really so intended, he could not have given this Power to his Ministers. But, my

---

* *Preservative*, p. 92.

Lord, who can see any Repugnancy in the Reason of the Thing itself? Is it not as easy to conceive, that our Lord should confer his Grace of Pardon by the Hands of his Ministers, as by Means of the Sacraments? And may not such Absolution be justly called *authoritative*, the Power of which is granted, and executed by his Authority?

Is it impossible for Men to have this Authority from God, because they may mistake in the Exercise of it? This Argument proves too much, and makes as short Work with every Institution of Christianity, as with the Power of Absolution.

For if it is impossible that Men should have Authority from God to absolve in his Name, because they are not infallible; this makes them equally incapable of being entrusted with any other Means of Grace; and consequently supposes the whole Priest's Office to imply a direct Impossibility in the very Notion of it.

Your Lordship's Argument is this: Christians have their Sins pardoned upon certain Conditions; but fallible Men cannot certainly know these Conditions: Therefore fallible Men cannot have Authority to *absolve*.

From hence I take Occasion to argue thus: Persons are to be admitted to the Sacraments on certain Conditions; but fallible Men cannot tell whether they come qualified to receive them according to these Conditions: Therefore fallible Men cannot have Authority to administer the Sacraments.

2ndly, This Argument subverts all Authority of the Christian Religion itself, and the Reason of every instituted Means of Grace. For if nothing can be authoritative, but what a Man is infallibly assured of, then the Christian Religion cannot be an authoritative Method of Salvation; since a Man, by being a Christian, does not become infallibly certain of his Salvation: Nor does Grace infallibly attend the Participation of the Sacraments. So that though your Lordship has formed this Argument only against this absolving Power, yet it has as much Force against the Sacraments, and the Christian Religion itself. For if it be absurd to suppose that the Priest should absolve anyone, because he cannot be certain that he deserves Absolution; does it not imply the same Absurdity, to suppose that he should have the Power of administering the Sacraments, when he cannot be *infallibly certain* that those who receive them are duly qualified? If a Possibility of Error destroys the Power in one Case, it as certainly destroys it in the other. Again, if Absolution cannot be authoritative, unless it be infallible; then it is plain that the Christian Religion is not an authoritative Means of Salvation; because all Christians are not infallibly saved: Nor can the

the Bishop of Bangor.   49

Sacraments be authoritative Means of Grace, because all who partake of them do not infallibly obtain Grace.

Your Lordship proceeds with your Laity by way of Expostulation : *If they amuse you with that Power which Christ left with his Apostles, Whose soever Sins ye remit, they are remitted unto them ; and whose soever Sins ye retain, they are retained unto them :**

But why *amuse*, my Lord ? Are the Texts of Holy Scripture to be treated only as Matter of *Amusement* ? Or does your Lordship know of any Age in the Church when the very same Doctrine which we now teach, has not been taught from the same Texts?

Do you know any Successors of the Apostles that thought the Power there specified did not belong to them ? But, however, your Lordship has taught your Laity to believe what we argue from this Text, all Amusement; and told them, *They may securely answer, that it is impossible for them to depend upon this Right as anything certain, till they can prove to you that everything spoken to the Apostles, belongs to Ministers in all Ages.*† The Security of this Answer, my Lord, is founded upon this false Presumption, *viz*, That the Clergy can claim no Right to the Exercise of any Part of their Office, *as Successors of the Apostles*, till they can prove that every Thing that was spoken to the Apostles, belongs to them.

This Proposition must be true, or else there is no Force or *Security* in the Objection you here bring for the Instruction of the Laity. If it is well founded, then the Clergy cannot possibly prove they have any more Right to the Exercise of any Part of their Office than the Laity. Do they pretend to ordain, confirm, to admit or exclude Men from the Sacraments? By what Authority is all this done ? Is it not because the Apostles, whose Successors they are, did the same Things ? But then, say your Lordship's well-instructed Laity, this is nothing to the Purpose : Prove yourselves Apostles ; prove that every Thing said to the Apostles belongs to you ; and then it will be allowed, that you may exercise these Powers, because they exercised them : But as this is impossible to be done, so it is impossible for you to prove that you have any Powers or Authorities, because they had them.

And now, my Lord, if the Case be thus, what Apology shall we make for Christianity, as it has been practised in all Ages? How shall we excuse the Noble Army of Martyrs, Saints, and Confessors, who have boldly asserted the Right to so many

---

* Page 93.   † Page 94.

Apostolical Powers? Could any Men in these Ages pretend, *that everything that was spoken to the Apostles, belonged to themselves?* False, then, was their Claim, and presumptuous their Authority, who should pretend any Apostolical Powers, because the Apostles had them; when they could not prove, *that everything that was spoken to the Apostles, belonged to them.*

Farther; To prove that the above-mentioned Text does not confer the Power of Absolution in the Clergy, you reason thus: *Whatever contradicts the Natural Notions of God, and the Design and Tenor of the Gospel, cannot be the true Meaning of any Passage in the Gospel: But to make the Absolution of weak and fallible Men so necessary, or so valid, that God will not pardon without them; or that all are pardoned who have them pronounced over them, is to contradict those Notions, as well as the plain Tenor of the Gospel.**

Be pleased, my Lord, to point out your Adversary; name any one Church of *England* Man that ever taught this romantic Doctrine which you are confuting. Who ever taught such a Necessity of Absolutions, that God will pardon none without them? Who ever declared that all are pardoned who have them pronounced over them? We teach the *Necessity* and *Validity* of Sacraments; but do we ever declare that all are saved who receive them? Is there no *Medium* between two Extremes? No such Thing, my Lord, as *Moderation!* Must every Thing be thus absolute and extravagant, or nothing at all?

In another Page we have more of this same Colouring: *But to claim a Right to stand in God's Stead, in such a Sense, that they can absolutely and certainly bless, or not bless, with their Voice alone: This is the highest Absurdity and Blasphemy as it supposeth God to place a Set of Men above himself; and to put out of his own Hands the Disposal of his Blessings and Curses.*†

If your Lordship had employed all this Oratory against worshipping the Sun or Moon, it had just affected your Adversaries as much as this. For who ever taught that any Set of Men could *absolutely* bless, or withhold Blessing, independent of God? Who ever taught, that the Christian Religion, or Sacraments, or Absolution, saved People on course, or without proper Dispositions? Whoever claimed such an absolving Power, as to set himself above God, and to take from him the Disposal of his own Blessings and Curses? What has such extravagant Descriptions, such romantic Characters of Absolution, to do with that Power the Clergy justly claim? Cannot there be a Necessity

---

* Page 93.   † Page 91.

in some Cases of receiving Absolution from their Hands, except they set themselves above God? Is God robbed of the Disposal of his Blessings, when, in Obedience to his own Commands, and in virtue of his own Authority, they admit some as Members of the Church, and exclude others from the Communion of it? Do they pretend to be Channels of Grace, or the Means of Pardon, by any Rights or Powers naturally inherent in them? Do they not in all these Things consider themselves as Instruments of God, that are made ministerial to the Edification of the Church, purely by his Will, and only so far as they act in Conformity to it? Now if it has pleased God to confer the Holy Ghost in Ordination, Confirmation, &c., only by them, and to annex the Grace of Pardon to the Imposition of their Hands, on returning Sinners; is it any *Blasphemy* for them to claim and exert their Power? Is the Prerogative of God injured, because his own Institutions are obeyed? Cannot he dispense his Graces by what Persons, and on what Terms he pleases? Is he deprived of the Disposal of his Blessings, because they are bestowed on Persons according to his Order, and in Obedience to his Authority? If I should affirm, that Bishops have the sole Power to ordain and confirm, would this be robbing God of his Disposal of those Graces that attend such Actions? Is it not rather allowing and submitting to God's own Disposal, when we keep close to those Methods of it which himself has prescribed?

Pray, my Lord, consider the Nature of Sacraments. Are not they necessary to Salvation? But is God therefore excluded from any Power of his own? Has he for that Reason, set Bread and Wine in the Eucharist, or Water in Baptism, above Himself? Has he put the Salvation of Men out of his own Power, because it depends on his own Institutions? Is the Salvation of Christians less his own Act and Deed, or less the Effect of his own Mercy, because these Sacraments in great measure contribute to effect it? Why then, my Lord, must that Imposition of Hands that is attended with his Grace and Pardon, and which has no Pretence to such Grace, but in Obedience to his Order, and in virtue of his Promise, be thus destructive of his Prerogative? Where is there any Diminution of his Honour or Authority, if such Actions of the Clergy are made necessary to the Salvation of Souls in some Circumstances, as their washing in Water, or their receiving Bread and Wine? Cannot God institute Means of Grace, but those Means must needs be above himself? They owe all their Power and Efficacy to his Institution, and can operate no farther than the Ends for which he instituted them. How then is he dethroned for being thus obeyed?

My Lord, you take no notice of Scripture; but in a new Way

of your own, contend against this Power, from the Nature of the Thing: Yet I must beg leave to say, this Power stands upon as sure a Bottom, and is as consistent with the Goodness and Majesty of God, as the Sacraments. If the annexing Grace to Sacraments, and making them necessary Means of Salvation, be a reasonable Institution of God; so is his annexing Pardon to the Imposition of Hands by the Clergy on returning Sinners. The Grace or Blessing received in either Case, is of his own giving, and in a Method of his own prescribing. And how this should be any Injury to God's Honour, or Affront to his Majesty, cannot easily be accounted for.

The Clergy justly claim a Power of reconciling Men to God, from express Terms of Scripture; and of delivering his Pardons to penitent Sinners. Your Lordship disowns this Claim, as making fallible Men the absolute Dispensers of God's Blessings, and putting it in their Power to damn and save as they please. But, my Lord, nothing of this Extravagance is included in it. They are only entrusted with a *conditional* Power; which they are to exercise according to the Rules God has given; and it only obtains its Effect when it is so exercised. Every instituted Means of Grace is *conditional;* and it is only then effectual, when it is attended with such Circumstances, as are required by God. If the Clergy, through Weakness, Passion or Prejudice, exclude Persons from the Church of God, they injure only themselves. But, my Lord, are these Powers nothing, because they may be exercised in vain? Have the Clergy no right at all to them, because they are not *absolutely infallible* in the Exercise of them?

Can you prove, my Lord, that they are not necessary, because they have not always the same Effect? May not that be necessary to Salvation, which is only effectual on *certain Conditions?* Is not the Christian Religion necessary to Salvation, though all Christians are not saved? Are not the Sacraments necessary Means of Grace, though the Means of Grace obtained thereby is only conditional? Is everyone necessarily improved in Grace, who receives the Sacrament? Or is it less necessary, because the salutary Effects of it are not more universal? Why then must the Imposition of Hands be less necessary, because the Grace of it is conditional, and only obtained in due and proper Circumstances? Is Absolution nothing, because if withheld wrongfully, it injures not the Person who is denied it; and if given without due Dispositions in the Penitent, it avails nothing? Is not this equally true of the Sacraments, if they are denied wrongfully, or administered to unprepared Receivers? But do they therefore cease to be standing and necessary Means of Grace?

The Argument therefore against this Power, drawn from the Ignorance or Passions of the Clergy, whereby they may mistake or pervert the Application of it, can be of no Force; since it is as conditional as any other Christian Institution. The Salvation of no Man can be endangered by the Ignorance or Passions of any Clergymen in the Use of this Power: If they err in the Exercise of it, the Consequences of their Error only affect themselves. The Administration of the Sacraments is certainly entrusted to them: But will anyone say, that the Sacraments are not necessary to Salvation; because they may, through Ignorance or Passion, make an ill Use of this Trust?

There is nothing in this Doctrine to gratify the Pride of Clergymen, or encourage them to lord it over the Flock of Christ. If you could suppose an Atheist or a Deist in Orders; he might be arrogant and domineer in the Exercise of his Powers: But who, that has the least Sense of Religion, can think it matter of Triumph, that he can deny the Sacraments, or refuse his Benediction to any of his Flock? Can he injure or offend the least of these; and will not God take Account? Or, if they fall through his Offence, will not their Blood be required at his Hands?

Neither is there anything in it that can enslave the Laity to the Clergy; or make their Salvation depend upon their arbitrary Will. Does anyone think his Salvation in danger, because the Sacraments (the necessary means of it) are only to be administered by the Clergy? Why then must the Salvation of *Penitents* be endangered, or made dependent on the sole Pleasure of the Clergy; because they alone can reconcile them to the Favour of God? If Persons are unjustly denied the Sacraments, they may humbly hope, that God will not lay the Want of them to their Charge. And if they are unjustly kept out of the Church, and denied Admittance, they have no Reason to fear but God will notwithstanding accept them, provided they be in other respects proper Objects of his Favour.

But to proceed, your Lordship says, *The Apostles might possibly understand the Power of remitting and retaining Sins, to be that Power of laying their Hands upon the Sick.*

Is this *possible*, my Lord? Then it is *possible*, the Apostles might think, that in the Power here intended to be given them, *nothing at all* was intended to be given them. For the Power of healing the Sick, was already conferred upon them. Therefore, if no more was intended to be given them in this Text, it cannot be interpreted, as having entitled them properly to any Power at all.

2. The Power mentioned here, was something that Jesus pro-

mised he would give them hereafter : Which plainly supposes they had it not then : But they then had the Power of *Healing;* therefore something else must be intended here.

3. The Power of the *Keys* has always been looked upon as the highest in the Apostolical Order. But if it related only to the Power of Healing, it could not be so : For the *Seventy*, who were inferior to the Apostles, had this Power.

4. The very Manner of Expression in this Place, proves, that the Power here intended to be given, could not relate to *Healing the Sick*, or to anything of that Nature ; but to some *spiritual Power*, whose Effects should not be *visible ;* but be made good by virtue of God's Promise. Thus, *whomsoever ye shall* heal *on Earth*, I will heal *in Heaven*, borders too near upon an Absurdity. There is no Occasion to promise to make *good* such Actions as are good already, and have antecedently produced their Effects. Persons who were restored to Health, to their Sight, or the Use of their Limbs, did not want to be assured, that the Apostles, by whom they were restored, had the Power to that End ; the Exercise of which Power proved and confirmed itself. There was no need therefore of a Divine Assurance, that a Person that was healed, was actually healed in virtue of it. But when we consider this Promise, as relating to a *Power* whose *Effects* are not *visible*, as the *Pardon of Sins*, the Terms whereby it is expressed, are most proper ; and it is very reasonable to suppose God promising, that the spiritual powers exercised by his Ministers on Earth, though they do not here produce their *visible Effects*, shall yet be made good and effectual by him in *Heaven*.

These Reasons, my Lord, I should think, are sufficient to convince anyone, that the Apostles could not *possibly* understand these Words in the Sense of your Lordship.

Let us now consider the Commission given to *Peter*. Our Saviour said to him, *Thou art Peter, and upon this Rock I will build my Church, and the Gates of Hell shall not prevail against it : And I will grant unto thee the Keys of the Kingdom of Heaven ; and whatsoever thou shalt bind on Earth, shall be bound in Heaven ; and whatsoever thou shalt loose on Earth, shall be loosed in Heaven.*

Now, my Lord, how should it enter into the Thoughts of *Peter*, that nothing was here intended, or promised by our Saviour, but a Power of Healing ; which he not only had before, but also many other Disciples, who were not Apostles ? *I will give unto thee the Keys of the Kingdom of Heaven ;* that is, according to your Lordship, *I will give thee Power to heal the Sick*. Can anything be more contrary to the plain obvious

Sense of the Words? Can anyone be said to have the *Keys* of the Kingdom of Heaven, because he may be the Instrument of restoring People to Health? Are Persons Members of Christ's Kingdom, with any regard to Health? How then can he have any Power in that Kingdom; or be said to have the *Keys* of it, who is only empowered to cure Distempers? Could anyone be said to have the *Keys* of a temporal Kingdom, who had no temporal Power given him in that Kingdom? Must not he therefore who has the *Keys* of a spiritual Kingdom, have some spiritual Power in that Kingdom?

Christ has told us, that his Kingdom is not of this World. Your Lordship has told us, that it is so foreign to everything of this World, that no *worldly Terrors* or Allurements, no Pains or Pleasures of the Body, can have anything to do with it. Yet here your Lordship teaches us, that he may have the *Keys* of this spiritual Kingdom, who has only a Power over Diseases. My Lord, are not Sickness and Health, Sight and Limbs, Things of this World? Have they not some relation to bodily Pleasures and Pains? How then can a Power about Things wholly confined to this World, be a Power in a Kingdom that is not of this World? The Force of the Argument lies here: Our Saviour has assured us, that his Kingdom is not of this World: Your Lordship takes it to be of so spiritual a Nature, that it ought not, nay, that it cannot be encouraged or established by any worldly Powers. *Our Saviour gives to his Apostles the Keys of this Kingdom:* Yet you have so far forgotten your own Doctrine, and the Spirituality of this Kingdom, that you tell us, he here gave them a temporal Power of Diseases; though he says, they were the *Keys of his Kingdom* which he gave them. Suppose any Successor of the Apostles should from this Text pretend to the Power of the Sword, to make People Members of this Kingdom: Must not the Answer be, that he mistakes the Power, by not considering, that they are only the *Keys* of a *spiritual*, not of a temporal Kingdom, which were here delivered to the Apostles.

I humbly presume, my Lord, that this would be as good an Answer to your Lordship's Doctrine, as to theirs who claim the Right of the Sword, till it can be shown that *Health* and *Sickness, Sight* and *Limbs*, do not as truly relate to the Things of this World as the Power of the Sword.

If this Power of the Keys must be understood, only as a Power of inflicting or curing Diseases; then the Words, in the proper Construction of them, must run thus: *Thou art Peter, and upon this Rock I will build my Church,* i.e., a peculiar Society of healthful People, *and the Gates of Hell shall never prevail against it*, i.e., they shall always be in a State of Health. *I will give unto thee the Keys of this Kingdom of Heaven*, i.e., thou shalt have the Power of inflicting and curing Distempers; *and whatsoever thou shalt bind on Earth, shall be bound in Heaven*, i.e., on whomsoever thou shalt inflict the Leprosy on Earth, he shall be a Leper in Heaven; *and whatsoever thou shalt loose on Earth, shall be loosed in Heaven*, i.e., whomsoever thou shalt cure of that Disease on Earth, shall be perfectly cured of it in Heaven.

This, without putting any Force upon the Words, is your Lordship's own Interpretation; which exposes the Honour and Authority of Scriptures as much as the greatest Enemy to them can wish. If our Saviour could mean by these Words, only a *Power of healing Distempers;* or if the Apostles understood them in that Sense, we may as well believe that when he said, *His Kingdom was not of this World,* that he meant, it was of this World; and that the Apostles so understood him too.

But, however, for the Benefit and Edification of the Laity, your Lordship has another Interpretation for them: You say, *if they* (the Apostles) *did apply this Power of remitting Sins to the certain Absolution of particular Persons, it is plain, they could do it upon no other Bottom but this; that God's Will and good Pleasure about such particular Persons was infallibly communicated to them.*

Pray, my Lord, how, or where is this so plain? Is it plain that they never baptized Persons till God had *infallibly communicated his good Pleasure to them about such particular Persons?* Baptism is an Institution equally sacred with this other, and puts the Person baptized in the same State of Grace *that Absolution* does the Penitent. Baptism is designed for the Remission of Sin. It is an Ordinance to which Absolution is consequent; but I suppose Persons may be baptized without such *infallible Communication* promised, as your Lordship contends for. If therefore it be not necessary for the Exercise of Absolution by Baptism, why must it be necessary for Absolution by the Imposition of Hands?

Can Pastors without Infallibility baptize Heathens, and absolve, or be the Instruments of absolving them thereby from their Sins? Are they not as able to absolve Christian Penitents, or restore those who have apostatised? If human Knowledge, and the common Rules of the Church, be sufficient to direct the Priest to whom he ought to administer the Sacraments; they are also sufficient for the Exercise of this other Part of the sacerdotal Office.

But your Lordship proceeds thus: *Not that they* themselves *absolved any.*

No, my Lord, no more than Water in Baptism of *itself* purifies the Soul from Sin. This baptismal Water is, notwithstanding, necessary for the Remission of our Sins.

Again, you say, *Not that God was obliged to bind and loose the Guilt of Men according to their Declarations, considered as their own Decisions, and their own Determinations.* No, my Lord, who ever thought so? God is not obliged to confer Grace by the *baptismal Water*, considered only as *Water;* but he is, considered as *his own Institution* for that End and Purpose. So if these Declarations are considered only as *the Declarations of Men*, God is not obliged by them: But when they are considered as the Declarations of *Men* whom he has especially authorised to make *such* Declarations in his Name, then they are as effectual with God, as any other of his Institutions whatever.

I proceed now to a Paragraph that bears as hard upon our Saviour, as some others have done upon his Apostles and their Successors; where your Lordship designs to prove, that though Christ claimed a Power of remitting Sins himself, or in his own Person, yet that he really had no such Power.

You go on in these Words: *If we look back upon our Saviour himself, we shall find, that when he declares that the Son of Man had Power upon Earth to forgive Sins, even he himself either meant by it the Power of a miraculous releasing Man from his Affliction; or if it related to another more spiritual Sense of the Words, the Power of declaring, that the Man's Sins were forgiven by God.*[*]

The Words of our Saviour, which we are to look back upon, are these: *Whether it is easier to say, thy Sins are forgiven thee; or to say, arise, take up thy Bed and walk? But that ye may know, the Son of Man hath Power on Earth to forgive Sins* (Mark ii. 9, 10); As if he had said, 'Is not the same Divine 'Authority and Power required? Is it not a Work as peculiar to 'God, to perform miraculous Cures, as to forgive Sins? The 'Reason therefore why I now choose to declare my Authority, 'rather by saying, *Thy Sins are forgiven thee*, than by saying, '*Arise and walk*, was purely to teach you this Truth, that the 'Power of the Son of Man is not confined to Bodily Cures; but 'that he has Power on Earth to forgive Sins.'

This, my Lord, is the first obvious Sense of the Words; and therefore I take it to be the true Sense. But your Lordship can look back upon them, till you find that Christ has not this Power, though he claims it expressly; but that he only intends a Power of doing *something or other*, which no more imports a

---

[*] *Preservative*, p. 94.

Power of forgiving Sins, than of remitting any temporal Debt or Penalty.

If our blessed Saviour had intended to teach the World that he was invested with this Power, I would gladly know how he must have expressed himself, to have satisfied your Lordship that he really had it? He must have told you, that he had not this Power, and then possibly your Lordship would have taught us, that he had this Power. For no one can discover any Reason why you should deny it him, but because he has in express Words claimed and asserted it. I hope your Lordship has not so low an Opinion of our Saviour's Person, as to think it unreasonable in the Nature of the Thing, that he should have this Power. Where does it contradict any Principle of Reason, to say, that a *King* should be able to pardon his Subjects? Since there is no Absurdity then in the Thing itself, and it is so expressly asserted in Scripture; it is just Matter of Surprise, that your Lordship should carry your Reader from a plain consistent Sense of the Words, to *either this or that, Something or other*, the Origin whereof is only to be sought for in your Lordship's own Invention; rather than not exclude Christ from a Power which he declared he had, and declared he had it for this very Reason, *that we might know that he had it.* Our Saviour has told us that the Way to Heaven is *narrow.* Your Lordship might as reasonably prove from hence, that he meant, it was *broad*, as that he did not mean that he could forgive Sins, when he said, *that ye may know, that the Son of Man hath Power on Earth to forgive Sins.*

Your Lordship has rejected all *Church Authority*, and despised the pretended *Powers* of the Clergy, for this Reason; because Christ is the *sole King, sole Lawgiver, and Judge in his Kingdom.* But, it seems, your Lordship, notwithstanding, thinks it now Time to depose him: And this *sole King* in *his own Kingdom*, must not be allowed to be capable of pardoning his own Subjects.

This Doctrine, my Lord, is delivered, I suppose, as your other Doctrines, out of a hearty Concern and *Christian* Zeal for the Privileges of the Laity; and to show that your Lordship is not only able to limit as you please the Authority of *temporal Kings;* but also to make Christ himself *sole King*, and yet *no King*, in his Spiritual Kingdom. For, my Lord, the Kingdom of Christ is a Society founded in order to the Reconciliation of Sinners to God. If therefore Christ could not pardon Sins, to what End could he either erect, or how could he support his Kingdom, which is only, in the great and last Design of it, to consist of absolved Sinners? He that cannot forgive Sins in a

Kingdom that is erected for the Remission of Sins, can no more be *sole King* in it, than he that has no *temporal Power*, can be *sole King* in a *temporal Kingdom.* Therefore your Lordship has been thus mighty serviceable to the Christian Laity, as to teach them that Christ is not only *sole King*, but *no King* in his Kingdom.

This is not the first Contradiction your Lordship has unhappily fallen into, in your Attempts upon *kingly Authority.* Nor is it the last which I shall presume to observe to the *common Sense* of your Laity.

Again, in this Account of our blessed Saviour, your Lordship has made no Difference between him and his Apostles, as to this *absolving Authority.* For you say, the *great Commission* given to them implied either a Power of releasing Men from their bodily Afflictions; or of declaring such to be pardoned, whom God had assured them that he had pardoned: And this *all* that you here allow to Christ himself.

Your Lordship's calling him so often *King*, and *sole King, &c.*, in his Kingdom, and yet making him a *mere Creature* in it, is too like the Insult, and designed Sarcasm of the *Jews*, who, when they had nailed him to the Cross, writ over his Head, *This is the King of the Jews.*

But to proceed: Your Lordship proves, That our Saviour had not the Power of *forgiving Sins;* because *His Way of Expression was, Thy Sins are forgiven thee. This was plainly to acknowledge, and keep up that true Notion, that God alone forgiveth Sins.*

Let us therefore put this Argument in Form. Christ hath affirmed, that he had Power to forgive Sins: But his Way was to say, *Thy Sins are forgiven thee:* Therefore Christ had not Power to forgive Sins. *Q. E. D.*

It is much your Lordship did not recommend this to your Laity, as another *invincible Demonstration.* For by the Help of it, my Lord, they may prove that our Saviour could no more *heal Diseases*, than *forgive Sins.* As thus; Christ indeed pretends to a Power of healing Diseases; but his usual Way of speaking to the diseased Person was, *thy Faith hath made thee whole;* therefore he had not the Power of *healing* Diseases. The Argument has the same Force against one Power, as against the other. If he did not *forgive Sins*, because he said, *Thy Sins are forgiven thee;* no more did he heal Diseases, because he said, *Thy Faith hath made thee whole.*

I have a Claim of several Debts upon a Man; I forgive him them all, in these Words, *Thy Debts are remitted thee.* A philosophical Wit stands by, and pretends to prove, that I had not the Power of remitting these Debts; because I said, *Thy Debts are remitted thee.* What can come up to, or equal such *profound Philosophy*, but the *Divinity* of one who teaches, our Saviour could not forgive Sins, because he said, *Thy Sins are forgiven thee?*

But your Lordship says, the Reason why our Saviour thus expresseth himself, *Thy Sins are forgiven thee,* 'was plainly to 'keep up that true Notion, that God alone forgiveth Sins.' Therefore, my Lord, according to this Doctrine, our Saviour was obliged not to claim any Power that was *peculiar* or *appropriated* to God *alone*. For if this be an Argument, why he should not *forgive Sins*, it is also an Argument that he ought not to claim any other Power, any more than this; which is proper to God, and only belongs to him. But, my Lord, if he did express himself thus, that he might not lay Claim to any Thing that was peculiar to God, how came he in so many other Respects to lay Claim to such Things as are as truly peculiar to God, as the Forgiveness of Sins? How came he in so many Instances to make himself equal to God? How came he to say, *Ye believe in God, believe also in me?* And that *Men should worship the Son, even as the Father?* That he was the Son of God, that he was the Way, the Truth, and the Life.

Are not evangelical Faith, Worship, and Trust, Duties that are solely due to God? Does he not as much invade the Sovereignty of God, who lays Claim to these Duties, as he that pretends *to forgive Sins?* Did not Christ also give his Disciples *Power and Authority* over Devils and unclean Spirits, and Power to heal all manner of Diseases?

Now if Christ did not assume a Power to *forgive Sins*, because God alone could forgive Sins, it is also as unaccountable that he should exercise other *Authorities* and Powers, which are as strictly peculiar to God as that of forgiving Sins. As if a Person should disown that Christ is omniscient, because Omniscience is an *Attribute* of God *alone;* and yet confess his Omnipotence, which is an Attribute equally *divine*.

But farther, my Lord: Did our Saviour thus designedly express himself, lest he should be thought to assume any Power which was divine, then it is certain (according to this Opinion) that if he had assumed any such Power, or pretended to do what was peculiar to God, he had been the Occasion of misleading Men into Error. For if this be a plain Reason why he expressed himself so as to disown this Power, it is plain that if he had owned it, he had been condemned by this Argument, as teaching false Doctrine.

Now if this would have been interpretatively false Doctrine in Christ, to take upon himself any Thing that was peculiar to God, the Apostles were guilty of propagating this false Doctrine. For there is scarce any known Attribute or Power of God, but they ascribe it to our Saviour. They declare him eternal, omnipotent, omniscient, &c. Is it not a *true Notion*, that God alone can create, and is Governor of the Universe? Yet the Apostles expressly assure us of Christ, that *all Things were created by him*, and that *God hath put all Things in Subjection under his Feet*. 'Tis very surprising that your Lordship should exclude Christ from this Power of *forgiving* Sins, though he has expressly said he could forgive Sins, because such a Power belongs only to God: When it appears through the whole Scripture, that there is scarce any divine Power which our Saviour himself has not claimed, nor any Attribute of God but what his Apostles have ascribed to him. They have made him the *Creator*, the *Preserver*, the *Governor* of the Universe, the Author of eternal Salvation to all that obey him; and yet your Lordship tells us, that he did not pretend to *forgive Sins*, because that was a Power peculiar to God.

Here is then (to speak in your Lordship's elegant Style) an *immovable Resting-place* for your Laity to set their Feet upon; here is an *Argument that will last them for ever*: They must believe that our Saviour did not forgive Sins, *because* this was a Power that belonged to God, though the Scriptures assure us, that every other divine Power belonged to Christ. That is, they must believe, that though our Saviour claimed all divine Powers, yet not this divine Power, *because* it is a divine Power. And, my Lord, if they have the common Sense to believe this, they may also believe, that though our Saviour took human Nature upon him, yet that he had not a human Soul, because it is proper to Man. They may believe, that any Person who has all kingly Power, cannot remit or reprieve a Malefactor, *because* it is an Act of kingly Power to do it; or that a Bishop cannot suspend any Offender of his Diocese, because it is an Act of episcopal Power to do it. All these Reasons are as strong and demonstrative, as that Christ who claimed all divine Powers, could not forgive Sins, *because* it was a *divine Power*.

Lastly, In this Argument your Lordship has plainly declared against the Divinity of Christ, and ranked him in the Order of Creatures. Your Lordship says, Christ did not forgive Sins, because it is God *alone who can forgive Sins*; as plain an Argument as can be offered, that in your Lordship's Opinion Christ is not God: For if you believed him, in a true and proper Sense, God, how could you exclude him from the Power of forgiving Sins, *because* God alone can forgive Sins? It is inconsistent with Sense and Reason to deny this Power to Christ because it is a divine Power, but only because you believe him not to be a divine Person. If Christ was God, then he might forgive Sins, though God alone can forgive Sins : But you say, Christ cannot forgive Sins, because God *alone* can forgive Sins ; therefore it is plain, that, according to your Lordship's Doctrine, Christ is not truly, or in a proper Sense, God.

Here, my Lord, I desire again to appeal to the *common Sense* of your Laity ; let them judge betwixt the Scriptures and your Lordship. The Scriptures plainly and frequently ascribe all divine Attributes to Christ : They make him the Creator and Governor of the World ; God over all, blessed for ever. Yet your Lordship makes him a Creature, and denies him *such* a Power, because it belongs only to God.

You yourself, my Lord, have allowed him to be absolute Ruler over the Consciences of Men ; to be an arbitrary Dispenser of the Means of Salvation to Mankind ; than which Powers, none can be more divine : And yet you hold, that he cannot forgive Sins, because Pardon of Sin can only be the Effect of a divine Power.

Is it not equally a divine Power (even according to your Lordship), to rule over the Consciences of Men, to give Laws of Salvation, and to act in these Affairs with an uncontrollable Power, as *to forgive Sins?*

My Lord, let their common Sense here discover the Absurdity (for I must call it so) of your *new Scheme* of Government in Christ's Kingdom. Christ is *absolute* Lord of it, (according to yourself) and can make or unmake Laws relating to it ; can dispense or withhold Grace as he pleases in this spiritual Kingdom, all which Powers are purely divine ; yet you say he cannot forgive Sins, though every express Power which you have allowed him over the Consciences of Men, be as truly a *divine Power* as that of *forgiving Sins.* Has not Christ a proper and personal Power to give Grace to his Subjects ? Is he not Lord over their Consciences ? And are not these Powers as truly appropriated to God ? And has not your Lordship often taught them to be so, as that of *Forgiveness of Sins?* Is it not as much the Prerogative of God to have any natural intrinsic Power, to confer Grace, or any spiritual Benefit to the Souls of Men, as to forgive Sins ? Has not your Lordship despised all the Administrations of the Clergy, because God's Graces can only come from himself, and are only to be received from his own Hands ? The Conclusion therefore is this, either Christ has a personal intrinsic Power to confer Grace in his Kingdom, or he has not; if you say he has not, then you are chargeable with the Collusion of making him a King in a spiritual Kingdom, where you allow him no spiritual Power: If you say he has, then you fall into this Contradiction, that you allow him to have divine Powers, though he cannot have divine Powers; that is, you allow him to *give Grace*, though it is a divine Power, and not to *forgive Sins*, because it is a divine Power. My Lord, I wish your Laity (if there be any to whom you can render it intelligible) much Joy of such profound Divinity. Or if there are others who are more taken with your Lordship's Sincerity, I desire them not to pass by this following remarkable Instance of it: Your Lordship has here as plainly declared, as Words can consequentially declare any Thing, that you do not believe Christ to be God, yet profess yourself Bishop of a Church, whose Liturgy in so many repeated Testimonies declares the contrary Doctrine, and which obliges you to express your Assent and Consent to such Doctrine. My Lord, I here call upon your *Sincerity;* either declare Christ to be perfect God, and then show why he could not *forgive Sins;* or deny him to be perfect God, and then show how you can sincerely declare your *Assent* and *Consent* to the Doctrine of the Church of *England*.

This, my Lord, has an Appearance of Prevarication, which you cannot, I hope, charge upon any of your Adversaries, who if they cannot think, that to be sincere is the only Thing necessary to recommend Men to the Favour of God, yet may have as much, or possibly more Sincerity, than those who do think so.

Before I take Leave of your Lordship, I must take Notice of a *Resting-place,* a *strong Retreat,* a *lasting Foundation,* i.e., *a Demonstration in the strictest Sense* of the Words, that all *Church-Communion* is unnecessary.

Your Lordship sets it out in these Words:

I am not now going to accuse you of a Heresy against Charity, but of a Heresy against the Possibility and Nature of Things. As thus, *Mr.* Nelson *(for Instance) thinks himself obliged in Conscience to communicate with some of our Church. Upon this you declare he hath no Title to God's Mercy; and you and all the World allow, that if he communicates with you whilst his Conscience tells him it is a Sin, he is self-condemned, and out of God's Favour. That Notion (viz.* the Necessity of Church-Communion) *therefore, which implies this great invincibe Absurdity, cannot be true.*

Pray, my Lord, what is this wondrous Curiosity of a *Demonstration,* but the common Case of an *erroneous Conscience?* Did the strictest Contenders for Church-Communion ever teach, *that any Terms* are to be complied with against Conscience? But it is a strange Conclusion to infer from thence, that there is no

Obligation to Communion, or that all Things are to be held indifferent, because they are not to be complied with against one's Conscience.

The Truths of the Christian Religion have the same Nature and Obligation, whatever our Opinions are of them, and those that are necessary to be believed, continue so, whether we can persuade ourselves to believe them or not. I suppose your Lordship will not say, that the Articles of Faith and necessary Institutions of the Christian Religion, are no other ways necessary, than because we believe them to be so, that our Persuasion is the only Cause of the Necessity; but if their Necessity be not owing merely to our Belief of them, then it is certain that our Disbelief of them cannot make them less necessary. If the Ordinances of Christ, and the Articles of Faith are necessary, because Christ has made them so, that Necessity must continue the same, whether we believe and observe them or not.

So that, my Lord, we may still maintain the Necessity of Church-Communion, and the strict Observance of Christ's Ordinances, notwithstanding that People have different Persuasions in these Matters, presuming *that our Opinions* can no more alter the Nature or Necessity of Christ's Institutions, than we can believe *Error* into *Truth*, *Good* into *Evil*, or *Light* into *Darkness*. I shall think myself no *Heretic against the Nature of Things*, though I tell a *conscientious Socinian*, that the Divinity of Christ is necessary to be believed, or a *conscientious Jew*, that it is necessary to be a Christian in order to be saved. But if your Lordship's Demonstration was accepted, we should be obliged to give up the Necessity of every Doctrine and Institution, to every Disbeliever that pretended Conscience. We must not tell any Party of People that they are in any Danger for being out of Communion with us, if they do but follow their own Persuasion.

Your Lordship's *invincible Demonstration* proceeds thus:

We must not insist upon the Necessity of joining with any particular Church, because then conscientious Persons will be in Danger either Way; for if there be a Necessity of it, then there is a Danger if they do not join with it, and if they comply against their Consciences, the Danger is the same.

What an inextricable Difficulty is here! How shall Divinity or Logic be able to relieve us?

Be pleased, my Lord, to accept of this Solution, in lieu of your Demonstration.

I will suppose the Case of a *conscientious Jew;* I tell him that Christianity is the only covenanted Method of Salvation, and that he can have no Title to the Favour of God, till he professes the Faith of Christ. What, replies he, would you direct me to do? If I embrace Christianity against my Conscience, I am out of God's Favour; and if I follow my Conscience, and continue a *Jew*, I am also out of his Favour. The Answer is this, my Lord; The *Jew* is to obey his Conscience, and to be left to the *uncovenanted, unpromised* Terms of God's *Mercy*, whilst the conscientious Christian is entitled to the *express and promised Favours of* God.

There is still the same absolute Necessity of believing in Christ, Christianity is still the only Method of Salvation; though the sincere *Jew* cannot so persuade himself; and we ought to declare it to all *Jews* and Unbelievers whatsoever, that they can only be saved by embracing Christianity: That a false Religion does not become a true one, nor a true one false, in Consequence of their Opinions; but that if they are so unhappy as to refuse the Covenant of Grace, they must be left to such *Mercy* as is without any Covenant. And now, my Lord, what is become of this mighty Demonstration? Does it prove that Christianity is not necessary, because the conscientious *Jew* may think it is not so? It may as well prove that the Moon is no larger than a Man's Head, because an honest ignorant Countryman may think it no larger.

Is there any Person of *common Sense*, who would think it a Demonstration that he is not obliged to go to Church, because a *conscientious* Dissenter will not? Could he think it less necessary to be a Christian, because a *sincere Jew* cannot embrace Christianity? Could he take it to be an indifferent Matter whether he believed the Divinity of Christ, because a *conscientious Socinian* cannot? Yet this is your Lordship's *invincible Demonstration*, that we ought not to insist upon the Necessity of Church-Communion, because a *conscientious Disbeliever* cannot comply with it.

A small Degree of *common Sense*, would teach a Man that true Religion, and the Terms of Salvation, must have the same obligatory Force, whether we reason rightly about them or not; and that they who believe and practise according to them, are in express Covenant with God, which entitles them to his Favour; whilst those who are sincerely erroneous, have nothing but the Sincerity of their Errors to plead, and are left to such Mercy of God, as is without any Promise. Here, my Lord, is nothing frightful or absurd in this Doctrine; they who are in the Church which Christ has founded, are upon Terms which entitle them to God's Favour; they who are out of it, fall to his Mercy.

But your Lordship is not content with the Terms of the

Gospel, or a Doctrine that only saves a particular Sort of People; this is a narrow View, not wide enough for your Notions of *Liberty*. Particular Religions, and particular Covenants, are *demonstrated* to be absurd, *because* particular Persons may disbelieve, or not submit to them.

Your Lordship must have Doctrines that will save all People alike, in every way that their Persuasion leads them to take: But, my Lord, there needs be no greater Demonstration against your Lordship's Doctrine, than that it equally favours every Way of Worship; for an Argument which equally proves every Thing, has been generally thought to prove nothing; which happens to be the Case of your Lordship's *important Demonstration*.

Your Lordship indeed only instances in a particular Person, Mr. *Nelson;* but your *Demonstration* is as serviceable to any other Person who has left any other Church whatever. The *conscientious Quaker, Muggletonian, Independent*, or *Socinian, &c.*, has the same Right to obey Conscience, and blame any Church that assumes a Power of censuring him, as Mr. *Nelson* had; and if he is censured by any Church, that Church is as guilty of the same *Heresy against the Nature of Things*, as that Church which censured Mr. *Nelson*, or any Church that should pretend to censure any other Person whatever.

I am not at all surprised that your Lordship should teach this Doctrine, but it is something strange that such an Argument should be obtruded upon the World as an unheard-of *Demonstration*, and that in an *Appeal to common Sense*. Suppose some Body or other in Defence of your Lordship, should take upon him to demonstrate to the World that there is no such Thing as Colour, because there are some People that cannot see; or Sounds, because there are some who do not hear them; He would have found out the only *Demonstration* in the World that could equal your Lordship's, and would have as much Reason to call those *Heretics against the Nature of Things*, who should disbelieve him, and insist upon the Reality of Sounds, as your Lordship has to call your Adversaries so.

For is there no Necessity of Church-Communion, because there are some who do not conceive it? Then there are no Sounds, because there are some who do not hear them; for it is certainly as easy to believe away the *Truth* and *Reality*, as the *Necessity* of Things.

Some People have only taught us the *Innocency of Error*, and been content with setting forth its harmless Qualities; but your Lordship has been a more hearty Advocate, and given it a *Power* over every Truth and Institution of Christianity. If we have but an *erroneous Conscience*, the whole Christian Dispensation is cancelled; all the Truths and Doctrines in the Bible are *demonstrated* to be unnecessary, if we do not believe them.

How unhappily have the several Parties of Christians been disputing for many Ages, who, if they could but have found out this *intelligible Demonstration* (from the Case of an erroneous Conscience), would have seen the Absurdity of pretending to necessary Doctrines, and insisting upon *Church-Communion;* but it must be acknowledged your Lordship's *new-invented Engine* for the Destruction of *Churches;* and it may be expected the *good Christians of no Church* will return your Lordship their Thanks for it.

Your Lordship has thought it a mighty Objection to some Doctrines in the *Church* of *England,* that the Papists might make some Advantage of them: But yet your own Doctrine defends *all* Communions alike, and serve the *Jew* and *Socinian, &c.,* as much as any other sort of People. Though this sufficiently appears, from what has been already said, yet that it may be still more obvious to the *common Sense* of everyone, I shall reduce these Doctrines to Practice, and suppose, for once, that your Lordship intends to convert a *Jew*, a *Quaker*, or *Socinian*.

Now in order to make a Convert of any of them, these Preliminary PROPOSITIONS are to be first laid down according to your Lordship's Doctrine.

Some *Propositions* for the Improvement of true Religion.

Proposition I. That we are neither more or less in the Favour of God, for living in any particular Method or Way of Worship, but purely as we are sincere. *Preserv.*, p. 90.

Prop. II. That no Church ought to unchurch another, or declare it out of God's Favour. *Preserv.*, p. 85.

Prop. III. That nothing loses us the Favour of God, but a wicked Insincerity. *Ibid.*

Prop. IV. That a conscientious Person can be in no Danger for being out of any particular Church. *Preserv.*, p. 90.

Prop. V. That there is no such Thing as any real Perfection or Excellency in any Religion, that can *justify* our adhering to it, but *that* all is founded in our personal Persuasion; which your Lordship thus proves: *When we left the Popish Doctrines, was it because they were* actually *corrupt?* No; *The Reason was, because we thought them so.* Therefore if we might leave the *Church of Rome*, not because her Doctrines were corrupt, but because we thought them so, then the same Reason will justify anyone else, in leaving any Church, how true soever its Doctrines are; and consequently there is no such Thing as any *real* Perfection or

Excellency in any Religion considered in itself, but is *right* or *wrong* according to our Persuasions about it. *Preserv.*, p. 85.

Prop. VI. That Christ is *sole* King and *Lawgiver* in his Kingdom, that no *Men* have any Power of Legislation in it; that if we would be good Members of it, we must show ourselves Subjects of Christ alone, without any Regard to Man's Judgment.

Prop. VII. That as Christ's Kingdom is not of this World, so when worldly Encouragements are annexed to it, these are so many Divisions against Christ and his own express Word. *Serm.*, p. 11.

Prop. VIII. That to pretend to know the Hearts and Sincerity of Men, is Nonsense and Absurdity. *Serm.*, p. 93.

Prop. IX. That God's Graces are only to be received immediately from himself. *Serm.*, p. 89.

These, my Lord, are your Lordship's own Propositions, expressed in your own Terms, without any Exaggeration.

And now, my Lord, begin as soon as you please, either with a *Quaker*, *Socinian*, or *Jew;* use any Argument whatsoever to convert them, and you shall have a sufficient answer from your own Propositions.

Will you tell the *Jew* that Christianity is necessary to Salvation? He will answer from *Prop.* I. *That we are neither more or less in the Favour of God for living in any particular Method or Way of Worship, but purely as we are sincere.*

Will your Lordship tell him, that the Truth of Christianity is so well asserted, that there is no Excuse left for Unbelievers? He will answer from Prop. V. *That all Religion is founded in personal Persuasion; that as your Lordship does not believe that Christ is come, because he is actually come, but because you think he is come; so he does not disbelieve Christ because he is not actually come, but because he thinks he is not come.* So that here, my Lord, the *Jew* gives as good a Reason why he is not a Christian, as your Lordship does why you are not a Papist.

If your Lordship should turn the Discourse to a *Quaker*, and offer him any Reasons for embracing the Doctrine of the *Church of England*, you cannot possibly have any better Success; anyone may see from your *Propositions*, that no Argument can be urged, but what your Lordship has there fully answered. For since you allow nothing to the *Truth* of Doctrines, or the *Excellency* of any Communion as such, it is demonstrable that no Church or Communion can have any Advantage above another, which is absolutely necessary in order to persuade any sensible Man to exchange any Communion for another.

Will your Lordship tell a *Quaker*, that there is any Danger in that particular Way that he is in?

He can answer from *Prop.* I., III., and IV. *That a conscientious Person cannot be in any Danger of being out of any particular Church.*

Will your Lordship tell him that his Religion is condemned by the universal Church?

He can answer from *Prop.* II. *That no Church ought to unchurch another, or declare it out of God's Favour.*

Will you tell him that Christ has instituted Sacraments as *necessary Means* of Grace, which he neglects to observe?

He will answer you from *Prop.* IX. *That God's Graces are only to be received* immediately from himself. And to think that *Bread* and *Wine*, or the sprinkling of Water, is necessary to Salvation, is as absurd, as to think any Order of the Clergy is necessary to recommend us to God.

Will your Lordship tell him that he displeases God, by not holding several Articles of Faith, which Christ has required us to believe?

He can reply from *Prop.* III. *That nothing loses us the Favour of God* but a *wicked Insincerity.* And from *Prop.* V. *That as* your Lordship believes such Things, not because they are actually to be believed, but because you think so; so he disbelieves them, not because they are actually false, but because he thinks so.

Will your Lordship tell him he is insincere?

He can reply from *Prop.* VI. *That to assume to know the Hearts and Sincerity of Men, is Nonsense and Blasphemy.*

Will your Lordship tell him that he ought to conform to a Church established by the Laws of the Land?

He can answer from *Prop.* VIII. That this very *Establishment* is an Argument against Conformity? *For as Christ's Kingdom is not of this World, so when worldly Encouragements are annexed to it, they are so many Decisions against Christ, and his own express Words.* And from *Prop.* VII. *That seeing Christ is sole King and Lawgiver in his Kingdom, and no Men have any Power of Legislation in it, they who would be good Members of it, must show themselves Subjects to Christ alone, without any Regard to Man's Judgment.*

I am inclined to think, my Lord, that it is now *demonstrated* to the common Sense of the Laity, that your Lordship cannot urge any Argument, either from the *Truth*, the *Advantage*, or *Necessity* of embracing the Doctrines of the *Church* of *England*, to either *Jew*, *Heretic*, or *Schismatic*, but you have helped him to a full Answer to any such Argument, from your own Principles.

Are we, my Lord, to be treated as *popishly* affected for

asserting some Truths, which the Papists join with us in asserting? Is it a Crime in us not to drop some necessary Doctrines, because the Papists have not dropped them? If this is to be *popishly* affected, we own the Charge, and are not for being such *true Protestants*, as to give up the *Apostles' Creed*, or lay aside the Sacraments, because they are received by the Church of *Rome*. I cannot indeed charge your Lordship with being *well affected* to the Church of *Rome*, or of *England*, to the *Jews*, the *Quakers*, or *Socinians;* but this I have *demonstrated*, and will undertake the Defence of it, that your Lordship's *Principles* equally serve them all alike, and do not give the least Advantage to one Church above another, as has sufficiently appeared from your *Principles.*

I will no more say your Lordship is in the Interest of the *Quakers*, or *Socinians*, or *Papists*, than I would charge you with being in the Interest of the Church of *England;* for as your Doctrines equally support them all, he ought to ask your Lordship's Pardon, who should declare you more a Friend to one than the other.

I intended, my Lord, to have considered another very obnoxious Article in your Lordship's Doctrines concerning the *Repugnancy of temporal Encouragements to the Nature of Christ's Kingdom;* but the Consistency and Reasonableness of guarding this spiritual Kingdom with human Laws, has been defended with so much Perspicuity and Strength of Argument, and your Lordship's Objections so fully confuted by the judicious and learned Dean of *Chichester*, that I presume this Part of the Controversy is finally determined.

I hope, my Lord, that I have delivered nothing here that needs any Excuse or Apology to the Laity, that they will not be persuaded, through any vain Pretence of Liberty, to make themselves Parties against the first Principles of Christianity; or imagine, that whilst we contend for the positive Institutions of the Gospel, the Necessity of Church-Communion, or the Excellency of our own, we are robbing them of their natural Rights, or interfering with their Privileges. Whilst we appear in the Defence of any part of Christianity, we are engaged for them in the common Cause of Christians; and I am persuaded better Things of the Laity, than to believe that such Labours will render either our Persons or Professions hateful to them. Your Lordship has indeed endeavoured to give an invidious Turn to the Controversy, by calling upon the Laity to assert their Liberties, as if they were in Danger from the Principles of Christianity.———But, my Lord, what Liberty does any Layman lose, by our asserting, that *Church-Communion* is necessary? What Privilege is taken from them by our teaching the Danger of certain Ways and Methods of Religion? Is a Man made a Slave because he is cautioned against the Principles of the *Quakers*, against *Fanaticism, Popery*, or *Socinianism?* Is he in a State of Bondage because the Sacraments are necessary, and none but episcopal Clergy ought to administer them? Is his Freedom destroyed because there is a particular Order of Men appointed by God to minister in holy Things, and be serviceable to him in recommending him to the Favour of God? Can any Person, my Lord, think these Things Breaches upon their Liberty, except such as think the Commandments a Burden? Is there any more Hardship in saying thou shalt keep to an episcopal Church, than thou shalt be baptized? Or in requiring People to receive particular Sacraments, than to believe particular Books of Scripture to be the Word of God? If some other Advocate for the Laity should, out of Zeal for their Rights, declare that they need not believe one-half of the Articles in the Creed, if they would but assert their Liberty, he would be as true a Friend, and deserve the same Applause, as he who should assert the Necessity of Church-Communion is inconsistent with the natural Rights and Liberties of Mankind.

I am, my LORD,

Your Lordship's most

Humble Servant,

William Law.

Postscript.

I HOPE your Lordship will not think it unnatural or impertinent, to offer here a Word or two in Answer to some Objections against my former Letter.

To begin with the Doctrine of the uninterrupted Succession of the Clergy.

I have, as I think, proved that there is a divine Commission required to qualify any one to exercise the priestly Office, and that seeing this divine Commission can only be had from such particular Persons as God has appointed to give it, therefore it is necessary that there should be a continual Succession of such Persons, in order to keep up a commissioned Order of the Clergy. For if the Commission itself be to descend through Ages, and distinguish the Clergy from the Laity; it is certain the Persons who alone can give this Commission, must descend through the same Ages, and consequently an uninterrupted Succession is as necessary, as that the Clergy have a divine Commission. Take away this Succession, and the Clergy may as well be ordained by one Person as another; a Number of Women may as well give them a divine Commission, as a Congregation of any Men; they may indeed appoint Persons to officiate in holy Orders, for the Sake of *Decency* and *Order;* but then there is no more in it, than an external *Decency* and *Order;* they are no more the Priests of God, than those that pretended to make them so. If we had lost the Scriptures, it would be very well to make as good Books as we could, and come as near them as possible; but then it would be not only Folly, but Presumption, to call them the Word of God. But I proceed to the Objections against the Doctrine of an uninterrupted Succession.

First, It is said, that there is no mention made of it in Scripture, as having any Relation to the Being of a Church.

Secondly, That it is subject to so great Uncertainty, that if it be necessary we cannot now be sure we are in the Church.

Thirdly, That it is a popish Doctrine, and gives them great Advantage over us.

I begin with the *first* Objection, that there is no mention made of it in the Scriptures, which though I think I have sufficiently answered in this Letter, I shall here farther consider.

Pray, my Lord, is it not a true Doctrine, that *the Scriptures contain all Things necessary to Salvation?* But, my Lord, it is nowhere expressly said, that *the Scriptures contain all Things necessary to Salvation.* It is nowhere said, that no other Articles of Faith need be believed. Where does it appear in Scripture, that the Scriptures were writ by any divine Command? Have any of the Gospels or Epistles this Authority to recommend them? Are they necessary to be believed, because there is any Law of Christ concerning the Necessity of believing them?

May I reject this uninterrupted Succession, because it is not mentioned in Scripture? And may I not as well reject all the Gospels? Produce your Authority, my Lord, mention your Texts of Scripture, where Christ *has hung the Salvation of Men* upon their believing that St. *Matthew* or St. *John* wrote such a Book seventeen hundred years ago. These, my Lord, are

Niceties and *Trifles* which are not to be found in Scripture, and consequently have nothing to do with the Salvation of Men.

Now if nothing be to be held as necessary, but what is expressly required in so many Words in Scripture, then it can never be proved that the Scriptures themselves are a *standing Rule of Faith in all Ages*, since it is nowhere expressly asserted, nor is it anywhere said, that the Scriptures should be continued as a Rule of Faith in all Ages. Is it an Objection against the Necessity of a perpetual Succession of the Clergy, that it is not mentioned in the Scripture? And is it not as good a one against the *Necessity* of making Scripture the *standing Rule of Faith in all Ages*, since it is never said that they were to be continued as a standing Rule in all Ages? If Things are only necessary for being said to be so in Scripture, then all that are not thus taught are equally unnecessary, and consequently it is no more necessary that the Scripture should be a fixed Rule of Faith in all Ages, than that there should be Bishops to ordain in all Ages.

Again, Where shall we find it in Scripture, that the Sacraments are to be continued in every Age of the Church? Where is it said that they shall always be the ordinary Means of Grace necessary to be observed? Is there any Law of Christ, any Text of Scripture, that expressly asserts, that if we leave the Use of the Sacraments, we are out of Covenant with God? Is it anywhere directly said, that we must never lay them aside, or that they will be *perpetually* necessary? No, my Lord, this is a *Nicety* and *Trifle* not to be *found in Scripture: There is no Stress laid there upon this Matter*, but upon Things *of a quite different Nature*.

I now presume, my Lord, that every one who has common Sense plainly sees, that if this Succession of the Clergy is to be despised, because it is not expressly required in Scripture; it undeniably follows, that we may reject the Scriptures, as not being a *standing Rule of Faith in all Ages;* we may disuse the Sacraments, as not the *ordinary Means of Grace in all Ages;* since these are no more mentioned in the Scriptures, or *expressly* required, than this uninterrupted Succession.

If it be a good Argument against the necessity of episcopal Ordainers, that it is never said in Scripture that there shall *always* be such Ordainers; it is certainly as conclusive against the Use of the Sacraments in every Age, that it is nowhere said in Scripture they shall be used in *all Ages*.

If no Government or Order of the Clergy is to be held as necessary, because no such Necessity is asserted in Scripture; it is certain, this concludes as strongly against *Government*, and *the*

Order itself, as against any *particular* Order. For it is no more said in Scripture that there shall be an Order of Clergy, than that there shall be any *particular* Order; therefore if this Silence proves against any *particular* Order of Clergy, it proves as much against *Order itself*.

Should therefore any of your Lordship's Friends have so much Church-Zeal, as to contend for the Necessity of *some Order*, though of no particular Order; he must fall under your Lordship's Displeasure, and be proved as mere a *Dreamer* and *Trifler*, as those who assert the Necessity of episcopal Ordination. For if it be plain that there need be no *episcopal Clergy*, because it is not said there shall *always* be episcopal Clergy; it is undeniably plain that there need be *no Order* of the Clergy, since it is nowhere said, there shall be *an Order* of Clergy: Therefore whoever shall contend for an Order of Clergy, will be as much condemned by your Lordship's Doctrine, as he that declares for the episcopal Clergy.

The Truth of the Matter is this; if nothing is to be esteemed of any Moment, but counted as mere *Trifle* and *Nicety* among Christians, which is not *expressly* required in the Scriptures; then it is a *Trifle* and *Nicety*, whether we believe the Scriptures to be a *standing Rule of Faith* in all Ages, whether we use the Sacraments in *all Ages*, whether we have any Clergy at all, whether we observe the Lord's Day, whether we baptize our Children, or whether we go to public Worship; for none of these Things are expressly required in so many Words in Scripture. But if your Lordship, with the rest of the Christian World, will take these Things to be of Moment, and well proved, because they are founded in Scripture, though not in *express Terms*, or under *plain Commands;* if you will acknowledge these Matters to be well asserted, because they may be gathered from Scripture, and are confirmed by the universal Practice of the Church in all Ages, (which is all the Proof that they are capable of,) I do not doubt but it will appear, that this *successive Order of the Clergy* is founded on the same Evidence, and supported by as great Authority, so that it must be thought of the same Moment with these Things by all unprejudiced Persons.

For, my Lord, though it be not expressly said, that there shall *always* be a *Succession of Episcopal Clergy*, yet it is a Truth founded in Scripture itself, and asserted by the universal Voice of Tradition in the first and succeeding Ages of the Church.

It is thus founded in Scripture: There we are taught that the Priesthood is a *positive Institution;* that no Man can take this Office unto himself; that neither our Saviour himself, nor his Apostles, nor any other Person, however extraordinarily endowed with Gifts from God, could, *as such*, exercise the priestly Office, till they had God's express Commission for that Purpose. Now how does it appear, that the Sacraments are positive Institutions, but that they are consecrated to such Ends and Effects, as of themselves they were no way qualified to perform? Now as it appears from Scripture that Men, *as such*, however endowed, were not qualified to take this Office upon them without God's Appointment; it is demonstratively certain, that Men so called are as much to be esteemed a *positive Institution*, as Elements so chosen can be called a *positive Institution*. All the personal Abilities of Men conferring no more Authority to exercise the Office of a Clergyman, than the natural Qualities of Water to make a Sacrament: So that the one Institution is as truly positive as the other.

Again, The Order of the Clergy is not only a *positive* Order instituted by God, but the different Degrees in this Order are of the same Nature. For we find in Scripture, that some Persons could perform some Offices in the Priesthood, which neither Deacons nor Priests could do, though those Deacons and Priests were inspired Persons, and Workers of Miracles. Thus *Timothy* was sent to ordain Elders, because none below his Order, who was a Bishop, could perform that Office. *Peter* and *John* laid their Hands on baptized Persons, because neither Priests nor Deacons, though Workers of Miracles, could execute that Part of the sacerdotal Office.

How can we imagine that the Apostles and Bishops thus distinguished themselves for nothing? That there was the same Power in *Deacons* and *Priests* to execute those Offices, though they took them to themselves? No my Lord; if three Degrees in the Ministry are instituted in Scripture, we are obliged to think them as truly distinct in their Powers, as we are to think that the Priesthood itself contains Powers that are distinct from those of the Laity. It is no more consistent with Scripture, to say that *Deacons* or *Priests* may ordain, than that the Laity are Priests or Deacons. The same divine Institution making as truly a Difference betwixt the Clergy, as it does betwixt Clergy and Laity.

Now if the Order of the Clergy be a *divine positive* Institution, in which there are different Degrees of Power, where some alone can ordain, *&c.*, whilst others can only perform other Parts of the sacred Office; if this (as it plainly appears) be a Doctrine of Scripture, then it is a Doctrine of Scripture, that there is a Necessity of such a Succession of Men as have Power to ordain. For do the Scriptures make it necessary that *Timothy* (or some Bishop) should be sent to *Ephesus* to ordain Priests, because the

Priests who were there could not ordain? And do not the same Scriptures make it as necessary, that *Timothy's* Successor be the only Ordainer, as well as he was in his Time? Will not Priests in the next Age be as destitute of the Power of ordaining, as when *Timothy* was alive? So that since the Scriptures teach, that *Timothy*, or Persons of his Order, could *alone* ordain in that Age, they as plainly teach, that the Successors of that Order can *alone* ordain in any Age, and consequently the Scriptures plainly teach a Necessity of an *episcopal Succession*.

The Scriptures declare there is a Necessity of a divine Commission to execute the Office of a Priest; they also teach, that this Commission can only be had from particular Persons: Therefore the Scriptures plainly teach, there is a Necessity of a *Succession of such particular Persons*, in order to keep up a truly *commissioned Clergy*.

Suppose when *Timothy* was sent to *Ephesus* to ordain Elders, the Church had told him, We have chosen Elders already, and laid our Hands upon them; that if he alone was allowed to exercise this Power, it might seem as if he alone had it; or that Ministers were the better for being ordained by his particular Hands; and that some Persons might imagine they could have no Clergy, except they were ordained by him, or some of his Order; and that seeing Christ had nowhere made an express Law, that such Persons should be necessary to the Ordination of the Clergy; therefore they rejected this Authority of *Timothy*, lest they should subject themselves to *Niceties* and *Trifles*.

Will your Lordship say, that such a Practice would have been allowed of in the *Ephesians?* Or that Ministers so ordained would have been received as the Ministers of Christ? If not, why must such Practice or such Ministers be allowed of in any After ages? Would not the same Proceeding against any of *Timothy's Successors* have deserved the same Censure, as being equally unlawful? If therefore the Scripture condemns all Ordination but what is episcopal, the Scriptures make a *Succession* of *episcopal Ordainers* necessary. So that I hope, my Lord, we shall be no more told that this is a Doctrine not mentioned in Scripture, or without any Foundation in it.

The great Objection to this Doctrine is, that this *episcopal Order of the Clergy* is only an apostolical Practice; and seeing *all* apostolical Practices are not binding to us, surely this need not.

In Answer to this, my Lord, I shall first shew, that though all apostolical Practices are not necessary, yet some may be necessary. *Secondly*, That the divine unalterable Right of Episcopacy is not founded *merely* on apostolical Practice.

To begin with the *first;* The Objection runs thus, *All apostolical Practices are not unalterable or obligatory to us, therefore no apostolical Practices are.* This, my Lord, is just as theological, as if I should say all Scripture-Truths are not Articles of Faith, or Fundamentals of Religion, therefore no Scripture-Truths are: Is not the Argument full as just and solid in one Case as the other? May there not be the same Difference between some Practices of the Apostles and others, that there is betwixt some Scripture Truths and others? Are all Truths equally important that are to be found in the Bible? Why must all Practices be of the same Moment that were apostolical? Now if there be any Way, either divine or human, of knowing an Article of Faith, from the smallest Truth, or most indifferent Matter in Scripture, they will equally assist us in distinguishing what apostolical Practices are of perpetual Obligation, and what are not. But it is a strange Way of Reasoning, that some People are fallen into, who seem to know nothing of *Moderation,* but jump as constantly out of one Extreme into another, as if there was no such Thing as a middle Way, or any such Virtue as *Moderation.* Thus either the Church must have an *absolute uncontrolable Authority,* or none at all; we must either hold *all* apostolical Practices necessary, or *none at all.*

Again, If no apostolical *Practices* can be unalterable, because all are not, then no apostolical *Doctrines* are necessary to be taught in all Ages, because all apostolical *Doctrines* are not; and we are no more obliged to teach the *Death, Satisfaction,* and *Resurrection* of *Jesus Christ,* than we are obliged to forbid the *eating of Blood and Things strangled.* If we must thus blindly follow them in all their Practices, or else be at Liberty to leave them in all, we must for the same Reason implicitly teach all their *Doctrines,* or else have a Power of receding from them all.

For if there be any Thing in the Nature of *Doctrines,* in the *Tenor* of Scripture, or the *Sense* of Antiquity, whereby we can know the Difference of some *Doctrines* from others, that some were *occasional temporary* Determinations, suited to particular States and Conditions in the Church, whilst others were such general *Doctrines* as would concern the Church in all States and Circumstances; if there can be this Difference betwixt apostolical *Doctrines,* there must necessarily be the same Difference betwixt apostolical *Practices,* unless we will say, that their *Practices,* were not suited to their *Doctrines.* For occasional *Doctrines* must produce occasional *Practices.*

Now may we not be obliged by some *Practices* of the Apostles, where the Nature of the Thing, and the Consent of Antiquity, shews it to be equally necessary and important in all Ages and

Conditions of the Church, without being tied down to the strict Observance of every Thing which the Apostles did, though it plainly appears that it was done upon *accidental* and *mutable* Reasons? Can we not be obliged to observe the *Lord's Day* from apostolical *Practice*, without being equally obliged to *lock the Doors* where we are met, because in the Apostle's Time they locked them for Fear of their Enemies.

My Lord, we are to follow the *Practices* of the Apostles, as we ought to follow every Thing else, with *Discretion* and *Judgment*, and not run headlong into every Thing they did, because they were Apostles, or yet think that because we need not practise after them in every Thing, we need do it in nothing. We best imitate them, when we act upon such Reasons as they acted upon, and neither make their *occasional* Practices *perpetual* Laws, nor break through such general Rules as will always have the *same Reason* to be observed.

If it be asked how we can know what Practices must be observed, and what may be laid aside? I answer, as we know *Articles* of Faith from *lesser Truths* ; as we know *occasional* Doctrines from *perpetual* Doctrines ; that is, from the Nature of the Things, from the *Tenor* of Scripture, and the *Testimony* of Antiquity.

Secondly, It is not true, that the *divine unalterable Right* of Episcopacy is founded *merely* upon apostolical Practice.

We do not say that Episcopacy cannot be changed *merely* because we have apostolical Practice for it, but because such is the Nature of the Christian Priesthood, that it can only be continued in that Method, which God has appointed for its Continuance. Thus Episcopacy is the *only* instituted Method of continuing the Priesthood ; therefore Episcopacy is *unchangeable*, not because it is an apostolical Practice, but because the Nature of the Thing requires it: A positive Institution being only to be continued in that Method which God has appointed ; so that it is the Nature of the Priesthood, and not the apostolical Practice alone, that makes it necessary to be continued. The apostolical Practice indeed shews, that Episcopacy is the Order that is appointed, but it is the Nature of the Priesthood that assures us that it is *unalterable*: And that because an Office which is of no Significancy, but as it is of divine Appointment, and instituted by God, can no otherwise be continued, but in that Way of Continuance which God has appointed.

The Argument proceeds thus: The Christian Priesthood is a divine positive Institution, which as it could only begin by the *divine Appointment*, so it can only descend to After-ages in such a Method as God has been pleased to appoint.

The Apostles (and your Lordship owns, Christ was in *all* that they did*) instituted Episcopacy *alone*, therefore this Method of Episcopacy is unalterable, not because an *apostolical Practice* cannot be laid aside, but because the Priesthood can only descend to After-ages in such a Method as is of divine Appointment.

So that the Question is not fairly stated, when it is asked whether Episcopacy, being an apostolical Practice, may be laid aside ? But it should be asked, whether an instituted particular Method of continuing the Priesthood be not necessary to be continued ? Whether an appointed Order of receiving a Commission from God be not necessary to be observed, in order to receive a Commission from him ? If the Case was thus stated, as it ought, to be fairly stated, anyone would soon perceive, that we can no more lay aside Episcopacy, and yet continue the Christian Priesthood, than we can alter the Terms of Salvation, and be in Covenant with God.

I come now, my Lord, to the second Objection, *That this uninterrupted Succession is subject to so great Uncertainty, that if it be necessary, we can never say that we are in the Church.*

I know no Reason, my Lord, why it is so uncertain, but because it is founded upon *historical Evidence*. Let it therefore be considered, my Lord, that Christianity itself is a *Matter of Fact* only conveyed to us by *historical Evidence :* That the *Canon of Scripture* is only made known to us by *historical Evidence ;* that we have no other Way of knowing what Writings are the Word of God ; and yet the Truth of our Faith, and every other Means of Grace depends upon our Knowledge and Belief of the Scriptures. Must we not declare the Necessity of the Succession of Bishops, because it can only be proved by *historical Evidence*, and that for such a long Tract of Time ?

Why then do we declare the Belief of the Scriptures necessary to Salvation ? Is not this equally putting the Salvation of Men upon a *Matter of Fact*, supported only by *historical Evidence*, and making it depend upon Things done seventeen hundred Years ago ? Cannot *historical Evidence* satisfy us in one Point, as well as in the other ? Is there any Thing in the Nature of this Succession, that it cannot be as well asserted by *historical Evidence*, as the Truth of the Scriptures ? Is there not the same bare Possibility in the Thing itself, that the Scriptures may in some important Points be corrupted, as that this Succession may be broke ? But is this any just Reason why we should believe, or fear, that the Scriptures are corrupted, because there is a physical

---

* *Answer to Dr.* Snape.

Possibility of it, though there is all the Proof that can be required of the contrary? Why then must we set aside the Necessity of this Succession from a *bare Possibility* of Error, though there is all the Proof that can be required, that it never was broken, but strictly kept up?

And though your Lordship has told the World so much of the *Improbability*, *Nonsense*, and *Absurdity* of this Succession, yet I promise your Lordship an Answer, whenever you shall think fit to show, *when*, or *how*, or *where*, this Succession broke, or *seemed* to break, or was *likely* to break.

And till then, I shall content myself with offering this Reason to your Lordship, why it is *morally impossible* it ever should have broken in all the Term of Years, from the Apostles to the present Times.

The Reason is this; it has been a received Doctrine in every Age of the Church, that no Ordination was valid but that of Bishops: This Doctrine, my Lord, has been a constant Guard upon the *episcopal Succession;* for seeing it was universally believed that Bishops *alone* could ordain, it was *morally impossible* that any Persons could be received as Bishops, who had not been so ordained.

Now is it not *morally impossible* that in our Church anyone should be made a Bishop without *episcopal Ordination?* Is there any Possibility of forging Orders, or stealing a Bishopric by any other Stratagem? No, it is *morally impossible*, because it is an acknowledged Doctrine amongst us, that a Bishop can only be ordained by Bishops. Now as this Doctrine must necessarily prevent anyone being a Bishop without *episcopal Ordination* in our Age, so it must have the same Effect in every other Age as well as ours; and consequently it is as reasonable to believe that the Succession of Bishops was not broke in any Age since the Apostles, as that it was not broke in our own Kingdom within these forty Years. For the same Doctrine which preserves it forty Years, may as well preserve it forty hundred Years, if it was equally believed in all that Space of Time. That this has been the constant Doctrine of the Church, I presume your Lordship will not deny; I have not here entered into the historical Defence of it; this, and indeed every other Institution of the Christian Church, has been lately so well defended from the ecclesiastical Records by a very excellent and judicious Writer.*

We believe the Scriptures are not corrupted, because it was always a received Doctrine in the Church, that they were the *standing Rule of Faith,* and because the Providence of God may

---

* *Original Draught of the Primitive Church.*

well be supposed to preserve such Books as were to convey to every Age the Means of Salvation. The same Reasons prove the great Improbability that this Succession should ever be broken, both because it was always against a received Doctrine to break it, and because we may justly hope the Providence of God would keep up his own Institution.

I must here observe, that though your Lordship often exposes the Impossibility of this Succession, yet at other times, even you yourself, and your Advocates, assert it. Thus you tell us, *That the Papists have one regular Appointment or uninterrupted Succession of Bishops undefiled with the touch of Lay-hands.**

Is this Succession then such an *improbable impossible* Thing, and yet can your Lordship assure us that it is at *Rome;* that though it be seventeen hundred Years old there, yet that it is a true one? Is it such *Absurdity*, and *Nonsense*, and every Thing that is *ridiculous*, when we lay Claim to it; and yet can your Lordship assure us that it is not only possible to be, but *actually* is in Being, in the Church of *Rome;* What Arguments or Authority can your Lordship produce, to shew that there is a Succession there, that will not equally prove it to be here?

You assert expressly, that there is a *true Succession* there; you deny that we have it here; therefore your Lordship must mean, that we have not episcopal Ordination when we separated from the Church of *Rome*. And here the Controversy must rest betwixt you and your Adversaries, *whether we had episcopal Ordination* then; for as your Lordship has expressly affirmed that there is this uninterrupted Succession in the Church of *Rome*, it is impossible that we should want it, unless we had not episcopal Ordination at the *Reformation*.

Whenever your Lordship shall please to appear in Defence of the *Nag's-Head Story*, or any other Pretence against our episcopal Ordination when we departed from *Rome*, we shall beg Leave to shew ourselves so far true Protestants, as to answer any *Popish* Argument your Lordship can produce.

Here let the *common Sense* of the Laity be once more appealed to: Your Lordship tells them that an *uninterrupted Succession* is improbable, absurd, and *morally* speaking, *impossible*, and, for this Reason, they need not trouble their Heads about it; yet in another Place you positively affirm, that this true *uninterrupted Succession* is actually in the Church of *Rome:* That is, they are to despise this Succession, because it never was, or ever can be; yet are to believe that it *really* is in the *Romish* Church. My Lord, this comes very near *saying* and *unsaying*, *to the great*

---

* *Preservative*, p. 80.

Diversion of the Papists. Must they not laugh at your Lordship's *Protestant Zeal*, which might be much better called the *Spirit* of Popery? Must they not be highly pleased with all your Banter and Ridicule upon an *uninterrupted Succession*, when they see you so kindly accept theirs: And think it only *Nonsense* and *Absurdity* when claimed by any other Church? Surely, my Lord, they must conceive great Hopes of your Lordship, since you have here rather chosen to contradict yourself, than not vouch for their Succession: For you have said it is *morally impossible*, yet affirm that it is with them.

The third Objection against this *uninterrupted Succession* is this, that it is a *Popish Doctrine*, and *gives* Papists *Advantage over us.*

The Objection proceeds thus, We must not assert the Necessity of this Succession, because the *Papists* say it is only to be found with them. I might add, because some mighty zealous *Protestants* say so too.

But if this be good Argumentation, we ought not to tell the *Jews*, or *Deists*, &c., that there is any Necessity of embracing Christianity, because the *Papists* say Christians can only be saved in their Church.

Again, we ought not to insist upon a true Faith, because the *Papists* say that a true Faith is only in their Communion. So that there is just as much Popery in teaching this Doctrine, as in asserting the Necessity of Christianity to a *Jew*, or the Necessity of a right Faith to a *Socinian*, &c.

I shall only trouble your Lordship with a Word or two concerning another Point in my former Letter. I there proved that your Lordship has put the whole of our Title to God's Favour upon Sincerity, *as such*, independent of every Thing else. That no Purity of Worship, no Excellence of Order, no Truth of Faith, no Sort of Sacraments, no Kind of Institutions, or any Church, *as such*, can help us to the least Degree of God's Favour, or give us the smallest Advantage above any other Communion. And consequently, that your Lordship has set sincere *Jews, Quakers, Socinians, Muggletonians*, and all *Heretics* and *Schismatics*, upon the same Bottom, as to the Favour of God, with sincere Christians.

Upon this, my Lord, I am called upon to prove that these several Sorts of People can be *sincere* in your Account of Sincerity. To which, my Lord, I make this Answer, Either there are some sincere Persons among *Jews, Quakers, Socinians*, or any kind of *Heretics* and *Schismatics*, or there are not; if there are, your Lordship has given them the same Title to God's Favour, that you have to the sincerest Christians; if you will say there are no sincere Persons amongst any of them, then your Lordship damns them all in the Gross; for surely Corruptions in Religion, professed with Insincerity, will never save People.

I have nothing to do to prove the Sincerity of any of them; if they are sincere, what I have said is true; if you will not allow them to be sincere, you condemn them all at once.

Again, I humbly supposed a Man might be sincere in his *religious Opinions*, though it might be owing to *some ill Habits*, or *something criminal* in himself, that he was fallen into such or such a Way of thinking. But it seems this is all *Contradiction;* and no Man can be sincere, who has *any Faults*, or whose *Faults* have any *Influence* upon his Way of thinking.

Your Lordship tells all the *Dissenters*, that they may be easy if they are sincere; and that it is the only Ground for Peace and Satisfaction. But pray, my Lord, if none are to be esteemed *sincere*, but those who have no Faults, or whose Faults have no Influence upon their Persuasions, who can be assured that he is *sincere*, but he that has the least Pretence to it, the *proud Pharisee?* If your Lordship, or your Advocates, were desired to prove your Sincerity, either before God or Man, it must be for these Reasons, because you have no ill Passions or Habits, no faulty Prejudices, no past or present Vices, that can have any Effect upon your Minds. My Lord, as this is the only Proof that any of you could give of your own Sincerity, in this Meaning of it, so the very pretence to it, would prove the Want of it.

A
REPLY
TO THE
Bishop of *BANGOR*'s
ANSWER
TO THE
REPRESENTATION
OF THE
COMMITTEE
OF
CONVOCATION.
Humbly addressed to his Lordship.

By *WILLIAM LAW*, M. A.

LONDON:
Printed for J. RICHARDSON, in Pater-noster-Row.

1762.

The Contents.

Of the Nature of the Church. *Page* 89

Of Church Authority. 113

A remarkable Evasion of his Lordship's in Relation to Church Authority. 132

Of Excommunication. 142

Of Church Authority, as it relates to external Communion. 165

Of Sincerity, and private Judgment. 184

Of the Reformation. 195

The Third Letter to the Bishop of *Bangor*.

My Lord,

I BEG leave to trouble your Lordship and the World once more with my Remarks upon the Doctrines you have lately delivered. Your *Sermon* and *Preservative* I have already considered in the most impartial manner I could; and shall now examine your Answer to the *Representation* of the Learned *Committee*, both as it is an Answer to that, and as it contains Opinions contrary to the fundamental Articles of Christianity.

I have less need of excusing to your Lordship this third Address, since you can so easily acquit yourself from the Trouble of making any Reply to whatever comes from me. It seems I have too small a Reputation to deserve your Notice; but if the *Dean of* Chichester *would but declare for the Doctrines delivered in my Letters, and put but a little of his Reputation upon the issue, then,* you say, *you would submit to the Employment* of an Answer.*

My Lord, I readily confess that I have neither *Reputation* nor *Learning*, nor any *Title* to recommend me to your Lordship's Notice; but I must own, that I thought the very *want of these* would, in your Opinion, qualify me to make better Enquiries into Religious Truths, and raise your Esteem of me as a Correspondent in these Matters. For you expressly declare, that *if* Learning *or* Literature *is to be interested in this Debate, then the most learned Man has certainly a Title to be the Universal Judge.*† So that no Man ought to shew any Regard to *Learning*, as a *Qualification* in religious Disputes, unless he will own that the most learned Man has a Title to be a Pope, or as you express it, the *Universal Judge.* Yet your Lordship, in spite of this Protestant Doctrine so lately delivered, has despised and

---

* *Answ. to Condit. of our Saviour vindicated*, p. 112.
† *Answ. to Repr.*, p. 99.

overlooked all my Opinions in Religion merely for my want of *Character* and *Learning*, and has promised to undertake the *needless* Task of examining those Opinions with another Gentleman, merely upon account of his *Character* and *Reputation*. So that though it is perfect Popery, and making the most learned Man the universal Judge, to allow anything to Learning; yet your Lordship is so *true a Protestant*, and pays so great a Regard to Learning, that you will not so much as examine a Doctrine with a Person of no Character for Learning.

Again you say; *Nothing has been seen to administer so many Doubts and Differences* (in Religion) *as Learning*,* and that *none are seen to be less secure from Error than learned Men*.

Now is it not strange, my Lord, that after this noble Declaration against *Learning*, as the greatest Cause of Doubts and Differences, this extraordinary Preference given to *Ignorance*, as a more likely Guide to Truth, you should despise anyone as below your Notice in religious Disputes, because he wants *that* Learning which so blinds the Understanding? Can you ascribe thus much Honour to Learning, which in your Opinion does so much Dishonour to Religion? Will you *interest* those Qualities in this Debate, which if they are allowed to have any *Interest* in it, will make the Man of the greatest Abilities the *Universal Judge*.

Again, As a farther Reason why you have taken no notice of me, you say, as *considerable a Writer as Mr.* Law *is, I hope the Committee*, as a Body, *are much more considerable in the Dean's Eyes; I am sure, they are in mine: And the Dean himself, I have thought a much more considerable writer than Mr.* Law, *and so have* spent all my time upon *Him* and the *Committee*.

Now, my Lord, though I readily acknowledge this to be exceeding true, and have so far at least a just Opinion of myself, as to be afraid to be compared to much less Persons than the Dean, or any of the learned Committee, yet, my Lord, this Reason, which, if urged by anyone else, might pass for a good one, cannot be urged by you, without contradicting a principal Doctrine maintained in your *Answer to the Representation*. For there you bid us *look into the Popish Countries; and see whether* one illiterate honest *Man be not as capable of judging for himself in Religion, as all their* learned *Men united; even supposing them met together in a* General Council, *with all possible Marks of Solemnity and Grandeur*.†

Here we see a Person merely for his want of *Literature* made as good a Judge in Religion, as a *General Council* of the most

---

* *Answ. to Repr.*, p. 98. † *Ibid.*, p. 98.

learned Men, acting with the utmost Solemnity. We see a Council in its utmost Perfection contemptuously compared to, and even made less considerable than a private illiterate Person. And this we may fairly suppose was intended to shew your Contempt of the *English Convocation*. But a few Weeks after, when you had another Design in your Head, you tell us to this purpose, that you disregarded the Writings of a single Person of no Figure in the learned World, to pay your respect to the Committee as a *Body, which, as such, is much more considerable in your Eyes*. So that here an *illiterate* Person is made a great Judge in Religion in regard to a Body of learned Men, because he is illiterate; and here that same Person is made of no Consideration in Points of Religion in regard to a *Body* of learned Men, merely because he is *private and illiterate*.

It wll be of no Advantage to your Lordship, to say that you have only replied to the *Dean*, in relation to me; in the *same* Words that he used to you, in relation to Mr. *Sykes*.

For, my Lord, that Reply might be proper enough from the Dean, if he judged right of Mr. *Sykes's* Performance; it being very reasonable to overlook an Adversary that has neither Truth, Abilities, or Reputation to support his Cause.

But though this might be right in the Dean, who pays a true Regard to the Authority and Learning of great Men, yet it cannot be defended by your Lordship. For though my *Learning* or *Reputation* were ever so low, they are so far from unqualifying me for Religious Enquiries, that if you would sincerely stand to what you have said, you ought, for the want of these very Accomplishments, to esteem me the more, and even choose me out as a Correspondent in this Debate.

But however, without any farther Regard to the Opinion your Lordship has either of me or my Abilities, I shall proceed to the most impartial Examination of your Book that I possibly can.

Of the Nature of the Church.

TO begin with your Lordship's Description of a Church; *The number of Men, whether small or great, whether dispersed or united, who truly and sincerely are Subjects to Christ alone in Matters of Salvation.**

The learned Committee calls this your Lordship's Description of a Church.

* *Serm.*, p. 17.

Your Lordship answers; *I wonder to hear this called my Description of* A Church; *whereas I pretend, in those Words to describe no other, but* The Universal Invisible Church. *It is a Description, not of* A Church, *in our modern way of speaking; but of* The Church, the Invisible Church of Christ.*

May not we also wonder, my Lord, that you should so describe *The* Church, that it will not bear being called *A* Church? If I should say it is a Description of no Church, I have your Lordship's Confession, that it is not *A* Church; so that it is something betwixt *a Church* and no Church, that is, it is *The Church.*

Suppose, my Lord, somebody or other should have a mind to be of your Church, if he betakes himself to *A Church*, he is wrong; you do not mean *A Church*, but *The Church.* Your Lordship owns that this is not a Description of a Church in the modern way of speaking; I humbly presume to call upon your Lordship to shew that it is a Description according to the ancient way of speaking. To call the Number of Believers the Invisible Church, is a way of speaking, no more to be found in the Scriptures, than the Company of *Præ-Adamites.*

There is, no doubt of it, an Invisible Church, *i.e.*, a Number of Beings that are in Covenant with God, who are not to be seen by human Eyes; and we may be said to be Members of this *Invisible Church*, as we are entitled to the same Hopes and Expectations. But to call the Number of Men and Women who believe in Christ and observe his Institutions, whether dispersed or united in this visible World, to call these *The Invisible Church*, is as false and groundless, as to call them the Order of *Angels*, or the Church of *Seraphims.* The Profession of Christians is as visible as any other Profession, and as much declared by visible external Acts. And it is as proper to call a Number of Men practising *Law* or *Physic*, an Invisible Society of *Lawyers* and *Physicians*, as to call the Church on Earth the *Invisible* Church. For all those Acts and Offices which prove People to be Christians, or the Church of Christ, are as visible and notorious, as those which prove them to be of any particular secular Employment. Would it be proper to call the Number of *Infidels* and *Idolaters* the Invisible Church of the Devil? Are they not visibly under the Dominion of the Powers of Darkness? Are they not visibly out of Christ's Church? Must it not therefore be as visible who is in this Church, as who is not in it?

If anyone should tell us that we are to believe *Invisible* Scriptures, and observe *Invisible* Sacraments, he would have just as much Reason and Scripture of his side, as your Lordship has

---

* *Answ. to Repr.*, p. 70.

for this Doctrine. And it would be of the same Service to the World to talk of these *Invisibilities*, if the *Canon* of Scripture was in dispute, as to describe this *Invisible* Church, when the Case is, with what *Visible* Church we ought to unite.

Our Saviour himself tells us, that *the Kingdom of Heaven is like unto a Net that was cast into the Sea, and gathered of every kind ; which, when it was full, they drew to shore and sat down, and gathered the good into Vessels, but cast the bad away.* And then says, *so shall it be at the end of the World.*[*]

This, my Lord, is a Description of the State of Christ's Church given us by himself. Is there anything in this Description that should lead us to take it for an *Invisible* Kingdom, that consists of one particular sort of People *invisibly* united to Christ ? Nay, is it not the whole Intent of this Similitude to teach us the contrary, that his Kingdom is to consist of a Mixture of good and bad Subjects till the End of the World ? The Kingdom of Christ is said here to gather its Members, as a Net gathers *all kinds* of Fish ; it is chiefly compared to it in this respect, because it gathers of *all kinds ;* which I suppose is a sufficient Declaration, that this Kingdom consists of Subjects good and bad, as that the Net that gathers of every kind of Fish, takes good and bad Fish. Let us suppose that the Church of Christ was this *Invisible Number* of People united to Christ by such internal invisible Graces ; is it possible that a Kingdom consisting of this one particular sort of People *invisibly good*, should be like a Net that gathers of *every kind* of Fish ? If it was to be compared to a Net, it ought to be compared to such a Net, as gathers only of one kind, *viz.* good Fish and then it might represent to us a Church that has but one sort of Members.

But since Christ who certainly understood the Nature of his own Kingdom, has declared that it is like a Net that gathers *of every kind of Fish ;* it is as absurd to say, that it consists only of *one kind* of Persons (*viz.*, the invisibly good) as to say, that the Net which gathers of *every kind*, has only of *one kind* in it. Farther ; *when it was full they drew it to shore, and gathered the good into Vessels, but cast the bad away ; so shall it be at the end of the World.* Now as it was the bad as well the good Fish which filled the *Net*, and the Church is compared to the *Net* in this respect ; so it is evident that bad Men as well as good are Subjects of this Kingdom. And I presume they are Members of that Kingdom which they fill up, as surely as the Fish must be in the *Net* before they can fill it. All these Circumstances plainly declare that the Church or Kingdom of Christ shall

---

[*] *Matth.* xiii. 47.

consist of a Mixture of good and bad People to the End of the World.

Again; Christ declares *that the Kingdom of Heaven is like to a certain King which made a marriage for his Son*, and sent his Servants out into the High-ways, who *gathered together all as many as they found, both good and bad, and the Wedding was filled with Guests.**

Nothing can be more evident than that the chief Intent of this Parable is to shew that the Church of Christ is to be a Mixture of good and bad People to the end of the World. It is like a *Feast* where good and bad Guests are entertained; but can it be like such a *Feast* if only the *invisibly* virtuous are Members of it? If the Subjects of this Kingdom are of one *invisible kind*, how can they bear any Resemblance to a *Feast* made up of *all kinds* of Guests? Nay, what could be thought of, more unlike to this Kingdom, if it was such a Kingdom as you have represented it?

How could our blessed Saviour have more directly guarded against such a Description of his Kingdom as your Lordship has given us, than he has done in these Parables? He compares it to a Quantity of good and bad Fish in a *Net*, to a Number of good and bad Guests at a *Feast*. Are there any Words that could more fully declare his Meaning to be, that his Kingdom consisted of good and bad Subjects? Could anyone more directly contradict this Account of our Saviour, than by saying that his Kingdom is an invisible Kingdom consisting of a particular sort of People invisibly virtuous?

Your Lordship professes a mighty Regard for the Scriptures, and a great Dislike to all Doctrines that are not delivered there; pray, my Lord, produce but so much as *one Text* of Scripture; tell us the *Apostle* or *Evangelist* that ever declared the *Number of Believers whether dispersed or united on Earth, to be the Universal Invisible Church;* shew us any one Passage in Scripture which teaches us, that none are of the Church of Christ, but those who have such *Invisible Virtues*, and cannot be known to be so.

There is as much Authority from Scripture to prove that the Church is a Kingdom without any Subjects, as that they are only of it, who have such Invisible Graces. And it is as easy to prove from those sacred Writings, that neither Christ or his Apostles were ever *Visible* on Earth, as that the Number of People on Earth who believe in Christ constitute the *Invisible Church*.

---

* *Matth.* xxii. 2.

In the Parables above mentioned it is out of all doubt that our Saviour describes his *Universal Kingdom* or *Church*: It is also certain that the *Universal* Invisible Church, which you call Christ's Church, cannot be this *Universal Church* that is made up of a Mixture of good and bad Members. I therefore beg of your Lordship to let us know where Christ has taught us, that he has two *Universal Churches* on Earth; for if you cannot shew that he has declared that he has these two Universal Churches, you must allow that this which you have described, is a Church of your own setting up, not only without any Authority, but even against the express Word of Scripture.

Your Lordship says that the Doctrines which the Learned Committee have condemned, if they be of that evil Tendency, must be so *either with Regard to the* Universal Invisible Church, *made up of all those who sincerely in their Hearts believe in Christ; or with respect to the* Universal Visible Church *made up of all, who in all Countries (whether sincerely or insincerely) openly profess to believe in Christ; or with respect to* some particular Visible Church.*

It may be justly expected, my Lord, that you should shew us some Grounds for this Distinction. Where does our blessed Lord give us so much as the least Hint that he has founded two Universal Churches on Earth? Did he describe his Church by halves when he likened it to a *Net* full of all kinds of Fish? Has he any where let us know that he has another Universal Kingdom on Earth besides this, which in the Variety of its Member is like a *Net* full of all sorts of good and bad Fish.

Let your Lordship, if you can, shew any Subtilties in *Popery* which are more of human Invention, or more contrary to Scripture than this refined Distinction. The *Opus Operatum* in the Sacraments, the *temporal* Satisfactions for Sins, Works of *Supererogation*, or any of the nicest Arts of *Jesuitism*, are not less founded in Scripture than this nice Distinction, of injuring either the *Universal Invisible*, or the *Universal Visible*, or a *particular Visible Church*. For, my Lord, the Church of Christ is as truly one and the same Church, as the Sacrament of Baptism is one and the same Baptism; and he no more instituted several sorts of Churches, than he instituted several kinds of Baptism.

Pray, my Lord, therefore be no longer angry at *Human Arts* in Religion; why may not *Popery* have its Peculiarities in Doctrine as well as your Lordship; the Church of *Rome*, with all its Additions and Corruptions, and pompous Ornaments, is as much like the Church as it was in the *Apostles'* Times, as your

---

* *Answ. to Repr.*, p. 5.

Invisible Church is like that which Christ declared to be his Church. When they set out the Church as *Infallible*, they do but *reason* like your Lordship, when you describe it as *Invisible*.

That there are good and bad Church-men, is past all doubt; but that People are of the Church by means of *Invisible Virtues*, is as false, as that only good Men came to the Feast in the Gospel. We are assured that *many are called, but few are chosen;* *i.e.*, that many shall be made Members of Christ's Church, but few shall be saved; and who these few are that truly work out their Salvation, may be *invisible* to us; but those many that were called, that is, who were in the Church, though they did not live up to all the Intents of Church-Communion, yet were as truly of the Church, as the bad Fish were really in the Net.

But to proceed; I shall Illustrate this Reply of your Lordship concerning an *Universal Visible, and Universal Invisible, and particular Visible Church*, with the following Instances.

Let us suppose any one was charged with writing against the *Sacraments;* if he should with your Lordship reply, that this Charge against him must either relate to the *Universal Visible Sacraments*, or *Universal Invisible Sacraments*, or *particular Visible Sacraments*, he would have just as much *Scripture* or *Reason* to support that Distinction, as your Lordship has for dividing the Church into *Universal Visible*, and *Universal Invisible*, and *particular Visible*. For the Profession of Christianity, or Church-Membership, is as external and visible a thing, as the Sacraments are external visible Institutions. So that it is as contrary to Scripture, and as mere an human Invention to make Pretence of an *Universal Invisible Church*, when the Dispute is concerning Christ's Church on Earth, as it is to have recourse to *Invisible Sacraments*, if the Question was concerning *Christ's Sacraments*.

They are both equally external and visible; and as the Sacraments may be received without any spiritual Advantage, so Persons may be of the Church and yet not be saved. And as the Sacraments are not less Sacraments, though they may not convey the designed Benefits to the Receiver; so neither are such a Number of People not of the Church, though they do not obtain that Salvation which is the intended Consequence of Church-Communion.

Your Lordship cannot give any one Reason for introducing this Distinction with Regard to the Church, which will not equally hold for the same Distinction in Regard to the Sacraments; and there is exactly the same *Quakery* and *Fanaticism* in one Doctrine as the other.

For as they are the *Sacraments* which chiefly constitute the

Church, so no *Distinctions* or *Divisions* can with any tolerable Propriety be applied to the Church, but such as may be also applied to the *Sacraments*, that constitute the *Church*. And therefore the Terms *Universal* and *Particular*, *Visible* and *Invisible*, have no more to do with Christ's Church which he has instituted in *this World*, than with the two Sacraments which he also instituted, *Baptism*, and the *Supper* of the Lord.

Again, If anyone was accused of writing against the *Christian Revelation*, he might answer with your Lordship, if this Accusation be true, it must be so either with regard to God's *Universal Visible* Revelation in all the *Canonical* Books, or with Regard to his *Universal Invisible Revelation* whereby he speaks inwardly to all *sincere* People, or with respect to some *particular* Part of his *visible Revelation*. Let all the World judge, whether if a Person so accused should make this Reply, it would not plainly appear, either that he was a downright *Enthusiast*, or a crafty Dealer in *Cant* and *artificial* Words. I am sure your Lordship cannot shew that you have more Authority to divide the Church on Earth into *Universal Visible*, and *Universal Invisible*, and *particular Visible*, than he had to divide the Christian *Revelation* into *Visible* and *Invisible*. Neither was it less to the purpose for such a one to talk of *Invisible* Scriptures, if he was accused of denying the *Gospel* of St. *John*, than it is for your Lordship under your present Accusation to have recourse to the *Invisible* Church; but your Lordship will find no Advantage in this Retreat.

Again; Suppose a Person was charged with writing *Treason* against the Government, and in his Defence should thus distinguish; *The Treason* that I am charged with against the Government, must relate either to *Universal* Government in this World, or to *Universal* Government in the *other World*, or to some *particular* Government in this World.

It would be as *ingenuous*, as *sincere*, and as *pertinent* for a Person thus accused to talk of Governments that had no relation to the Case, but in his own Imagination, as for your Lordship in the present Dispute to talk of *Universal Visible*, and *Universal Invisible*, and *particular Visible* Churches. For besides this, that there is no Foundation for such a Distinction, yet if there was such an Invisible Church, how is it possible your Lordship should hurt it? How is it possible the *Learned Committee* should mean to charge you with injuring it? They might as well think your Lordship capable of forming a Design to arrest a Party of *Spirits*, as to attack an Invisible Church that neither you nor they know anything of, or where to find.

Your Lordship saith, *That if you have unjustly laid anything* *down in this Description of the Invisible Church, to the Prejudice or Injury of any Particular Visible Church,* you acknowledge that it is your part to answer for it.*

I believe it appears already that your Lordship has a great deal to answer for upon this Head; and I shall now farther shew, that you have set up this *Invisible Church* in Opposition to *all other* Churches *whatever*. This will appear from the following Passage in your Sermon; *This Inquiry will bring us back to the first, which is the only true Account of the Church of Christ or Kingdom of Christ in the Mouth of a Christian,* viz. *the Number of Men whether small or great,*† &c.

We have your Lordship's Confession that you only here pretend to describe the *Universal Invisible* Church of Christ; you also here plainly declare, that *it is the only true Account of Christ's Church or Kingdom in the Mouth of a Christian.*

Is not this, my Lord, expressly declaring, that *any other* Account of Christ's Church is not a true one; for you say this is the *only true* one? Is it not directly affirming that any other Description of Christ's Church cannot become the Mouth of a Christian; for you say that this is the *only true one in the Mouth of a Christian?* So that if we call the Universal Visible Church, the Church of Christ, we give a false Account of Christ's Church, and such a one as is unfit for the Mouth of a Christian.

Could your Lordship have thought of anything more shocking, than to say that the Description of your *Invisible Church is the only true Account* of Christ's Church, and fit for the Mouth of a Christian, when our Saviour has given us a quite contrary Account of it from his own Mouth? He compares it to a *Net* full of good and bad Fish, to a *Feast* full of good and bad Guests; this surely, my Lord, is not an Account of your *Invisible* Church, where there are only Invisible Members. Your Lordship cannot say that Christ has here described the *Invisible Church;* you directly say that your Description of the Invisible Church, is the only true Account of Christ's Church in the Mouth of a Christian; and consequently this Account which our Saviour himself has given of his Church, stands condemned by your Lordship as a false Account of Christ's Church unfit for the Mouth of a Christian. I appeal to the common Sense of every Reader, whether I have laid anything to your Charge, but what your own express Words amount to. The short is this; If Christ has in these Parables described the *Universal Church* as Visible, then it is plain that this Account of Christ's Church is a false one in the Mouth of a Christian; for you say your

---

* *Answ. to Rep.*, p. 70. † P. 16.

Account of the Invisible Church *is the only true Account of Christ's Church in the Mouth of a Christian;* so that nothing can secure this Account which our Saviour has given of his Church from your Lordship's Censure, but shewing that it is the very *same Account of the Invisible Church* that you have given; which I believe is more than your Lordship will undertake to prove; it being as hard to prove that a Net full of good and bad Fish, or a Feast full of good and bad Guests, should represent an Invisible Kingdom of only one sort of Subjects, as that the Net and Feast, though both *full*, should represent a Kingdom that had not *one* Subject in it.

If a *Fanatic* should describe the Christian Sacraments, as *Spiritual* and *Invisible* Sacraments, and then affirm that that was the *only true Account of Christian* Sacraments *in the Mouth of a Christian,* could we charge him with less than writing against *all* Sacraments but *Invisible* Sacraments? It is just thus far that your Lordship has proceeded against the *External Visible* Church; you have declared the Invisible one to be the *only true Church,* fit to be spoken of by a Christian, which I think is laying down a Position highly injurious to the Visible Church, since it is here condemned as false in the Mouth of a Christian.

From all this it appears, that the *Learned Committee* have justly disliked your Lordship's Description of the Church of Christ.

First; As you describe it as an Invisible Church, directly contrary to the Scripture Representations of it, as given by our Saviour himself.

Secondly; As it is in Disparagement of the *Article* of our Church, which gives quite another Description of the Church.

That the Church described in the *Article* falls under your Lordship's Censure, is very plain. For you declare that your Description of the Invisible, is the only true Account of Christ's Church; therefore the Description in the Article cannot be a true one, because it is different from yours, which is the only true one.

Secondly; You declare that you consider the Church under this Description, *viz.* as *Invisible*, because every other Notion of it, is made up of inconsistent Images:* Therefore the Account of the Church in the Article is thus inconsistent.

Now what does your Lordship answer here? Only this, *that the Article speaks of* the Visible Church, *and you speak of the Invisible one.*†

This Answer, my Lord, proves the Charge upon you to be

---

* *Serm.,* p. 10.   † *Answ. to Repr.,* p. 78.

just. For since you own that you describe another Church than that which is described in the *Article*, and expressly affirm that your Account of this other Church is the only *true Account of Christ's Church in the Mouth of a Christian;* you plainly declare that the other Church is a false one in the Mouth of a Christian. Yet your Lordship rests satisfied with this Reply, as if you had cleared yourself by it. Whereas this is the very Charge itself, That you have described the Church otherwise than it is in the Article, and have called this *different* and *new* Account of it, the *only true Account* of it; and if it be the only true one, then that which is given in the *Article* must be a false one.

Your Lordship goes on, *The Article declares what it is, that makes every such Congregation, the* Visible Church *of Christ; and I describe what it is that makes every particular Man, a Member of Christ's* Universal Invisible Church. *The Article describes those* outward Acts, *which are necessary to make a Visible Church; and I describe that* inward Sincerity, *and Regard to Christ himself, which make Men Members of the Invisible Church of Christ. And where is the* Contradiction *contained in all this?**

Suppose, my Lord, anyone should affirm that there is a *Sincere, Invisible* Bishop of *Bangor*, who is the *only true* Bishop of *Bangor* in the *Mouth of a Christian*. Would your Lordship think here was no Reflection intended upon yourself? Would you think this Account no *Contradiction* to your *Right* as Bishop of *Bangor?* Does your Lordship believe such an Assertion could come from anyone that owned your Right to your *Bishopric*, and was a Friend to you in it? Would you imagine that nothing was meant against you, because the other Bishop was said to be *Invisible?* Your Lordship cannot but know, that though he is said to be Invisible, yet if he is the *only true Bishop of* Bangor *in the Mouth of a Christian*, then *any* other Bishop of *Bangor*, whether *Visible* or *Invisible*, must be a *false one in the Mouth of a Christian*.

Thus it is your Lordship has dealt with the *Visible* Church; you have set another up as the *only true Church*, and yet think all is well: that there is no Contradiction, because you call this other an *Invisible Church*, whereas if it be the only true Church, it contradicts every other Church in the highest Sense. And though it does not contradict it as a *Visible* Church, yet it does as a *True* Church, which is of more Consequence.

Your Lordship here puts a Question in favour of the *Visible* Church. *Can it be supposed by this learned Body, that a Man's*

---

* *Answ. to Repr.*, p. 79.

being of the Invisible Church of Christ, is inconsistent with his joining himself with any Visible Church?*

No, my Lord, it cannot be supposed. It cannot be supposed by any Body that *a Man's being of the Invisible Church,* is inconsistent with his joining himself to the *Royal Society,* or *College of Physicians.* But pray, my Lord, is this all that your Invisible Church will allow of? Dare your Lordship proceed no farther, than only to grant that it is *no Inconsistency, no Contradiction* for a Member of your *Invisible* Church to join with any *Visible* Church? If you would *sincerely* shew that you have said nothing to the Prejudice of the *Visible* Church, you ought to declare that the Members of your *Invisible* Church, may not only *consistently* join with that which is Visible, but that it is their *Duty,* and that they are *obliged* to join with it in order to be of yours that is *Invisible.* For if you have set up an *Invisible* Church, which will excuse its Members from being of any that is Visible, then you have plainly destroyed it, by making it useless. And it is but a poor Apology for it to say, there is no *Inconsistency* in joining with it, after you have made it needless and unnecessary to join with it. And it will be pretty difficult to give a *consistent* Reason, why any Person should join himself to a needless Church.

Your Lordship has here made great Discoveries of the Nature of your *Invisible* Church, which appears to have nothing *visible* or *external* in it.

For first, you declare that the Article describes one Church, and you another. But how does this appear? How does your Lordship prove this? 1st. *Because the Article declares what it is that makes every such Congregation the* Visible *Church.*† Now, my Lord, if this shews that the Article does not describe your Church, then it is plain that the Article here describes *something* that does not belong to your Church; for if it *equally* belonged to your Church, it could be no *Proof* that it did not describe your Church. But you expressly say that it describes a different Church from yours; therefore it must describe *something* that does not belong to yours.

Now if that which makes any Congregation the Visible Church, be not necessary to make Persons Members of your Church, it follows that they may be Members of yours, without being of *any Visible* Church.

Again; Another Reason why the Article does not describe your Invisible Church is this; Because it describes *those outward Acts, which are necessary to make a Visible Church.* These out-

---

* *Answ. to Repr.,* p. 79.   † *Answ. to Repr.,* p. 70.

ward Acts are, the *Preaching the pure Word of God, and administering the Sacraments.* Now, my Lord, seeing these *outward Acts* shew that the Church here described is not your *Invisible Church*, does not this evidently declare that such outward Acts are not necessary to your Church? For if they did equally belong to both Churches, and were alike necessary to them, how could they more describe one than another? But you say, it is the mentioning of these *outward Acts*, that shews that your *Invisible Church* is not described; therefore it is plain, that you do not include these *outward Acts* as essential to your Invisible Church, and consequently it is a Church to which neither *public Worship*, nor *visible Sacraments are necessary*. For if these outward Acts are necessary to your *Invisible* Church, why does not your Lordship mention them as such? You own *you describe what it is that makes every particular Man a Member of the Invisible Church;* yet you not only take no notice *of these outward Acts*, but say that the Article describes not your Church, because it mentions *these outward Acts*, which is a *Demonstration*, that these *outward Acts do not belong to your Church*.

Farther; When the *Learned Committee* has charged your Lordship with the Omission of *preaching the Word and administering of the Sacraments*, you answer, *they might have added, He omits likewise the very public Profession of Christianity. And is not the Reason plain? because I was not speaking of the* Visible *Church; to which* alone, *as such*, visible outward Signs, *and* verbal *Professions belong: but of the* Universal *Invisible Church*.*

My Lord, the Reason is very plain, and it is as plain that is not a good Reason. For if the *preaching* of the Word, the *administering* of the Sacraments, and the public Profession of Christianity, be necessary to make anyone a Member of *your Invisible Church*, then there was as good Reason to mention them in your Description, as if you had been describing the Visible Church.

If they are not necessary, then you have set up a Church *exclusive* of the Visible Church. The Case stands thus; If these outward Acts be as necessary to make Persons be of the *Invisible* as of the *Visible Church*, then they ought to come equally into the Description of both Churches, being equally necessary to both: If you say they are not equally necessary, then you must allow that there is no Necessity that the Members of your Church should be in *any external* Communion.

It is therefore no Apology, to say that you describe the

---

* *Answ. to Repr.*, p. 80.

Invisible Church, unless you will say that a Man may be of it, without *any outward Acts*, or *Communion* with *any Visible* Church. If a Person may be of this *Invisible* Church without having anything to do with Visible Sacraments, or Worship in a Visible Communion, then you have an Excuse, why you did not mention these *outward Professions* in your Description of the Church; but if he cannot be of this Invisible Communion without observing these *outward Ordinances*, then it was as necessary to mention these *outward Ordinances* in your Account of this Church, as if you had been describing a Church, which consisted of nothing else but outward Ordinances.

So that the short of the Case is this; If the Observation of external Ordinances be not necessary to make Men Members of your *Invisible Church*, then indeed there is a plain Reason why your Lordship should omit them; and it is also plain, that this Doctrine sets aside the Gospel, if this *Invisible Church*, the *only true Church in the Mouth of a Christian*, be excused from *Gospel* Ordinances. But if these external Ordinances be necessary to constitute the Invisible Church, then there was as plain a Reason to mention them, in the Description of your Church, as if you had been describing the *Visible Church*.

So that if your Lordship will give a good plain Reason why you have omitted these *outward Acts*, it must be because they do not belong to it; for otherwise the calling it Invisible is no Excuse, unless it has no occasion for such *outward* Performances.

And indeed this has appeared to be your Doctrine in almost every Page, that you set up this *Invisible* Church in Opposition to *Outward and Visible* Ordinances. For you all along set out the Opposition or Difference betwixt the Visible and Invisible Church in respect to external Ordinances: Thus the one is Visible, *because to it alone belong external Signs, or verbal Professions.** The other is Invisible for the *want* of *these*. Yet this Invisible Church thus destitute, and even necessarily destitute of external Ordinances, is by you called, the *only true Church in the Mouth of a Christian*.

One may, I acknowledge, easily conceive in one's Mind a Number of People, whose Internal and Invisible Graces may entitle them to the Favour of God; and these may be called an *Invisible Number*, or *Congregation*, or *Church*, because it is Invisible to us where it is, or how great it is. But then, my Lord, it is a great Mistake if this Invisible Church is opposed to, or distinguished from the *Visible Church* in respect of *external*

---

* *Answ. to Repr.*, p. 81.

Ordinances. For in these things they are both *equally* obliged to be Visible. And the Invisible Church is not so called, in *Contradistinction* to those who attend *Visible* Communions, and observe external Ordinances, but in *Contradistinction* to those who are *invisibly bad*, and are not what their external Profession promises. This is the only *Number* of People or *Church*, which the *Invisible* Church is opposed to. For as the Invisible Church intends a Number so called, because of their *Invisible* Graces; so this Invisibly good Church can be *truly* opposed only to the *Invisibly* bad Church, or such as are not such Persons *inwardly*, as they profess to be *outwardly*.

But, contrary to this, your Lordship has all along considered and described this *Invisible* Church in Opposition to the *Visible*, and made those outward Acts which are *necessary* to the Visible Church, so many *Marks* to distinguish it from that which is Invisible. Thus you say, *that you were not speaking of the Visible Church, to which alone, as such, visible outward Signs, or verbal Professions belong: but of the Universal Invisible Church.**

Here you plainly make *external Signs*, and *outward Professions*, distinguish the Visible from the Invisible Church; whereas it is not *Invisible* in this respect, as being *without* these *external* Professions, or in *Contradistinction* to a *Visible* Church; but it is only Invisible in those Graces, which human Eyes cannot perceive. Thus they are said to be the Invisible Church, because they are a Number of Men, who are such *inwardly*, as they profess to be *outwardly*. But this shews, that they cannot be so called in *Contradistinction* to *outward* Professions, since they must have an *outward* Profession themselves before they can be inwardly *sincere* in it; and consequently they are not opposed to, or distinguished from a Number of *outward Professors*, for this they are obliged to be themselves, but from a Number of outward Professors, who are *not sincere* in what they *outwardly* profess.

If I should describe *charitable* Men to be an *Invisible Church* of Persons *sincerely* well affected to Mankind, and this in Contradistinction to others who are *externally* charitable, and perform *outward* Acts of Love; or if I should describe *chaste* Men to be an *Invisible Church* of Persons *inwardly chaste* and pure, and this in Contradistinction to others *externally chaste* and *visibly* pure as to *outward Acts;* I should just have the same Authority either from Reason or Scripture to set up these *Invisible* Churches of *charitable* and *chaste* Men, in Opposition to persons *outwardly* charitable and chaste, as your Lordship has to set up this

---

* *Answ. to Rpr.*, p. 81.

invisible sincere Church, in *Contradistinction* to the visible external Church. For, first, this *Sincerity* no more makes a *Church*, than *Charity* and *Chastity* make a Church, or than *Honesty* makes a Man a *Member* of a Corporation, or an *Officer* in the Army; these, being private personal Virtues, do not constitute a *Church* or *Society*, but concern Men, as Men, in every Estate of Life.

Secondly, *Outward* Ordinances and *Visible* Professions, are as necessary to make Men true Christians, as *outward* Acts of Love and external Purity are necessary to make Men *charitable* or *chaste*. For Christianity as truly implies *external Acts* and *Professions*, as Chastity implies *outward* Purity.

Now, my Lord, suppose the Question was, whether *Adultery* or *Fornication* or any other Impurity was lawful, and that the World was divided upon this Controversy; Would he not be an excellent Preacher of Chastity, that should never tell us whether any or all of these were unlawful, but should pretend to decide the Controversy, by telling the World, that *chaste* Men, are an *Invisible* Church of Persons *inwardly pure*, and this in *Contradistinction* to Persons *externally* pure? Suppose he should tell them, that their Title to Chastity did not depend upon their being or not being of the Number of any *outwardly* pure or impure Persons, but upon their *inward* Purity; What Apology could even Charity itself make for such a Teacher?

The Controversy on foot is this; Whether external Communion with any sort of Fanatics be lawful? Whether it be as safe to be in one external visible Communion as in another? The Word is divided upon this Subject; and your Lordship comes in to end the Controversy. But how? Is it by examining the Merits of the contending Parties? Is it by telling us what is right and what is wrong in the different Communions? Is it by telling us that one external Communion is better than another? Is it by shewing us that any is dangerous? Is it by directing us, with which we ought to join, or indeed that we ought so much as to join with any? No: This right and wrong, or good and bad in *external* Communions, though it was the *whole Question*, is wholly skipped over by your Lordship; and you preach up an *Invisible Church* as the *only true Church in the Mouth of a Christian*, and this in *Contradistinction* to all *Visible* Churches: And only declare, that our Title to God's Favour cannot depend upon our being or continuing in any particular Method, but upon our *Sincerity*.

Your Lordship says; *I have laid down a Description of the Universal Invisible Church or Kingdom of Christ.** Your Lord-

---

* P. 78.

ship had been as well employed if you had been painting of *Spirits*, or weighing of *Thoughts*. *The main Question*, you say, *is whether this Description be true and just.**

This, my Lord, is not the *main Question;* nor indeed does it concern us at all whether your Lordship is ingenious, or not, in this Description.

For suppose your Lordship had been describing an *Invisible King* to the People of *Great Britain*, do you think the *main Question* amongst the *Lords* and *Commons* would be, whether you had hit off the Description well? No, my Lord, the *main Question* would be, To what Ends and Purposes you had set up such a King, and what Relation the Subjects of *Great Britain* had to him; whether they might leave their *Visible*, and pay only an *internal Allegiance* to your *Invisible King?* If your Lordship should farther describe him as the *only true King in the Mouth of a* Britain, I believe it would be thought but a *poor Apology* to appeal to your fine Painting, that you had described him *justly*, and set him out as *Invisible*. The Application is here very easy; it is a very trifling Question, and only concerns your Lordship's *Parts*, Whether your Description of your Invisible Church be just or not? But it is the Use and the End of setting up this Church, which is any Matter of Question to us. Your Lordship might erect as many Churches as you please, if you did it only for *speculative Amusement*, and to try your Abilities in fine Drawing; but if you pretend to unsettle the Christian Church, by your new Buildings, or to destroy the Distinction between the *Church* and *Conventicle*, by your *Invisibles*, we must beg your Lordship's Excuse, and can no more admire the *Beauty* or *Justness* of your fine Descriptions, than you would admire a *just Description* of an *Invisible Diocese*, if it was set out in order to receive your Lordship.

You add; But *of this* (Description) they (*the Committee*) have not said one word; *but rather chosen to* go off *to an article of the Church of* England, which defines not the *Universal Invisible Church*. And your Lordship might as well observe, that they have not said one word about *Plato's Republic*. For how they should imagine that you were describing an *Invisible* Church, or if they did, why they should trouble their Heads with such a Description, is not easily conceived.

For, my Lord, if it was your primary Intention only to appear in Defence of an *Universal Invisible Church*, what can we conceive in our Minds more surprising? What can be more extraordinary, than that a Visible Bishop at a *Visible* Court, should

---

* P. 78.

with so much Solemnity preach in Defence of a Church which can neither be defended nor injured? Are there any Rights in your Invisible Church which can possibly be lost? If not, to what purpose does your Lordship come in as a Defender? Can the Sight of any Men find it, the Malice of any Men attack it, or the Good-will of any Men support it? No: Yet though it is as invisible as the *Centre* of the Earth, and as much out of our reach as the *Stars*, yet your Lordship has very pathetically preached a Sermon, and published some Volumes, lest this Invisible Church, which nobody knows where to find, should be run away with.

Should the same Christian Zeal induce your Lordship to appear, at some other solemn Occasion, in the Cause of the *Winds*, your Pains would be as well employed; for it would be as reasonable to desire that they might *rise* and *blow* where they list, as that an Invisible Church, nowhere to be known or found by us at present, may not be injured.

If therefore the *Learned Committee* had so far forgot that Visible Church of which they are Members, as to have engaged with your Lordship about your *Invisible Church*, the Dispute would have been to as much purpose, as a *Trial* in *Westminster Hall* about the *Philosopher's Stone*.

But you complain that they rather chose to *go off* to an Article of the Church of *England*. My Lord, this is very hard indeed, that they should *go off* to the Church of *England*, when you had an *Invisible Church* ready for them; or that this Learned Body cannot dispute about Churches, but they must needs bring the *Church of England* into the Question.

Suppose, as in the above-mentioned Instance, your Lordship should lay down a *fine* and *just* Description of your *Invisible* King of *Great Britain*, a Number of Tories should, instead of examining the Truth of your Description, *go off* to the *Act of Settlement*, which declares a *Visible* King of *Britain*: This would be to use your Lordship just as the *Learned Committee* have done; who, instead of dwelling upon the Beauty and Justness of this Description, have *gone off* to an old Article in the *Church of England*, which indeed only describes an old-fashioned *Visible* Church, as Churches went in the Apostles' Days: That is, a *Congregation of faithful Men, in which the pure Word of God is preached, and the Sacraments duly administered.**

I am of Opinion, that the *Apostolical* Church would not have thought themselves too *Invisible* to be thus described, or that

---

* *Artic.* 19.

this was too *Visible* a Description of the Church of Christ to take in its *sincere* Members.

Whether therefore your Lordship has given a true Description of the *Invisible* Church, that is, a Church of *Thoughts* and *Sentiments*, I shall not consider, but thus much I must observe, that it is a very false Description; first, as it pretends to describe THE Church,* *and the only true Church in the Mouth of a Christian.* For the Church of Christ, as has been shewn, is as truly a *Visible external* Society, as any Civil or Secular Society in the World: And it is no more distinguished from such Societies by the *Invisibility*, than by the *Youth* or *Age* of its Members.

The holy consecrated *Elements* differ from common *Bread* and *Wine*, but they do not so differ from it, as to cease to be as *Visible*, as common Bread and Wine. Thus the Holy Catholic Church, the Kingdom of Christ, differs from worldly Societies and Kingdoms, but not in point of *Visibility*, but in regard to the *Ends* and *Purposes* for which it is erected, viz., the eternal Salvation of Mankind.

Secondly, This Description contradicts the nineteenth Article of the *Church of England*. For though it is not set up as another *Visible* Church, so as to contradict it in point of *Visibility*, yet seeing it is described as THE Church, and *the only true Church*, it plainly contradicts it in point of Truth; for if it be the only true Church, every other must be a false one.

Thirdly, This Description is a mere *speculative Conjecture*, a *Creature* of the Imagination, which can serve no Purposes, but is entirely foreign to the present Dispute, and must be so to any Dispute which ever can arise between contending Communions. It no more serves to inform anyone, whether he should go to the *Visible* Church, or *Visible* Conventicle, than whether he should study the *Law* or *Physic*. It may indeed serve to make Persons regardless of any *Visible Church*, but can be of no use to them, if they desire to know with what *Visible* Church they ought to join.

It may now be worth our while to observe, how your Lordship came by this Account of Christ's Kingdom, which you say is the *only true* one. *Jesus answered, my Kingdom is not of this World*, is the Text to your Sermon. You say, *you have chosen these Words in which our Lord declares the Nature of his Kingdom.*†

Now, my Lord, one would imagine, that you hereby mean, that our Lord has in *these* Words declared what his Kingdom is; for without this, it cannot be true that he hath declared the

---

* *Answ. to Repr.*, p. 70. † *Serm.*, p. 10.

Nature of his Kingdom. Whereas it is so far from being true, that he hath in *these Words* declared what his Kingdom is, that he has only, and that in one particular Respect, declared *what it is not.* If he had said that his Kingdom was not a *Jewish* Kingdom, would this be declaring the Nature of his Kingdom? If a Person should say that his Belief was not the Belief of the Church of *England*, would he in *these Words declare the Nature of his Belief?* Would it not still be uncertain whether he was an *Arian* or *Socinian*, or something different from them both? Thus our Saviour's saying that his *Kingdom is not of this World*, no more declares the Nature of his Kingdom, than a Person by saying *such* a one was not his Son, would in *these Words* declare how many Children he had.

My Kingdom is not of this World, are very indeterminate Words, and capable of several Meanings, if we consider them in themselves. But as soon as we consider them as an Answer to a particular Question, they take one determinate Sense. The Question was, whether our Saviour was the (Temporal) *King of the Jews? Jesus answered, my Kingdom is not of this World.* Now as these Words may signify no more than the Denial of what was asked; as there is nothing in them that necessarily implies more, than that he was not a King as the *Jewish* or other Temporal Kings are; as the Question extends the Answer no farther than this Meaning; so if we enlarge it, or fix any other Meaning to it, it is all human Reasoning, without any Warrant from the Text.

Now, taking the Words in this Sense, what a strange Conclusion is this that your Lordship draws from it: That because Christ said his Kingdom was not a Temporal Kingdom as the *Jewish* and other Kingdoms were; therefore his Kingdom is *Invisible*. Is it denied to be a Temporal Kingdom, *because a* Temporal Kingdom is Visible? If not, it will by no means follow, that it must be *Invisible*, because it is said not to be Temporal. Must it be in every respect contrary to a Temporal Kingdom, because it is said not to be Temporal? Then it must have no Subjects, because in Temporal Kingdoms there are Subjects; then there must be no King, because in such Kingdoms there are Kings. I suppose the Sacraments may in a very proper Sense be said to be not *Temporal Institutions*, though they are as external and *Visible* as any thing in the World; and consequently the Church may be not Temporal in a very proper Sense, without implying that it must therefore be *Invisible*. Indeed I cannot conceive how your Lordship could have thought of a more odd Conclusion, than this which you have drawn from them. If you had concluded that because Christ's Kingdom is not a Temporal Kingdom, therefore its Members are all of an Age; it had been as well as to say, therefore they are *Invisible*.

Nothing can be more surprising, than to see your Lordship throughout your whole Sermon describing this Kingdom, with all the Accuracy and Exactness imaginable, and even *demonstrating* every particular Circumstance of its Nature, from this little *Negative, that it is not a Temporal Kingdom*. Your Lordship must be very excellent at taking a *Hint*, or you could never have found out this *Kingdom* of God so exactly from so small a Circumstance. It seems, had this *little Text* been all the Scripture that we had left in the World, your Lordship could have revealed the rest by the help of it. For there is nothing that relates to this Kingdom, or the Circumstances of its Members, but you have purely by the Strength of your Genius, unassisted by any other Scripture proved and demonstrated from this single Passage.

If a Foreigner should tell your Lordship, that his House in his own Country was not as the Houses are in this Kingdom, would it not be very wonderful in your Lordship, to be able to *demonstrate* its Length and Breadth, to tell how many Rooms there are on a Floor, and to describe every Beauty and Convenience of the Structure, merely from having been told that it was not like the Houses in this Kingdom? But it would not be more wonderful, than to see your Lordship describe the Nature of Christ's Kingdom, and explain every Circumstance that concerns its Members, from having been told this Negative Circumstance. Nor indeed is it much to be wondered, seeing you set out upon this bottom, if you give as false an Account of Christ's Kingdom, as you would do of an House, that you only knew what it was not.

Again, you say, *As the Church of Christ is the Kingdom of Christ, he himself is King; and* in this *it is implied that he is himself the sole Law-giver to his Subjects, and himself the sole Judge of their Behaviour* in the Affairs of Conscience and Salvation.*

What a pretty fine-spun Consequence is this, to be drawn from the above mentioned Text. Your Lordship here advances a mere human Speculation founded upon no other Authority, than the uncertain Signification of the Words, *King* and *Kingdom;* you say it is *in this implied that* because *Christ is King* of his *Kingdom, he is the sole Law-giver to his Subjects*. Pray, my Lord, why is it *in this* implied? Do the Words, *King* and *Kingdom* always imply the *same* thing? Has a King in one

---

* *Serm.*, p. 11.

Kingdom the *same* Powers, which every King hath in another Kingdom? Has the King of *England* the same Power, which a King of *France*, or any Sovereign hath in his Kingdom? Would it be any reason why the King of *England* should be *sole* Law-giver to his Subjects, because there are Kings who are sole Law-givers to their Subjects? Now if the word, *King*, does not necessarily imply the *same* Power in every Kingdom, how can there be any Conclusion, that *because* Christ is King of his Kingdom, he is sole Law-giver to his Subjects? Yet your Lordship's whole Argument is founded upon this weak and false bottom, that the word, *King*, is to be taken in one absolute and fixed Sense: For you expressly say, it is *in this* implied, that *because* he is King, he is sole Law-giver. Now it is impossible it should be implied *in this*, unless the word, *King*, always implies the same Power: For if there be any Difference in the Constitutions of Kingdoms, though they all have Kings, then it is plain nothing certain as to the Nature and Condition of any Kingdom, can be drawn from its having a King. But your Lordship has described the Constitution of Christ's Kingdom, the Circumstances of its Subjects, and in short everything that can concern it, as absolutely, and with as much Certainty, from Christ's being King of it, as if the word, *King*, had but one Meaning, or every King the same Power.

Again, you tell us; *The grossest Mistakes in Judgment, about the Nature of Christ's Kingdom or Church, have arisen from hence, that Men have argued from other Visible Societies, and other Visible Kingdoms of this World, to what ought to be Visible and Sensible in his Kingdom.*

Is it thus, my Lord? Are all our gross Errors owing to this way of Reasoning? How then comes your Lordship to fall into this grossest of Errors? How come you to state the very Nature of Christ's Kingdom from the Consideration of Temporal Kingdoms, or *Absolute* Monarchies? How come you to argue from the Relation between a King and his Kingdom, to what ought to be in Christ's spiritual Kingdom? Are not Kings and Kingdoms Temporal Institutions? Is not the Relation betwixt a King and his Kingdom a Temporal Relation? How then can you argue from these Temporal Kingdoms, to anything concerning Christ's Kingdom? Why will your Lordship fall into so gross an Error, as to assert that Christ must be *sole* Law-giver to his Subjects, because there are some Temporal *Kings* who are sole Law-givers to their Subjects? Is there any Consequence in this Argument? Nay, are not all our Errors owing to this mistaken way of arguing?

The only way to know the Constitution of this Kingdom, is

not to reason from what is implied in the Words *King* and *Kingdom*, for they do not imply *any fixed, or absolute* Sense, but from the Laws and Institutions of it, whether they admit of or require the Authority of under Magistrates. Thus, if it appears that Christ has commissioned others to act in his Name, to exercise Authority in his Kingdom, and govern his Subjects in such a manner as he has commissioned them to govern; Is it any Answer to this, to say that *the Church is a Kingdom, and Christ is a King, and consequently sole Law-giver in it?* Is there nothing in this Text, *Whatsoever ye shall bind on Earth shall be bound in Heaven, &c.*, because Christ is King of his Church?

The whole Scheme of all your Doctrines is raised out of this single Text, *My Kingdom is not of this World;* which certainly implies no more, than if Christ had said, *I am not the Temporal King of the Jews.* Let us therefore see how your Lordship's Doctrines appear, if we bring them to the Principle from whence you had them: As thus, *Jesus is not the Temporal King of the Jews*, therefore there is no such thing as Church-Authority, no Obligation to join in any particular Communion. *Jesus* is not the Temporal King of the *Jews*, therefore *Absolutions*, *Benedictions*, and *Excommunications* are *Dreams* and *Trifles;* therefore no Succession or Order of Clergy is better than another.

Jesus is not the Temporal King of the *Jews*, therefore the *Invisible Church* is the *only true Church in the Mouth of a Christian;* therefore Sincerity alone, exclusive of any particular Communion, is the *only Title* to God's Favour. Now if the Papists should say, *Jesus is not the Temporal King* of the *Jews*, therefore there is a *Purgatory*, therefore we are to pray to *Saints;* they would shew as much true *Logic* and *Divinity*, as your Lordship has shewn in the Proof of your Doctrines from the above-mentioned Text. And I dare say, that every Reader of this Controversy knows, that you have not pretended to any other Proof from the Scriptures for your Doctrine, than what your Oratory could draw from this single Text.

This therefore, I hope, every Reader will observe, that all which you have advanced against the Universally Received Doctrines of Christianity, is only an *Harangue* upon this single Text, which everyone's common Sense will tell him, contains nothing in it that can possibly determine the Cause, which you are engaged in. For who can imagine, that it is as well to be a sincere *Turk* as a sincere *Christian*, or that a sincere *Quaker* is as much in the Favour of God as a sincere *Churchman*, because our blessed Lord told *Pilate*, that *his Kingdom was not of this World;* and that in such a manner, and upon such an occasion, as only to imply that he was not that King which he enquired after? Who can conceive that there is no particular Order of the Clergy necessary, no Necessity of any particular Communion, no Authority in any Church, nor any Significancy in the sacerdotal Powers, for this reason, because there is a Text in Scripture, which denies that Christ was the *Temporal King of the Jews*.

Your Lordship has said much of the Plainness and Simplicity of the Gospel, and of its peculiar Fitness to be judged of, by the ordinary common Sense of Mankind; you have also interposed in this Controversy, to deliver them from the Authority of the Church, and turn them loose to the Scriptures. But, my Lord, if this Text, *My Kingdom is not of this World*, which seems to common Sense to contain only the Denial of a particular Question, contains, as you have pretended, the whole Christian Religion; and every other seemingly plain Part of the Gospel is to take its Meaning from this Passage; if it be thus, my Lord, what can we conceive more mysterious than the Scripture? Or more unequal to the common, ordinary Sense of Men?

For how should it come into a plain honest Man's Head, that this Text, which is nothing but the *Denial* of a *certain Question*, should be the *Key* to all the rest of Scripture? How should he know that the plainest Texts in Scripture were not to be understood in their apparent Meaning, but in some Sense or other given them from this Text? Thus, when it is said, *Go ye and disciple all Nations; and lo I am with you to the end of the World:* The first apparent Sense of these Words is this, that as Christ promised to be with the Apostles in the Execution of their Office, both as to *Authority* and *Power*, so he promises the same to their Successors, the Bishops, since he could no otherwise be with them to the End of the World, than by being with their Successors. Now, my Lord, how should an ordinary Thinker know that this plain Meaning of the Words was to be neglected, and that he was to go to the above-mentioned Text, to learn to understand, or rather disbelieve them? For what is there in this Text, *My Kingdom is not of this World*, to shew either that Christ did not authorise the Apostles to ordain Successors, who should have his Authority, or that the Bishops alone, are not such Successors? Is there anything in this Text which can any way determine the Nature, the Necessity, or the Significancy of such a Succession?

Again it is said, that *There is no other Name under Heaven given unto Men, whereby they may be saved but Jesus Christ.* Now how should a Man that has only common Sense imagine, that he must reject this plain Meaning of the Words, and believe that a *sincere Turk* is as much in the Favour of God as a *sincere Christian*, for this only reason, because *Christ's Kingdom is not of this World?* It must not be common ordinary Sense which can reason and discover at this rate.

Lastly, it is said, *Whatsoever ye shall bind on Earth, shall be bound in Heaven, &c.* Now how shall anyone that has only *sober* Sense find out, that there is nothing at all left in this Text, that it only gave *something or other to the Apostles*, but gives no Authority to any Persons now, because the *Kingdom of Christ is not of this World.*

Our Saviour told his Disciples, that *they were not of this World*, but is that an Argument that they therefore became immediately invisible? Was neither St. *Peter*, nor St. *Paul, &c.*, ever to be seen afterwards? Why then must the Kingdom of Christ become immediately invisible, because it is said not to be of this World, any more than its first Members were Invisible, who were also declared to *be not of this World?*

Had St. *Peter* or St. *Paul* no visible Power and Authority over the Presbyters and Deacons, because *they were not of this World?* If they had, why may not some Persons have Authority over others in Christ's Kingdom, though *it is not of this World?*

For our blessed Lord's saying that his Disciples *were not of this World*, does as strictly prove that St. *Peter* and St. *Paul* had no distinct Powers from Presbyters and Deacons, as his saying, that *his Kingdom was not of this World*, proves that there is no real or necessary Difference betwixt Bishops and Presbyters in his Kingdom. And it is as good Logic, to say the Disciples of Christ were not of this World, therefore there was no Necessity, that some should have been *Apostles*, and others *Presbyters, &c.*, as to say Christ's Kingdom is not of this World, therefore there is no Necessity that some should be Bishops and others Presbyters in it.

I have been the more particular in examining the Text to your Sermon, and bringing your Doctrines close to it, that every Reader who has common Sense, may be able to perceive that they have no more Relation to that Text from which you would be thought to have them, than if you had deduced them from the first Verse in the first Chapter of *Genesis*.

And yet thus much every Reader must have observed, that it is your Explication of this Text alone, which has led you to condemn all that Authority, to censure all those Institutions as *Dreams* and *Trifles*, which the holy Scriptures, and the first and purest Ages of Christianity, have taught us to esteem as sacred in themselves, being ordained by God; and of the greatest Benefit to us, being means of obtaining his Grace, and Favour.

Thus far concerning the Nature of Christ's Church.

Of Church Authority.

I COME now to consider what your Lordship has delivered upon the Article of *Church Authority*, as it is invested in the Governors of the Church. And here I have little else to do, but to clear it from those *false Characters*, under which you have been pleased to describe it.

Thus you begin; *If there be an Authority in any to judge, censure, or punish the Servants of another Master, in Matters purely relating to Conscience and eternal Salvation; then Christ has left behind Judges over the Consciences and Religion of his People; then the Consciences and Religion of his People are subject to them whom he has left Judges over them; and then there is a Right in some Christians to determine the Religion and Consciences of others. And what is more, if the Decisions of any Men can be made to concern or affect the State of Christ's Subjects with regard to the Favour of God, then the Salvation of some Christians depends upon the Sentence passed by others.**

Here is the Sum of what you have advanced from *Reason* and the *Nature* of the Thing against the Authority of Church Governors; which you would have pass for a strict Proof, that if they have any Authority in *Matters purely* relating to *Conscience* derived to them from Christ, that then their Authority can *damn* or *save* at pleasure.

But, my Lord, in this *same strict* way of Reasoning, and by only using your own Words, I will as plainly prove that a *Father* hath not Authority even to send his Children of an *Errand*.

For, 'If the Christian Religion authorises a *Father* to judge
'the Servants of another Master in *Matters purely* relating to
'*Motion*, then Christ has left behind him Judges *over* the *Motion*
'of his People, then the *Motion* of his People is subjected to *them*
'whom he has left Judges over *it;* and then there is a *Right* in
'some *Christians* to determine the *Motion* of others. And what
'is more, if the *Determinations* of any Men can concern or affect

---

* *Answ. to Repr.*, p. 27.

'the State of Christ's Subjects with regard to *Motion*, then the 'Lives of some Christians depend upon the Determination passed 'by others; because they may determine them to move from the '*top* of a Precipice to the *bottom*.'

Here, my Lord, I freely leave it to the Judgment of *common Sense*, whether I have not in your *own Words* proved it as absurd and unreasonable, that a *Father* should have any Power over his Son, so as to send him of an *Errand*, as to allow the Church to have Authority in Matters of *Conscience* and *Salvation ;* and the Consequence, according to your Argument, is *equally* dreadful in both Cases : For it is as plain that if *Fathers* have Authority in Matters of *Motion*, then they may *move* their Sons to the *bottom* of a *Precipice ;* as that if the *Church* hath Authority in *Matters of Salvation*, then it may *save* or *damn* at pleasure; and it is as well proved, that *Fathers* have no Authority in Matters of *Motion*, because they have no Authority to command their Children to *destroy* themselves, as that the Church hath no Authority in Matters of *Conscience* and *Salvation*, because they have not an Authority to *damn* People for ever : For there is the same room for *Degrees* in the Authority of the Church, which there is for *Degrees* in the Authority of *Parents ;* and it is as justly concluded that *Parents* have no Authority in Matters of any *particular Nature*, because they have not *unlimited* Authority in things of that *particular Nature*, as that the *Church* hath no Authority in *Matters of Conscience and Salvation*, because it has not an absolute unlimited Authority in *these Matters*.

Yet this is the whole of your Argument against *Church Authority*, that it cannot relate to Matters of Conscience and Salvation, because an Authority in *these Matters*, is an *absolute Authority* over the Souls of others; which is just as true, as if anyone should declare that a *Father* hath no Authority in *Matters* purely relating to the *Body* of his Son, because an *Authority* in *these* Matters, is an *absolute* Authority to dispose of his *Body* as he pleases.

Suppose it should be said, that a *Father* hath Authority over his Son in *Civil Affairs ;* Will it be an Argument that he has no such Authority, because he has not *all*, or an *unlimited* Authority in *Civil Affairs ?* Will it be an Argument that he has no Authority in *such Matters*, because his Son is not *wholly* and *entirely* subjected to him in such Matters ? Has a Father no Right to choose an *Employment* for his Son, or govern him in several things of a *Civil Nature*, because he cannot oblige him to resign his *Title* to his *Estate*, or take from him the Benefit of the *Laws* of the *Land ?*

If he has an Authority in these Matters, though not *all*, why cannot the Governors of the Church have an Authority in *Matters of Conscience*, though they have not *all*, or an *unlimited* Authority in Matters of Conscience? How does it follow that they have no such Authority, because Christians are not *wholly* and *absolutely* subjected to them in *such* Matters? Why can there not be *Bounds* to an Authority in *Matters of Conscience*, as well as *Bounds* to an Authority in *Civil Affairs?* And if a *Father* may have Authority over his *Son* in *Civil Affairs*, though that Authority is limited by the *Laws* of the Land, and the superior Authority of the *Civil Magistrate;* why may not the Church have an Authority in *Matters of Conscience* and Salvation, though that Authority is *limited* by the *Scriptures*, and the supreme *Authority* of God?

He therefore who concludes the Church hath no Authority in Matters of *Salvation*, because it cannot *absolutely* save or damn People, reasons as *strictly*, as he who concludes a Person has *no Authority* in *Civil Affairs*, because he cannot grant or take away *Civil Privileges* of the *highest* Nature.

What therefore your Lordship has thus *logically* advanced against the *Authority* of the Church, concludes with the *same Force* against *all* Authority in the World. For if the Church hath no Authority in Matters of Conscience, for this *demonstrative Reason*, because it hath not an *unlimited* Authority in *Matters of Conscience;* then it is also *demonstrated* that no Persons have any Authority in *any particular* Matters, because they have not an *absolute unbounded Authority* in those *particular Matters*.

As thus; A *Prince* hath no Authority to oblige his Subjects to make *War* against *such* a People, because he hath not an *unlimited* Authority to oblige his Subjects to fight *where*, and *when*, and with *whom* he pleases.

A *Father* has no Authority over the *Persons* or *Affairs* of his *Children*, because he cannot dispose of the *Persons* and *Affairs* of his Children in what manner he will.

Masters have no Authority to command the *Assistance* of their *Servants*, because they cannot oblige them to *assist* in a *Rebellion* or *Robbery*.

Thus are all these *particular Authorities*, as plainly confuted by your *Argument*, as the Authority of the Church is confuted by it.

But now, my Lord, have neither *Masters*, nor *Fathers*, nor *Princes*, any Authority in these *particular* Matters, because they have no Authority to command at *any rate*, or as they please in these Matters? If they have, why may not the Governors of the *Church* have an Authority in *Matters of Conscience*, though they cannot oblige Conscience at *any rate*, or as they please? Why may not they have an Authority in Matters of Salvation, though they have not Power absolutely to damn or save?

Your Lordship would therefore have done as much Justice to Truth, and as much Service to the World, if, instead of calling Christians from the Authority of the *Church*, you had publicly declared that neither *Masters*, nor *Fathers*, nor *Princes*, have, *properly speaking*, any *real* Authority over their respective *Servants*, *Sons*, and *Subjects*, and that because they are none of them to be obeyed but in *such* and *such* Circumstances, and upon certain supposed Conditions. For you have plainly declared there is no Authority in the Church, that it has no power of obliging, because we are only to obey upon *Terms* and *certain supposed Conditions*. If therefore this *conditional* Obedience proves that there is, *properly speaking*, no *Authority* in the Church, then that conditional Obedience of *Servants*, *Sons*, and *Subjects*, proves that neither their *Masters, Fathers,* or *Princes, have* any Authority *properly speaking*.

You say ; *If there be a Power in some OVER others in Matters of Religion, so as to determine these others ; then all Communions are upon an equal foot, without any regard to any intrinsic Goodness ; or whether they be right or wrong ; then no Religion is in itself preferable to another, but all are alike with respect to the Favour of God.**

Now, my Lord, all this might, with as much Truth, be said of any other Authority, as of Church Authority.

As thus ; ' If there be a *Power* in the *Prince*, or in *some* over
' others in *Matters of War and Fighting*, so as to determine
' those others ; then all *Wars* and *Fightings* are upon an *equal*
' foot, without any regard to any intrinsic Goodness ; or whether
' they be *right or wrong ;* then no *Wars* or *Fightings* are in
' themselves preferable to others, but all are alike with respect to
' the Favour of God.'

And now, my Lord, what must we say here? Has the Prince no *Right* or *Power* to command his Subjects to wage War with such a People? Or if he has this Power over them, does this make *all* Wars *alike* ? Does this Authority leave nothing to the *Justice* or *Equity* of *Wars*, but make all Wars *exactly* the same with regard to the *Favour* of God?

Does this Authority of the *Prince* make all *Engagements* equally lawful to the Subject that engages by his Authority? Is he neither *more* or *less* in the Favour of God, for whatever Cause

---

* *Answ. to Repr.*, p. 114.

he fights in, because he has the Authority of his Prince? Is it as pleasing to God that under such Authority he should make War upon the *Innocent,* plunder and ravage the *Fatherless* and *Widows,* as engage in the Cause of *Equity* and *Honour?*

Now, my Lord, if *all Wars* are not alike to the Persons who are concerned in them, *as to the Favour of God;* if there can be *any Cases* supposed, where it is not only *lawful,* but *honourable* and *glorious* for Soldiers to disobey the *Orders* of their *Prince;* then it is past doubt, that Soldiers *may* and *ought* to have some regard to the *Nature* and *Justice* of the *Orders* they have from their Prince.

But we have your Lordship's Assurance, that if they may have *any* regard to the *Nature* and *Justice* of their *Orders,* then *there is an end of all Authority,* and an *end of all Power of one Man over another in such Matters.*

So that you have as plainly confuted *all Authority* of the *Prince* over his Soldiers in *Matters purely* Military, as you have confuted all Authority of the *Church* in *Matters purely* of Conscience. For it is plain to every Understanding, that if there is an end of all Authority in Religion, because Persons may have some regard to the *intrinsic Goodness of things,** that therefore there is an end of all *Regal Authority* over Soldiers, if Soldiers may have any regard to the *Nature* and *Justice* of their *Military Orders.*

Your Argument against Church Authority consists of two Parts; the *first Part* is taken from the *Nature* of *Authority,* and proceeds thus: *If there be an Authority in Matters of Conscience, it must be an absolute Authority over Conscience, so as to be obeyed in all its Commands of what kind soever;* which is as false as if it were said, that if a Father hath Authority over the *Person* of his Son, then he hath an *absolute* Authority to do what he will with his *Person;* or if he hath Authority over his Son in *Civil Affairs,* then he hath an *absolute unlimited* Authority in the *Civil Affairs* of his Son.

The *other Part* of your Argument, is taken from the *Nature* of *Obedience,* and proceeds in this manner: *If Persons may have some regard to the intrinsic Goodness of things* in Religion, then there is an end of *all Authority* in Matters of Religion; which is as false as to say, that if a *Soldier* may have *some regard* to the *Nature* and *Justice* of the *Military Orders* of his *Prince,* then there is an end of all Authority of the *Prince* over his Soldiers in *Military Affairs;* or if a Servant may have *some regard* to the

---

* *Answ. to Repr.,* p. 115.

Lawfulness of the *Commands* of his Master, then there is an end of *all Authority* of Masters over their Servants as to such Matters.

So that if there be any such thing as Authority either in *Masters*, or *Fathers*, or *Princes*, then *both Parts* of your Argument are confuted; for none of these have any other than a *limited* Authority, nor do their respective *Servants, Sons*, or *Subjects*, owe them any other *active* Obedience, but such as is *conditional*.

Now if it can be any way proved that *Obedience* to our *Masters, Parents*, and *Princes* is a very great *Duty*, and *Disobedience* a very great *Sin;* though they cannot oblige us to act against the Laws of God, or the Laws of our *Country;* then it will follow that *Obedience* to our *Spiritual* Governors may be a very great *Duty*, and Disobedience a very great *Sin;* though they cannot oblige us to submit to their *sinful* or *unlawful* Commands.

And if *common* Reason, the *Laws* of God, and our *Country* be sufficient to direct us, where to *stop* in our *active* Obedience to our *Masters, Fathers*, or *Princes*, though they have Authority from God to demand our Obedience; the *same Guides* will with the *same Certainty* teach us where to *stop* in our Obedience to the Authority of the Church, though that Authority be set over us by God himself.

Though this might be thought sufficient to shew the Weakness of your Arguments against the Authority of the Church, yet I shall beg leave to examine them a little farther in another manner.

You say the Authority which you deny, is only an *Authority in Matters relating purely to Conscience and eternal Salvation*, an Authority whose Laws and *Decisions affect the State of Christ's* Subjects with regard to the Favour of God; and the reason of your denying it is this, that if this Authority, or *Laws*, or *Decisions of Men can concern or affect the State of Christ's Subjects with regard to the Favour of God, then the eternal Salvation of some Christians depends upon the Sentence passed by others.*[*]

In order to lay open the Weakness of this Reasoning, I shall state the Meaning of the Propositions of which it consists.

And, first, I suppose an Authority may be properly said to affect the *State* of People with regard to the *Favour* of God, when their *Obedience* to such an Authority procures his Favour, and their *Contempt* of it raises his displeasure; and I believe that this is not only a proper Sense, but the *only* proper Sense which the Words are capable of.

---

[*] *Answ. to Repr.*, p. 28.

It is certainly true that the Authority of our blessed Saviour, was an Authority which *affected* the *State* of the *Jews* with regard to the *Favour* of God ; but yet it no otherwise affected their State, than as their Obedience to his Authority was pleasing to God, and their Disobedience to it, the Cause of his farther Displeasure. This is the *only* way in which the Authority of Christ affected the *State* of People with regard to the Favour of God ; and therefore is the *only* manner in which any other Authority can be supposed to affect Persons with regard to the Favour of God.

Secondly ; Any *Things* or *Matters* may be properly said to relate to *Conscience* and *eternal Salvation*, when the Observance of them is a *Means* of obtaining Salvation, and the Neglect of them, an *Hindrance* to our Salvation. Thus *Baptism* and the *Supper* of the Lord, are Matters relating to *Conscience* and eternal *Salvation*, but then they are only so, for this reason, because the partaking of these Sacraments, is a *Means* of obtaining Salvation, and the Refusal of them, is an *Hindrance* of our Salvation. He therefore who hath Authority in *such things*, as by our observing of them we promote our Salvation, and by our neglecting of them, we hinder our Salvation, he has in the utmost Propriety of the Words, an *Authority in Matters of Conscience and Salvation.*

Hence it appears that it is not peculiar or appropriate to the Authority of the Church *alone*, to relate to Matters of Conscience and eternal Salvation, but *equally* belongs to every other Authority which can be called the *Ordinance* of God.

Now all lawful Authority, whether of *Masters, Fathers,* or *Princes*, is the *Ordinance* of God, and the respective Duties of their *Servants, Children*, and *Subjects*, are as truly Matters of *Conscience* and eternal *Salvation*, as their Observance of any Part of the Christian Religion is a Matter of *Conscience* and eternal *Salvation:* And it is not more their Duty to receive the *Sacrament*, or worship God in any particular manner, than to obey their respective Governors ; nor does it more *concern* or *affect their State* with regard to the *Favour* of God, whether they neglect *those Duties* which particularly regard his *Service*, or *those Duties* which they owe to their *proper* Governors. So that *Conscience* and eternal Salvation are *equally* concerned in *both* Cases.

For *things* may as well be Matters of *Conscience* and eternal *Salvation*, though they are of a Civil or Secular Nature, as the *positive Institutions* of Christ are Matters of *Conscience* and *Salvation.*

For *Baptism* has no more of Religion in its *own Nature*, nor has of *itself* any more concern with our Salvation, than any Action that is merely *Secular* or *Civil*. But as Baptism by *Institution* becomes our *Duty*, and so is a Matter of *Conscience* and *Salvation;* so when Actions merely *Secular* and *Indifferent*, are by a *Lawful* Authority made our *Duty*, they are as truly Matters of *Conscience* and *Salvation*, as any Parts of Religion.

The Difference betwixt a *Spiritual* and *Temporal* Authority does not consist *in this*, that one relates to Matters of *Conscience* and Salvation, and *concerns* and *affects* our *State* with regard to the *Favour* of God, and the other does not; but the Difference is this, that *one* presides over us in things relating to Religion and the *Service* of God, the *other* presides over us in things relating to *Civil Life;* and as our Salvation depends as *certainly* upon our Behaviour in things relating to *Civil Life*, as in things relating to the *Service* of God, it follows that they are *both equally Matters* of *Conscience* and *Salvation:* And as the *Temporal* Authority is the *Ordinance* of God, to which we are to submit, not only *for Wrath,* but also for *Conscience'* sake, it undeniably follows, that this *Temporal* Authority as *truly concerns* and *affects* our State with regard to the *Favour* of God, as any Authority in Matters *purely* relating to Religion. For such an Authority could in *no other* Sense *affect* our State with regard to the *Favour* of God, than by our Obedience or Disobedience to it; but our State with regard to the Favour of God is as *truly affected* by our *Obedience,* or *Disobedience* to our Lawful Sovereign, as by our observing or neglecting any Duty in the World; and consequently the *Temporal* Authority as *truly affects* our *State* with regard to the *Favour* of God, as any Authority in Matters of Religion.

Seeing therefore, by an Authority in Matters of *Conscience* and *Salvation,* by an Authority which can *affect* our *State* with regard to the *Favour* of God, nothing more is implied, than an Authority to which our Obedience is a *Duty*, and our Disobedience a *Sin*, which is the Case of every Lawful Authority; it plainly appears, that all those *frightful* Consequences, those *Dangers* to the Souls of Men which you have charged upon such *Church Authority,* are as truly chargeable upon *Masters, Fathers,* and *Princes,* and make their several Authorities as dangerous Powers over the Salvation of others, as the Authority of the Church.

Thus, when your *Demonstration* proceeds in this manner: *If there be an Authority in some over others in Matters* purely *relating to Conscience and Salvation, then the Salvation of some People will depend upon others.* Which, if we set it in a true Light, ought to proceed thus; *If there be an Authority in Matters of Religion, to which our Obedience is a Duty, and our Disobedience a Sin, then the Salvation of some People depends upon others.*

But, my Lord, what a Sagacity must he have who can see this dismal Consequence? Who can see that *Masters, Fathers,* and *Princes,* have a Power over the Souls *of others,* either to *damn* or *save* them, because Obedience to their Authority is a *Duty,* and Disobedience a *Sin?*

Your Lordship cannot here say, that *an Authority* in *Matters purely relating to Conscience* and *eternal Salvation,* is not expressed *high* enough, by being described as an *Authority to which our Obedience is a Duty, and our Disobedience a Sin.* For, my Lord, no Authority, however concerned in things of the greatest Importance in *Religion* and *Salvation,* can possibly be an Authority of an *higher* Nature, than that *Authority to which our Obedience is a Duty, and our Disobedience a Sin.* It was in this *Sense alone,* that the Authority of our *Saviour* himself *affected* the state of the *Jews* with regard to the *Favour* of God; his Authority was of an *high* and *concerning* Nature to them only for this Reason, because their Obedience to it was their Duty, and their Disobedience their Sin.

If we now consider this Authority in the Church, in this true Manner in which it ought to be considered, your Lordship's Argument against it, either proves a deal too much, or nothing at all.

Thus, if the Consequence be just, that if it be Sin to disobey the Church, then the Church hath a Power of damning us; then it is as good a Consequence in regard to other Authority; as thus, *It is a Sin to disobey our Parents, therefore our Parents have a Power of damning us;* it is a Sin to disobey our *Prince,* therefore *our Prince has a Power of damning us.* These Consequences are evidently as *just* and *true,* as that other drawn from Church Authority; so that all those *dismal Charges* which you have fixed upon *Church Authority,* are as false Accounts of it, as if you had asserted that every *Father,* or *Master,* or *Prince,* who demands Obedience from his *Child, Servant,* or *Subject,* in point of *Duty,* or by declaring that their Disobedience is a *Sin,* does thereby prove himself to be a *Pope,* and to have the Souls of others at his Disposal. For it is out of all doubt, that if the *Governors* of the Church by demanding Obedience to them in point of *Duty,* or by declaring Disobedience to be *Sin,* do thereby assert the Claims of *Popery,* and assume a Power to dispose of the Souls of the People; that any other Authority which requires this Obedience as a *Duty* of Conscience, and forbids Disobedience as *Sin,* does thereby claim the Authority of the *Pope,* and pretend to a Power over the Souls of others.

So that if your Lordship has destroyed Church Authority, which pretends Obedience to be a *Duty*, as a *Popish Claim;* you have also as *certainly* destroyed every other Authority which demands Obedience as a *Duty*, as being equally a *Popish Presumption*.

Whenever therefore you shall please to call away *Servants, Children*, or *Subjects* from their respective *Masters, Fathers*, and *Princes*, you have as many *Demonstrations* ready to prove them *all Papists*, if they will stick by their Obedience to them as a *Duty of Conscience*, and to prove their Governors *all Popes*, if they declare their Disobedience to be *Sin*, as you have to prove Church Authority to be a *Popish Claim*. And I must beg leave to affirm, that they are as much misled who follow your Lordship against the Authority of the Church, as if they should follow you in the *same Argument* against owning any Authority of their *Parents* and *Princes*.

The Intent of all this is only to shew, that though there is an Authority in the Church, to which our Obedience is a *Duty* and our Disobedience a *Sin* (which is as high an Authority as can be claimed) yet this Authority implies no more a *frightful* Power of *disposing* of our Souls, than any other Lawful Authority, which it is a *Sin* to disobey, implies such a Power.

For where is the Danger to our Souls? How is our Salvation made subject to the Pleasure of our Church Governors, because God has appointed them to direct us in the manner of worshipping him, and to preside over things relating to Religion, and made it our Duty to obey them? How does this imply a dangerous Power over our Salvation? If we sin against this Authority, we endanger our Salvation as we do by neglecting *any other Ordinance* of God; and our Damnation is no more affected by any *Power* in the Persons, whom we may be damned for disobeying, than a Person that is *damned* for *killing* his Father, is damned by any *Power* of his *Father's*.

Neither is it in the Power of the Governors in the Church, though they have Authority in Matters of Salvation, to make our Salvation any more difficult to us, than if they had no *such* Authority.

For all their Injunctions must be either *Lawful*, or *Unlawful;* if they are *Lawful*, then by our Obedience to an *Ordinance* of God, we recommend ourselves to the Favour of God; and sure there is no harm in this Authority thus far. And if their Commands are *Unlawful*, then by our not obeying them, we still please God, in choosing rather to obey him than Men, where *both cannot* be obeyed. And where, my Lord, is the

Terror of this Authority so much complained of? How does this make our Salvation lie at the Mercy of our *Church Governors?* We are still as truly saved or damned by our own Behaviour, as though they had no *such Authority* over us; and though we may make their Authority the *Occasion* of our Damnation, by our rebelling against it, yet it is only in such a manner as anyone may make *Baptism,* or the *Supper* of the Lord, the *Occasion* of his Damnation, by a profane Refusal of them.

Upon the whole of this Matter, it appears, First, that when the Authority of the Church is said to be an *Authority* in *Matters of Conscience and Salvation,* or an Authority which *concerns* and *affects our State* with *regard to the* Favour of God; that this is the only true Meaning of those Propositions, *viz.,* an *Authority in Matters of Religion, to which Obedience is a Duty, and Disobedience a Sin.*

Secondly, That this Authority to which we are *thus obliged,* is as consistent with our working out our own Salvation, and no more puts our Souls into the Disposal of such Authority, than our Salvation is at the Mercy of our *Parents* and *Princes,* because to obey their Authority is a *great Duty,* and to disobey it, a *great Sin.*

Your Lordship has yet another Argument against *Church Authority,* taken from the Nature of our Reformation, which it seems cannot be defended, if there was then this *Church Authority* we have been pleading for.

Thus you say; *If there be a Church Authority, I beg to know, how can the Reformation itself be justified.**

My Lord, I cannot but wonder this should be a Difficulty with your Lordship, who has writ so *famous* a Treatise to inform People, *how* they not only *may,* but *ought* in point of *Duty* to get rid of a *real* Authority; I mean in your Defence of *Resistance.*

I suppose it is taken for granted, that *James* the Second was King of *England,* that he had a *Regal* Authority over all the People of *England,* and that they all of what Station soever were his *Subjects;* yet granting this *Regal* Authority in him, and this State of *Subjection* in all the People of *England,* your Lordship *knows how to set aside* that Government, and set up another Government; and even to make it our *Duty* as *Men* and *Protestants* to set up another Government.

Now since you know how to get rid of this Authority in so *Christian* and *Protestant* a manner, one cannot but wonder

---

* *Answ. to Repr.,* p. 117.

how you should be at a loss to justify the *Reformation*, without supposing that the Church at *that time* had no Authority.

For did you ever justify the *Revolution*, because *James* the Second had no *Kingly Authority*, or that the People of *England* were not his *Subjects?* Nay, did you not defend it upon the quite contrary Supposition, that though *James* the Second had a *Regal* Authority, though all the People of *England* were his *Subjects*, and had sworn to be his *faithful* Subjects, yet in spite of all these Considerations, did you not assert that they not only *might*, but *ought* to set him aside and choose another Governor in his stead?

And yet after all this, you *know not how* to defend the *Reformation*, it is a perfectly lost Cause, and not a word to be said for it, unless we suppose that there was no *Authority* in the Church when we *reformed* from it. Surely if your Lordship loved to defend the *Reformation*, as well as you loved to defend the *Revolution*, you would not have so *many* Reasons for one, and *none* for the other.

For supposing an Authority in the Church, will not *Tyranny*, *Breach* of *Fundamentals*, and *unlawful Terms* of Communion, defend our Departure from a *real* Authority in the Church, as well as any *Grievances* or *Oppressions* will defend our leaving a *real* Authority in the State?

What a *pitiful* Advocate, what a *Betrayer* of the *Rights* of the People would you reckon him, who should say, *If there was any Regal Authority in* James *the Second, if the People of* England *were his* Subjects; *I beg to know, how can the* Revolution *itself be justified?*

Yet just such an *Advocate* are you, just such a *Betrayer* of the *Reformation*, you cannot defend it, it has no bottom to stand upon; and if there was any *Authority* in the Church before the *Reformation, you beg to know,* how the *Reformation itself can be justified?*

My Lord, I do not urge this to shew either that the *Revolution* and *Reformation* are equally justifiable, or that they both are to be justified upon the *same* Reasons; but to shew that your Lordship from *your own Principles*, needed not to have wanted as good Reasons for the *Reformation*, as you have produced for the *Revolution*, even supposing the Church of *Rome* had as *real* an Authority over us as *James* the Second had, and that we were as truly in a State of Subjection to that Church before the *Reformation*, as we were in a State of Subjection to that King before the *Revolution*.

Again, you proceed thus; *For there was then* (at the Time of the Reformation) *a* Church, *and an Order of* Church-men, *vested* with all such spiritual Authority, as is of the Essence of the Church. There was therefore a Church Authority to oblige Christians; and a Power in some over others. What was it therefore to which we owe this very Church of England?*

Now, my Lord, I hope you will grant, that just at the Time of the *Revolution*, 'there was then a *King*, vested with all such Civil 'Authority as is of the Essence of a *King*. There was therefore 'a *Regal Authority* to oblige the People of *England*, and a Power 'in one over others. What was it therefore to which we owe this 'very *Revolution* in *England*?'

I suppose you will say that we owe it, not to any *Want* of Authority in the late King *James*, but to his *Abuse* of his Authority: Why therefore is it not as easy to account for the *Reformation*, not from the *Want*, but the *Abuse* of Authority in the Church of *Rome*? Is it an Argument that the People of *England* were no *Subjects*, under no Government, nor had any *King*, because they would no longer submit to the *Oppressions* and *Grievances* of a late Reign, but asserted their *Liberties* and appealed to the Conditions of the *Original Contract*?

If not, why is it an Argument that the Church had *no Authority*, because some Years ago the People of *England* would no longer submit to the *Corruptions*, and *unlawful* Injunctions of the Church of *Rome*, but appealed to the *Scriptures*, and the Practice of the *first* and *purest* Ages of Christianity?

If your Lordship was so entirely consistent with yourself as you tell us you are; if you never pursued an Argument farther than the plain Reason of it led you; how is it possible that you, who have so strenuously defended the *Resistance* of People against a *Legal King*† (for so you expressly call him), should declare that our Separation from the Church of *Rome* cannot be *justified*, without supposing that the Church of *Rome* had never any Authority over us?

For supposing that Church had been really our Sovereign in Affairs of Religion, is it not strange that you, who have asserted that our *present Settlement is owing entirely to the taking up Arms, and adhering to such as were in Arms against* their Sovereign,‡ should yet declare that our opposing the Church of *Rome*, cannot be justified but by supposing, that she never had any *Sovereignty* over us?

Is it not yet stranger, that you, who have defended the *Revolution* by comparing it to the *Reformation*, should yet declare that the *Reformation* cannot be justified without supposing that

---

* *Answ. to Repr.*, p. 118.
† *Sev. Tracts*, p. 332.   ‡ *Ibid.*, p. 366.

the Church of *England* was under no Authority of the Church of *Rome* ?

For, my Lord, if the Church of *England* had not been under the *Authority* of the Church of *Rome*, how could our *opposing* that Church be compared to the *resisting* of King *James* ? How could our *Separation* from that Church be a Defence of our *withdrawing* our *Allegiance* from King *James*, without supposing that the Church before that *Separation*, had as *Real* and *Legal* Authority as that King had before the *Revolution* ?

Your Words are these ; *Why should that (i.e.,* Resistance*) be absolutely and entirely condemned, as a damnable Sin, any more than* Church Separation, *by which we got rid of the* Tyranny *of* Rome ? And again, *All* Church Reformation *is not Church* Destruction ; *Why therefore must* all Resistance *be called* Rebellion ?*

Now is it not very strange, my Lord, that after this, you should assert that the Church had *no Authority* before the *Reformation ;* and that if it had any Authority, then our *Separation* from it cannot be *justified ?* Is not this very strange, after you had used it as an Argument to justify the withdrawing of our Allegiance from King *James* the Second ?

For let us suppose with you, that there was *no Church Authority* at the time of the *Reformation*, and then see how excellent an Argument you have found out in Defence of the *Revolution*, which, upon this Supposition, must proceed in this manner.

The Church of *England might* separate from the Church of *Rome*, who had *no Authority* over her ; therefore the People of *England* might resist their *Legal* King, who had a Regal Authority over them. Again, The Clergy of *England*, who were *no Subjects* of the Church of *Rome*, *might* separate from that Church ; therefore the People of *England*, who were *Subjects* to King *James* the Second, might withdraw their *Allegiance* from him.

Thus absurd is your Argument made, by supposing that the Church had not as real and rightful an Authority before the *Reformation*, as *James* the Second had before the *Revolution*.

Farther ; Let us suppose with your Lordship, that *if there was a real Authority in the Church at the time of the Reformation*, then the Reformation *has no bottom, but is altogether unjustifiable;* let us suppose that this Doctrine is true, and then see how *consistently* you have argued upon this Supposition.

You say the *Reformation* cannot be justified ; it has no *bottom* to stand upon, if the Church of *Rome* had a real Authority ; yet

---

* *Sev. Tracts*, p. 334.

this *Opposition*, which is so entirely *wrong*, because an *Opposition* to Authority, is brought by you as a *parallel Case* to prove that the *Resistance* against the *Authority* of King *James* was entirely *right*. This *Reformation*, which if it was brought about against any *Church Authority*, is said to be for that *very Reason* without any *bottom*, and to have no *Foundation*, is used by your Lordship to point out the *true Bottom* and *firm Foundation* of the *Revolution*.

And here let all the World judge, whether *Reason* and *Religion* alone can induce anyone to maintain the *Truth*, the *Justice*, the *Honour*, the *Christianity* of the Revolution, as founded upon Resistance to a Legal King ; and yet condemn at the same time the *Reformation*, as having neither *Reason*, nor *Truth*, nor *Justice* to support it, as founded upon a Departure from a real Authority in the Church of *Rome*. For *Reason* and *Religion* do as plainly give leave to depart from the *highest* Authority in the Church, when the Laws of God cannot be observed without departing from it, as in any other Case ; and there is no more Necessity of supposing or proving that there was no rightful Authority in the Church, to justify our departing from it, than it is necessary to prove such a Person not to be my *Father*, or to have no *Authority* over me, in order to justify my disobeying his *unlawful Commands*.

Again, your Lordship is farther at a loss about the *Reformation*, which cannot possibly be justified, if afterwards, an *Authority* in Matters of *Conscience* and *Salvation*, be still claimed.

Thus you say ; *Nor can I ever understand, upon this bottom* (viz., the claiming such Authority) *what it was that could* move or justify *those, who broke off from the Tyranny of the Church of* Rome ; *unless it be sufficient to say, that it was only* that Power might change Hands.*

Here your Lordship cannot conceive anything more unjustifiable than the *Reformation*, if *Church Authority* is still to be kept up ; nor can you upon this Claim assign any other Pretence for *reforming*, but *only* that Power might change Hands.

Did your Lordship then never hear of the *Justice* of removing one Authority, and setting up another ? Can you think of no Case, where *Equity*, *Honour*, and *Duty*, called upon a People to *resist* one Power, and yet make another to succeed ?

Now if this Practice can be equitable and honourable, and is asserted to be so by your Lordship, can it be conceived, that *Reason alone* should induce you to load the *Reformation* with so much *Guilt* and *Injustice*, to condemn it as so groundless an

---

* *Answ. to Repr.*, p. 48.

Undertaking; because though it set aside the *Tyrannical* Authority of the Church of *Rome*, yet it asserted a true Church Authority, and made Obedience to it necessary to obtain the Favour of God.

Suppose some Friend to the *Revolution*, after hearing that the *Prince* of *Orange* was proclaimed King, and a *Regal* Authority set up, should then have said in your Lordship's Words, *I can never understand, upon this bottom, what it was that could move or justify those, who broke off from the Tyranny of the late King* James; *unless it was sufficient to say, that it was only* that Power might change Hands.

I appeal to your Lordship, whether anything could be more *extravagant* and *senseless*, than such a Declaration as this from a Friend to the *Revolution*.

And I as freely appeal to the *common Sense* of everyone, whether your *own Declaration* expressed in the *same* Words with regard to the *Reformation*, sets you out to any better Advantage in relation to that.

For it is full as good Sense to say, where is the *Justice* of the *Revolution*, or what *Foundation* has it in the Reason of Things, if there is still a *King* to be acknowledged, and a *Regal Authority* to be submitted to? as to call out for the *Justice*, and *Equity*, and *Reason* of the *Reformation*, if there is still a *Church Authority* which we are obliged to obey. And it is as certainly the *Shame* and *Reproach* and *Injustice* of the *Revolution*, that a Government and *Regal* Authority is still maintained, as it is the *Shame*, and *Reproach*, and *Injustice* of the *Reformation*, that a *Church Authority* is still asserted.

And there was no more Necessity in the Nature or Reason of the Thing, that the *Reformation* should disown all *Authority* properly so called, in Matters of *Religion*, than that the *Revolution* should have rejected all Authority properly so called in *Civil Affairs*. Neither does the *Reformation* any more contradict itself, or undermine its own Foundation, and give the *Papists* an Advantage over it, by claiming and asserting a *Church Authority*, than the *Revolution* contradicted itself, or conspired its own Ruin, by setting up a *King*, and maintaining a *Government* in the State. And it had been just as *wise*, as *prudent*, and *politic* Management, if the *Revolution* had set up no Government, but left every Man to himself in *Civil Affairs*, in order to have prevented the Return of the late King *James;* as if the *Reformation* had maintained no Church Authority, but left every Person's Religion to himself, in order to keep out *Popery*. And it is just as much Matter of Joy and Triumph to the *Papists*, to see this Authority asserted in the Church of *England*, as it was Matter of Joy to the late King *James*, to find that a *Regal Authority* was set up against him.

But to go on ; your Argument, when put in form, will proceed in this manner.

The Church of *England* departed from the Authority of the Church of *Rome*, therefore we may *lawfully* depart from any Church Authority. And again ; at the *Reformation* we *lawfully* separated from the *Communion* of the *Church* of *Rome*, therefore we may as *lawfully* separate from any particular *Communion*.

And now, my Lord, can any Argument be more trifling, or draw more absurd Consequences after it, than this? And yet, absurd as it is, it is one of your best, and which you seem to take great Delight in : Thus are we told in almost every Page, that if we will stand by the *Reason* and *Justice* of the *Reformation*, we must give up *all Authority* in Matters of Religion ; and not pretend to a Necessity of being of any *particular* Church, if we would justify our leaving the *Romish* Church.

But pray, my Lord, you have told us, that the People of *England* of all *Stations* did *lawfully* and *honourably*, &c., resist the late King *James;* but does it therefore follow, that they may as *lawfully* and *honourably* resist King *George?* If not, how does it follow, that because we might *justly* separate from the Church of *Rome*, therefore others may as *justly* separate from the Church of *England?*

Is it inconsistent with the Principles of the *Revolution* to declare Men *Rebels*, because it was founded (as you affirm) upon Resistance? If not, why must it be inconsistent with the Principles of the Church of *England*, to declare any people *Schismatics*, because she separated from the Church of *Rome ?* Now if you will say that all who take *Arms* at *any* time against *any* King, are justified by those, who took Arms against the late King *James;* then you would have some Pretence to make our *Separation* from the Church of *Rome* a Justification of *every* other *Separation* in the World. But since you cannot say this, but have pretended to demonstrate the contrary, that though sometimes *Resistance* is not *Rebellion*, yet sometimes *Resistance* certainly is *Rebellion*, you are particularly hard to the *Reformation*, to make it either unjustifiable in itself, or else to be a *Justification* of every other pretended *Reformation*.

But however, as hard as you are upon the *Reformation* in this Place, making it, considered as a *Separation*, a Defence of all other *Separations* from the Church of *England;* yet you yourself, to shew your equal regard to both sides of a Contradiction, have asserted the contrary, and declared that as all *Resistance is not Rebellion*, so neither *is all Separation Schism*.

Now, I suppose, when you say that *all Resistance* is not *Rebellion*, it is certainly implied that *some Resistance* may be *Rebellion;* and likewise by declaring in the *same* manner *all Separation* not to be *Schism*, it must as necessarily be implied that *some Separation* may be *Schism*. Here therefore you plainly teach us, that some *Separation* may be *Schism*, and some *Separation* may not be *Schism;* yet your present Argument is founded upon the contrary Supposition, that either all Separations are *Lawful*, or none are *Lawful;* for it is the constant Complaint in every Chapter of your Book, that the Church of *England* should assert any Necessity or Obligation upon others of conforming to her, when she herself denied the Necessity of her conforming to the Church of *Rome*. So that the *Lawfulness* or *Justice* of her *Separation* from *Rome*, is urged to shew the equal *Lawfulness* and *Justice* of all *Separations* from the Church of *England;* which Argument is plainly founded upon this Proposition, that all Separations from any Churches, are either equally *Lawful*, or equally *Unlawful*. Which is directly contrary to this other Proposition, that some Separation may be *Schism*, and some Separation may not be *Schism*. Which Contradiction is just as palpable, as if you had said, all Resistance is not the Sin of Rebellion ; yet all Resistance is either *equally* lawful, or *equally* unlawful.

But to go on, you say that *all* Resistance is not Rebellion, and for a Proof of it, say, that all *Church Separation* is not *Schism;* which plainly implies, that there is *at least* as much Difference betwixt some *Separations* from *different* Churches, as there is betwixt some armed *Resistances* against *different* Kings. Now if, according to your Lordship, there is as much Difference betwixt *Resistances,* as there is betwixt an Action that is a *Duty*, and an Action that is a *Sin*, and you have proved this Difference, by comparing those *Resistances* to different sorts of *Separations*, then it will necessarily follow that there may be, nay must be, as much Difference betwixt one *Separation* and another *Separation*, as there is betwixt one Action that is a *Duty*, and another Action that is a *Sin*. This being the true State of the Case, your Lordship's Argument in Defence of the *Separatists*, taken from our *Separation* from the Church of *Rome*, will stand thus.

We separated from the Church of *Rome*, because *such Separation* was our *Duty*, therefore the *Fanatics* may separate from the Church of *England*, though *such Separation* is a *Sin* : Which is as rational an Argument, as if it should be said, such a one killed a Man *lawfully*, therefore anyone else may kill a Man *unlawfully*. For if some Separation may be a *Duty*, and some

Separation a *Sin*, it is as false and ridiculous to infer, that if *our* Separation is just, it justifies *all other* Separations; as to conclude, that because we may do our *Duty*, others may transgress their *Duty*. For there is manifestly, and from your own Acknowledgment, this great Difference between one Separation and another Separation, that one *Separation* in such Circumstances, will no more justify a Separation in other Circumstances, than the Lawfulness of killing a Man in some Cases, will prove it lawful to kill a Man in all other Cases.

Now if your Lordship has any *Demonstrations* ready, to show that *Resistance* in some Circumstances is a *Christian Duty*, and *Resistance* in some other Circumstances is a *damnable Sin;* and that it may be as great a Sin to resist some Princes, as it is a Duty to resist others; if you can help us to any plain Rule, any certain Signs to know an honest Christian *Resister*, from a *Resister* who is a *Rebel* and in danger of *Damnation;* I hope there may be found as plain Rules to shew us who separates *lawfully*, and who separates *unlawfully* from any particular Church. If you can give any Reasons why the late King *James* might be resisted *then*, and yet show it a Sin to resist King *George now*, it is something strange that you cannot find any Reasons, why it was our *Duty* to separate from the Church of *Rome then*, and yet shew it a *Sin* to separate from the Church of *England now*.

For I would suppose at least, that there is as much Difference between separating from the Church of *England* and separating from the Church of *Rome*, as there is betwixt Resistance against a *good* King, and Resistance against a *Tyrannical* Oppressor; and if there be this Difference, then you must allow, that it is as false to argue from the *Lawfulness* of separating from one Church, to the *Lawfulness* of separating from the other, as it would be to argue, that because oppressive Tyrants may be resisted, therefore just and good Kings may be resisted. I have been the longer in examining this Doctrine, in this particular View in relation to *Resistance*, that it may be seen with how much Truth you say, you have *recommended such Principles as serve to establish the Interest of our common Country and our common Christianity, of human Society and true Religion, upon one* uniform, steady, and consistent Foundation.*

For it is evident that these Principles, if put in Practice, directly tend to the utter Ruin of our common Country, and our common Christianity; for I have shewn that all the Arguments which you have advanced against Church Authority, if they

---

* *Pref. to Com. Rights of Subjects.*

have any Force, conclude with the same Force against all sorts of Authority in the World.

I shall now proceed to a most remarkable evasive Denial of everything you have said relating to Church Authority, from your own Mouth.

A Remarkable Evasion of your Lordship's in relation to Church Authority.

THE *Learned Committee* charged your Lordship with *denying all Authority to the Church, and leaving it without any Authority to judge, censure, or punish Offenders in the Affairs of Conscience and eternal Salvation.** To support this Charge, they quoted these Words of your Sermon ; *Christ is sole Lawgiver to his Subjects, and himself sole Judge of their Behaviour in the Affairs of Conscience and Salvation; in these Points he hath left behind him no visible human Authority.*

Now how is it that your Lordship has cleared yourself from this Charge? Why truly by declaring, that by a Denial of *all Church Authority*, you only meant to deny to the Governors of the Church a Power of passing the *irreversible Sentence*, or that Christ has left no visible Authority here to *judge* People at the last Day. When you talked so much of Church Authority in Matters of Religion, and of *an Authority left behind*, it was very reasonable to think that you were speaking of an Authority which related to the Church in this World. But it seems, all you have denied in relation to Church Authority, is only this, that anyone but Christ shall *pass the irreversible Sentence*, or judge us at the last Day.

For you say ; *As Christ is to pass the irreversible Sentence, thus he is judge alone.* And *what I affirm of him, I deny of others in the same Sense in which I affirm it of him : And in no other Sense can I be supposed to deny it, because it answers no Purpose.*†

Therefore when you say no Men have any Authority in Affairs of *Religion* and *Conscience*, you only say that no Men have Authority to pass the *irreversible Sentence* at the last Day. For you declare that thus it is that Christ alone is Judge, and you only deny that of others, which you affirm of him, and con-

---

* *Repres.*, p. 4.   † *Answ. to Repr.*, p. 33.

sequently the only Authority which you deny them, is that of judging the World at the *last Day*.

Strange! my Lord, that after so many elaborate Pages for ecclesiastical Liberty, so many Compliments received for your successful Attacks upon *Church Authority;* that after all, you should declare, that you have not so much as touched upon *Church Authority*, but have only been labouring to *demonstrate* that the *Judgment of the last Day is committed to Christ alone.*

Christ, you say, *is in no other Sense Judge of the Behaviour of Christians in these Points, than as their Condition must and will be determined by his* Sentence. *And when I deny this of Men, I do not, I cannot, mean to deny this of them in any other Sense, but that in which I affirm it of Christ.**

So that when you in plain Words seem to deny all Authority in the Church, as by saying, that *Christ alone is Judge of the Behaviour of Christians, in Matters of Religion*, and that he left behind him *no visible human Authority in these Points;* and such like Phrases, as seem to ordinary Understandings to deny all *Rule* and *Authority* in the Church; you only mean, that *no* one but Christ is to pass the *Sentence* at the last Day. This is the *Key* your Lordship has given us to your Writings, which indeed gives them quite another Face, and makes them such a Course of *Amusements*, as exceeds all which have yet been seen in that kind; as will appear from the following Particulars.

Thus when you say, that *in the Affairs of Conscience and Salvation, Christ hath left no visible human Authority behind him.* The Meaning is this, that *Christ hath left no body behind him in this World, to pass the irreversible Sentence in the next World, i.e.*, hath left no one to do that *here*, which cannot be done till *hereafter.* This is the *sublimest* Sense which this Passage is capable of, from your own Construction.

Again, you say, the *Church of Christ is the Number of Persons who are sincerely and willingly Subjects to him as their Lawgiver and Judge;†* which according to this new *Key*, is to be thus understood; The *Church of Christ is the Number of Persons who will sincerely and willingly submit to the Sentence of Christ at the last Day.* For you say, we are to submit to him as our Judge; and you expressly say, he is *in no other Sense judge of the Behaviour of Christians*, than as he is to pass the *irreversible Sentence;* therefore if we are to be *willingly* and *sincerely* subject to him *as Judge*, our Obedience or Subjection to him as Judge, can be no otherwise expressed, than by our Submission to his Sentence then pronounced.

---

* *Answ. to Repr.*, p. 46. † *Serm.*, p. 25.

So that this Definition comes at last to signify a Number of Persons, who sincerely and willingly submit, some to be saved, and some to be damned at the last Day; for this will be the Effect of Christ's Sentence as Judge.

This is as sound Divinity, as if I should define the Church of Christ, to be a *Number of Persons, who sincerely and willingly submit, some to live, and some to die.*

Again, you say, that *your Doctrines relating to the Authority of the Church*, is the very Foundation *on which the Church of* England *stands; and that they are so necessary for its continuance, that without them it is impossible to defend its Cause against the* Roman *Catholics*.

Now your Doctrine concerning Church Authority, you have over and over declared to be only this, *that Christ alone shall judge the World at the last Day*. For you expressly say, that you deny the Church an Authority of judging in *no other Sense*, than in the Sense in which you affirm it of Christ.

Now, my Lord, how comes this Doctrine to be the Support of the Church of *England*? How can it possibly have any relation to the Merits of the Cause? Does it follow that the *Pope* had no Legal Authority in *England*, that *Transubstantiation* is false, that *Purgatory* is a groundless Fiction, and *Prayers* to Saints are unlawful, because *Christ alone shall judge the World?* This is what you have affirmed of Christ, this is all which you have denied of Men; and this Doctrine it seems about *Church Authority*, as you are pleased to call it, is the *only Support* of the Church of *England*, and *the very Foundation on which it stands*.

A *Roman* Catholic tells me that *Transubstantiation* is true; I answer him no, that cannot be, and that for this reason, because no Order of Men shall judge us at the last Day; Christ alone should do it. Could anything be more extravagant, or more foreign to the Purpose, than such an Answer as this to a *Roman* Catholic? And yet, according to your Account of the Matter, this is the only Answer which can be defended. For you have denied *no Authority* to the Church, but that which peculiarly belongs to Christ *as Judge at the last Day;* and yet you say that your Doctrine relating to Church Authority, is the very Foundation and Support of the *Reformation*.

Now if this Doctrine be our only Defence against the Church of *Rome*, and what alone supports us against that Church, then the *Presbyterians*, the *Independents, Quakers*, and all sorts of *Fanatics*, who own this Doctrine, that *Christ alone shall pass the last Sentence*, are by it as well defended against the Church of *England*, as she is against the Church of *Rome;* so that it makes us as much wrong in regard to the *Dissenters*, as it makes us right in regard to the *Papists*; and though it should give us *Victory* over the *Papists*, yet it makes us fall a Conquest to the *Fanatics*. For it is certainly as proper for a *Quaker* to reply to the *Church* of *England*, that his Reformation is justified against the Authority of the *Church* of *England*, because Christ alone shall judge the World at the last Day; as for the Church of *England* to make that Answer to the Church of *Rome*.

Your Lordship says, for you to deny Church Authority in any other Sense, *answers no Purpose*. Pray, my Lord, what Purpose does this manner of denying answer? Here is a Dispute about Church Authority, and the Powers of Ecclesiastical Governors: Your Lordship interposes, and declares that no Man shall *pass the irreversible Sentence at the last Day*. To what Purpose, my Lord, is this Declaration? Does it strike any Light into the Controversy, or any way point out the Merits of the Cause? Does this inform us whether there is any such thing as Church Authority, or where it is seated? If two *Families* were trying their Title to the same Estate, and the Judge should pretend to determine the Matter, by saying that *God alone is sole Proprietor of all Things*, it would be as much to the Purpose, as to tell us in the Controversy about Church Authority, that *Christ alone shall judge the World*. Does this any way prove that there is no human Authority in the Church, or that Christians are no way concerned with it? What an excellent Argument is this? *Christ alone* shall judge the World, therefore no Men have *any Authority* in Religion, therefore it can no way affect you with regard to the Favour of God, whether you submit or not, to such human Authority?

Whether your Lordship is forced upon this Method of explaining yourself, by any other Motives than those of Sincerity and Conviction, is what I shall not presume to say; but I believe, if a Person should be called to account for saying the *King* had no Right to *create Peers*, and should afterwards defend himself, by saying that he only meant he could not *create* in that Sense, in which *God alone* could create; I am apt to think such a Defence would be no great Recommendation of his Sincerity. But, my Lord, it would be as proper and as ingenuous for a Person so accused to make such a Defence, or rather such an Escape, as for your Lordship, after the most express repeated Denials of *all Church Authority*, to declare that you only meant to exclude it from passing the *irreversible Sentence* at the last Day. And the Nature of Church Authority is as much settled and determined by this Declaration, as the King's Power in his Kingdom, as to the Creation of *Peers*, is declared by saying that *God alone* can create.

For is it any Argument that no Persons have any particular Authority to baptize others, to admit to the holy Sacrament, and exclude unworthy Persons from it, because they are not to judge the World at the last Day? Is it a Proof that Bishops have no Authority to ordain, to confirm; no Commission from God to take care of Religious Matters, and see that all Things in the Divine Service be done decently and in order, because Christ alone is to pass Judgment upon all at the last Day? Does it follow that Men are under no Church Authority, but may choose any Government, or no Government as they please, because Christ alone shall call the World to Judgment? There is as much Logic in saying that *Jesus Christ* suffered under *Pontius Pilate*, therefore Bishops have no more Authority than Laymen; as to say they have no Authority in Religious Affairs, because Christ is to judge the World.

Yet you say this was the only proper Sense in which you could be supposed to deny it. Now, my Lord, I should have thought it had been more to the Purpose, to have denied Church Authority in some such Sense, as it had been falsely claimed by somebody or other, that it might have been said that you had an Adversary somewhere or other. But in this Matter, you have not so much as an Adversary in this World; for no one pretends to be Judge, as Christ is Judge, or sets up the *Authority* of the Church in Opposition to the last *Tribunal;* yet this is the *only manner* of Judging, the *only sort* of Authority, which you say you have denied to others; therefore you have only denied that which was never claimed; you have only denied that which no more relates to *Church Authority*, than it relates to Church *Music*. The *Pope* himself neither pretends to pass Sentence at the last Day, nor that his Judgments here will have any Effect in the next World, but conditionally, that is, *Clave non errante.* Now this is not a Sense in which Christ alone is Judge, therefore it is not a Sense in which you have denied it to others. So that notwithstanding this long elaborate Treatise against Church Tyranny and Popish Claims, *Popery* itself is as safe and sound as ever it was. For you have denied this Power of Judging in *no other Sense*, than as you have affirmed it of Christ, as he is to pass the last *irreversible* Sentence at the Day of Judgment; but the *Pope* does not claim it in that Sense, therefore the *Papal Power* is untouched by your Lordship.

Here I must observe, how your Lordship has evaded the great Points in Dispute, both concerning the *Nature* of the Church, and Church Authority. When you were charged with describing the

Church contrary to *Scripture* and the *Article* in the Church of *England;* your Answer was, that you had only described the *Invisible Church;* which was saying in other Words, that in a Dispute amongst *Visible Churches,* and about Church-Communion, you described a Church which had no relation to the Matter, nor ever can have to any Dispute amongst Christians. This, my Lord, to speak tenderly of it, may be called only an *Evasion.*

Again, as to Church Authority, your Lordship has been charged with denying it all, and leaving it no right to judge or censure in the Affairs of Conscience. Your Answer is this, that you have only denied that Christ has left any Men here to judge us at the last Day. That is, in a Controversy about the *Existence* of Church Authority, the *Extent* and *Obligation* of its Laws, you have only denied such an Authority as nobody claims, nor ever will be executed, till *all Visible* Churches, and Disputes about them, will be at an end, *viz.,* at the Day of Judgment.

This, my Lord, is another Evasion, and that in the very chief Point in Dispute, where Sincerity should have obliged you to have been open, clear, and express. But no sooner are you touched upon this Point, but you fly into the Clouds, and the very Dissenters themselves lose sight of you.

Thus when you had plainly said, that *Christ hath left behind him no visible human Authority in the Affairs of Conscience,* the Dissenters might justly think they had nothing to be charged with for their Disobedience to Bishops; they might well think that they were left to any Government, or no Government in Religion, as they pleased, since Christ had left *no visible human Authority;* but then how must they be astonished, my Lord, to find that your Assertion about Church Authority, does not at all relate to the Church in *this World,* but to the Exercise of a certain Authority in the *next World,* after all Churches on the Earth are at an end? To find that you have denied no Authority to any Men, but that which peculiarly belongs to Christ at the last Day? That is, that you denied no Authority which ever was claimed either by *Protestant* or *Popish* Churches, or indeed which relates to the Church in this World?

Suppose, when his Majesty was last at *Hanover,* anyone should have asserted, that the *Regency* had no Authority in Civil Matters; would the Regency have thought it any Excuse, if he had said that he only meant they were not the Governors of *Hanover?* Yet, my Lord, it would be as proper an Apology for him who had denied the Power of the Regency in *Great Britain,* to say he only meant they had not the supreme Power in *Hanover,* as for your Lordship, after a Denial of *all Visible*

Church Authority in this World, to say you only denied an Authority to pass the irreversible Sentence in the next World.

Thus has your Lordship left the Dispute, and only pretended to deny that which nobody ever claimed, viz., *that any Men have Authority to judge the World in Christ's stead, or pass the irreversible Sentence at the last Day.* Your Lordship is here apprehensive, that you shall be charged with *fighting without an Adversary*, and therefore you point out several, and say, *I meant it against those, who are so very free in declaring others of Christ's Subjects out of God's Favour; and in obliging Almighty God, to execute the Sentences of Men.*

There has been indeed, my Lord, a Number of Men, ever since Christianity appeared in the World, who have been *very free* in declaring *Heretics* and *Schismatics* out of God's Favour, and who have maintained that these Heretics and Schismatics, when censured by the Church, cannot be received into God's Favour, but by their submitting to, and returning to the Church. But now, if your Lordship means your Doctrine against these, you are still *without an Adversary*, and might as well mean it against no Body; for these Men never pretended to *judge others in Christ's stead, or to erect an Ecclesiastical Authority in Opposition to the Great Tribunal, which is the only Authority you pretend to deny.*

You go on: *If we had not such amongst Protestants;* yet it might be pardonable to guard *our People against the Presumptions of the* Roman Catholics; *who assume to themselves that Power of Judgment, which Christ alone can have.*

Surely your Lordship must have so great an Aversion to Popery, that you never could so much as look into their Books; for otherwise I cannot conceive how you should not know, that the *Roman* Catholics pretended to no Power of Judging so as to affect People, but upon certain Conditions, as *Clave non errante;* but I suppose this is not a Power of Judging which belongs to our Saviour; *Clave non errante* has no Place in his Judgments. How then can your Lordship charge the *Papists* with assuming his Power, when that which they assume, cannot be ascribed to him without Blasphemy? So that, my Lord, it is just as pardonable to guard your People against these Presumptions, as it is to alarm them with false and imaginary Dangers.

Again you say; *But how lately is it, that we have had People terrified with this very Presumption, even by Protestants; and the Terms of Church Power, and the spiritual fatal Effects of Church Censures, made use of to frighten Men into a separate Communion?*

My Lord, I shall not here enter into the Merits of that Controversy, which your Lordship here points at; it being the Doctrine itself which your Lordship blames, and not the Misapplication of it. Thus you censure them, not because they would draw People from a *true* Church to a *false* one, but because they pretend to frighten Men out of one Communion into another. This is your Lordship's heavy Charge against them, that they should presume to talk of the Differences of Communions, and prefer one Communion to another. So that whoever thinks any way of Worship to be dangerous, and endeavours to withdraw People from it, is here censured by your Lordship, as pretending to judge in Christ's stead, and setting up an Authority in Opposition to the last Day.

Your Lordship saith, it is with this *very Presumption* (*viz.*, that they can pass the irreversible Sentence) *that these Men have endeavoured to frighten People into a separate Communion.* If I should say, that it is upon *Presumption* that Christ never appeared in the World, that your Lordship has delivered your late Doctrines, I should freely submit to the Charge of Calumny; and I am sure your Lordship has ventured as far, in saying that it was with *this very Presumption* that these Men delivered such Doctrines. And your Lordship has as much reason to charge them with *Atheism*, as with this *very Presumption;* for they no more presume *to judge in Christ's stead,* or pass the *irreversible Sentence*, than they presume there is no God.

Your Lordship has still, it seems, another Adversary, a late Writer (the Dean of *Chichester*) *who has spoken unwarily of the Effects of the spiritual Punishments, the Church inflicts, being generally suspended till the Offender comes into the other World.**
This first Censure is very modest, carrying it no farther than an *unwary* Expression; but presently the Charge advances; *and*, you say, *if it be thus, you confess you think the Condition of Christians much worse than the Condition in which St.* Paul *describes the Heathens, who are left to their own Consciences and the righteous Judgment of God.* So that at last it comes to this, that the Dean has taught such Doctrine, as makes it more desirable to be a *Heathen* than a *Christian*.

Let us therefore try how this Charge is supported: The *Dean* has said, *the Effects of spiritual Punishments are generally suspended till the Offender* comes into another World ;† therefore, says your Lordship, *the Condition of Christians is much worse than that of Heathens,* and the Reason is this, *because Heathens are left to their own Consciences and the righteous Judgment of God;* so that if spiritual Punishments signify anything to

---

* *Answ. to Repr.*, p. 35.   † *Serm.*, p. 8.

Offenders in the other World, or *have any Effect there*, then such People are in your Lordship's Judgment, not *left to their own Consciences and the righteous Judgment of God*.

Pray, my Lord, how does it follow that if spiritual Punishments have any Effect in *the other World*, that then Offenders *are not left to the righteous Judgment of God?*

Is it an Argument that People are not *left to the righteous Judgment of God*, because they are to be punished in the other World? Or is it an Argument that they are excluded from God's righteous Judgment, because they are not punished till they come thither? I should have thought it a plain Argument for the direct contrary, and that one could not give a stronger Proof that such Offenders were left *to the righteous Judgment of God*, than by saying that the Effects of such Punishments are not felt till the Offender comes into the other World; I should have thought this a manifest Declaration that the Offender was to fall to the *righteous Judgment of God*, since he was not to feel any Punishment till he was fallen into God's Hands. If the *Dean* had intended to teach that Church Punishments have no Effect, but such as the *righteous Judgment of God* gives them, how could he have better signified his Intention, than by declaring, that *the Effects of such Punishments are generally suspended till the Offender comes into the other World?* How could the *Dean* more expressly guard against any horrible Apprehensions of Church Censures, or more directly refer the Cause to God, than he has done here? His Words are a plain Declaration, that such Offenders must fall to the *righteous Judgment of God*, since they are to fall into his Hands before they feel the Effects of such Punishment.

If any discontented Offender against the *Church* should tell me, that if the Censures of the Church can signify anything to him, he should be glad to be a *Heathen*, and have his Fate amongst them; would it not be sufficient Matter of Satisfaction to tell him, that these Punishments will have no Effect but in the other World, where there can be no Injustice; and that it is the same God who judges the Heathens, who will judge Christians?

Yet this Declaration, which is the only Ground for Satisfaction to Men of Conscience, under the Censures of the Church, is by your Lordship pretended to be such an Evil, as to make us rather resign our Christianity, than submit to it. This is all which the *Dean* has said to make it more desirable to be a *Heathen* than a *Christian*.

Suppose, my Lord, the Matter had been worded stronger, and instead of saying that the *Effects of spiritual Punishments are generally suspended till the Offenders come into the other World*, it had been said, *the spiritual Censures* of the Church shall *rise in the Judgment and condemn Offenders.* If it had been thus expressed, what Complaints might you not have made against such *unwary* Expressions? What Cruelties and Hardships might you not have charged on such Doctrine? And how advantageously might you have compared the Felicity of *Heathenism* to such *Christianity?*

But, my Lord, that *Divine Person* who has reserved to himself the righteous Judgment of the World, has yet declared to a certain *Generation*, that the Men of *Nineveh* shall *rise up in the Judgment with them and condemn them, because those repented at the preaching of* Jonas, *but these did not, though a greater than* Jonas *was with them.**

Now, my Lord, here lies the same Objection against this Doctrine, which there does against the *Dean's.* For is it not full as hard that the *Repentance* of the Men of *Nineveh*, or anywhere else, should have any Effect upon the Impenitent at the Day of Judgment, as that the *Censures* of the Church should have any Effect upon Offenders in the other World? Is it not as cruel that the Impenitent shall have their Guilt aggravated by other People's *preaching* or *Repentance*, as by other People's *Censures?* And would it not be as proper here to say, if this be so, happy they who never heard of *Preaching* or *Repentance*, as to set forth the Happiness of *Heathens*, because they are free from *Church Censures?* If the *Sentence* of the Church will rise in Judgment and condemn Offenders, then you say such Persons do not fall to the righteous Judgment of God. But is not this as true of the Men of *Nineveh*, that if they shall rise up in Judgment and condemn the Impenitent, that then such Persons are not left to the *righteous Judgment of God?*

So that had you been one of our Saviour's Hearers, you must have been as much astonished at his Doctrine, as at the Dean's *unwary Expression*, and have been obliged to say then, as you have said now, *that you have such Notions of the Goodness of God, and of his gracious Designs in the Gospel, that you think it your Duty to declare your Judgment, that the Supposition is greatly injurious to the Honour of God and of the Gospel, and the thing itself impossible to be conceived.*†

Your Lordship has here only advanced this Argument against the *Significancy* of Church *Censures*, but anyone else may as justly, and to as much Purpose urge it against every Part of Christianity.

---

* *Matth.* xii. 41.   † *Answ. to Repr.*, p. 36.

Thus it may serve to prove that it would be better never to have had the Scriptures; for if any Texts of Scripture shall rise in Judgment and condemn those who disbelieved them, or disregarded their Doctrine, then it may be said, much happier are the Heathens, who have nothing of this to fear from any Scriptures, but are left to their own *Consciences and the righteous Judgment of God.*

Again; As this Argument proves even the Scriptures to be an Unhappiness, so will it prove every Advantage in human Life to be a Misery.

For it is certain that the *Examples* of religious Men, the good *Advice* of our *Friends*, and the virtuous *Commands* of our *Parents* and *Governors*, will, if neglected, *affect* our Condition; and though, like the spiritual *Corrections* of the Church, they may not be felt here, yet hereafter they will rise in Judgment and condemn us. May I not here say with your Lordship, *if the Case be thus;* if other People's *Wisdom, Virtue, Advice* or *Commands*, can affect our *State* in the next World, then more happy are those who never saw a *good* or *wise* Man in their Lives, and who have nothing to fear from the *Advice* or *Commands* of any, but *are left to their own Consciences and the righteous Judgment of God.*

So that you cannot condemn the *Dean's* Doctrine as *horrible*, without condemning it as an *horrible* thing, that the Men of *Nineveh* should rise in Judgment and condemn the impenitent *Jews;* or an *horrible* thing that the *Light* of the *Gospel*, the *Blessings* of Christianity, and the *Advantages* of Education, should have *any Effect* in the next World upon those, who despised them in this World.

Of the Authority of the Church, as it relates to Excommunication.

IN order to vindicate this Doctrine thoroughly, and shew upon what bottom it is founded, I shall, as briefly as I can, state the *Nature* and *Intent* of spiritual Punishments, and shew what Effects they have upon Offenders in the other World; from whence, I persuade myself, it will farther appear, that such Effects do no more exclude Persons from the righteous Judgment of God, than the Heathens are excluded from his righteous Judgment.

Now that corrupt Members may be cut off from Christian

Communion, till by their Amendment they recommend themselves to a Re-admission, is plain from Scripture. This is even granted by your Lordship, that *Christians may set a Mark upon Notorious Offenders, even by refusing to them the peculiar Tokens and Marks of Christian Communion, as well as by avoiding their Company and Conversation.** But then your Lordship makes no more of it, *than a Right which all Christians have to avoid an open, wilful, and scandalous Sinner;*† so that *this Excommunication, considered as a Church Act*, is only the same Power in a Body or Society, of avoiding Persons they abhor; which is the common Privilege of every single Person, whether in or out of the Church, to shun those he dislikes.

And all the Excommunication you allow, is this, that as private Persons have a Right to shun and avoid those they dislike, so the Church may exclude such Members as are disapproved of; and that this judging, or excommunicating, is a Right equally invested in all Christians, and entirely without any Effect upon the Person excommunicated, so as to make his Condition either better or worse before God.

I shall therefore, my Lord, beg leave to shew that the Power of Excommunication, is a *Judicial Power*, which belongs to particular Persons, which they have a Right to exercise from the Authority of Christ; and that Persons so excommunicated, are not to be looked upon as Persons who are only to be abhorred and avoided by Christians, as any Man may avoid those he dislikes, but as Persons who are to be avoided by Christians, because they lie under the *Sentence* of God, and are by his *Authority* turned out of his Kingdom.

That Excommunication is a Power which belongs only to particular Persons, will appear from the Nature of the Thing itself, as it is an Exclusion of Persons from the Christian Worship: for as only particular Men can *officiate* in the Christian Worship, and admit People into Communion; so only those Persons can refuse the Sacrament, and exclude Offenders from Communion. Nothing can be more plain, than that those who can alone administer the Sacrament, can alone exclude Men from it.

All Persons are admitted conditionally into the Christian Covenant, and have only a Title to the Benefits of it, or the ordinary Means of Grace, as they perform the Conditions of their Admission; and those same Persons who have alone the Authority to admit them into the Church upon those Conditions, have alone the Authority to exclude them for Non-performance.

---

* Page 39. † Page 43.

And their Act of Exclusion is *as effectual* towards the taking from them all the Privileges of Christians, and as truly makes them *Aliens* from the Kingdom of God, as their Act of Admission at first entitled them to all the Benefits of Church-Communion. For as they have as much Authority to exclude some, as they have to admit others into the Church, the Authority being the same in both Cases, it must be in both Cases *equally* effectual.

If your Lordship will say that all People, are equally qualified to admit Persons into the Church, that, *Go ye, and baptize all Nations*, conferred the same Powers on all Christians; then indeed it must be granted that Excommunication, or Exclusion from the Church, is a Right equally invested in all Christians. But as sure as Christ gave peculiar Powers to his Apostles, as sure as they left particular Men to succeed them in their Powers, so sure is it that only such Successors can either admit or exclude Persons from Christian Communion.

Secondly; That Excommunication belongs to particular Persons, will appear from the Institution of it in Scripture.

If thy Brother shall trespass against thee, go and tell him his Fault between thee and him alone. But if he will not hear thee, then take with thee one or two more. And if he shall neglect to hear them, tell it unto the Church; but if he neglect to hear the Church, let him be unto thee as an Heathen Man, and a Publican. Verily I say unto you, whatsoever ye shall bind on Earth, shall be bound in Heaven; and whatsoever ye shall loose on Earth, shall be loosed in Heaven.*

Here, my Lord, is as plain an Institution of *Excommunication*, as can well be conceived; and he who can doubt of it, may doubt whether Baptism be instituted in Scripture.

First, We may observe that here is an Authority given to the Church over the Offender, and that *such* an Authority, as neither belonged to private Men, either separate or united together; for the Offender here had first been admonished, by a single Person, then by *one or two more*, *i.e.*, an indefinite Number, but still here is nothing granted but Admonition; but as soon as he is brought before the Church, there an Authority appears, and the Offender is to feel its Sentence, *let him be unto thee as an Heathen.*

Secondly; That this Authority did not belong to the Church, considered *only* as a greater Number of Christians, but as it signified particular Persons who had this Authority from Christ, for the Edification of his Church.

---

* *Matth.* xviii. 15.

For Christ expressly declares in the following Verse, that *where two or three are met together in his Name, there is He in the midst of them.*

Here is the Description of that Church before whom the Offender was to be brought, and whose Authority Christ promises to support; it is *two or three met together in his Name.*

Now the Church had not this Authority over the Offender, considered as a *Number, i.e.,* as two or three; for we see that the Offender had been already before *such* a Church; he had been before *two or three;* and after Neglect of them, he was brought before another *two or three,* met together *in Christ's Name.* Which is a plain Proof that the Offender was not censured by the Church, as it signifies a Number of Christians, but as it implies particular Persons acting in the *Name* of Christ, and with *his Authority.*

Thirdly; We may observe that the Authority here granted to the Church is a *Judicial Authority*, such an Authority as *affects* and *alters* the *Condition* of the Person excommunicated, implied in these Words, *Let him be unto thee as an Heathen;* that is, as the Bishop of *Oxford* observes, *in the most natural and common Sense of the Words, they should look upon him no longer as a Member of the Church, but place him amongst Infidels;** and again, *as reduced into the State of Heathens.*†

Now unless it can be said, that a Person who is turned out of the Kingdom of God, and reduced into the State of Heathens, is in the same Condition which he was, when he was in the Church, and had a Right to all the Benefits of Communion; unless we can say that a Person thus rejected from the Means of Grace, by the *Commission* of Christ, is in the same Condition with him, who is continued in the Church by the *same Commission* of Christ; it must be allowed that here is a *Judicial* Power granted to the Church, and such as affects the Condition of the Offender in the Sight of God.

Fourthly; It is to be observed, that this Authority of the Church is made *Judicial* by the express Promise of God to ratify and confirm it. For after it is said, *let him be unto thee as an Heathen,* it is declared, that *whatsoever they should* thus *bind on Earth, should be bound in Heaven.*

From all this, it plainly appears, that Excommunication is as truly a Divine *Positive Punishment*, as Baptism is a Divine *Positive Blessing;* and that the one as certainly *excludes* us from the Kingdom of God, as the other *admits* us into it. For since

---

* *Chur. Gov.*, p. 351. † *Ibid.*, p. 356.

here is as plainly Christ's *express Authority* to take from some Men the ordinary Means of Grace, and exclude them from the common Benefits of Christianity, as there is his Authority *to go and baptize all Nations;* I desire to know, why one is not as truly a Divine *Positive Institution* as the other? Is not Christ's Authority as effectual and significant in excluding, as in admitting Persons into his Kingdom? Is not that same Power as able to take away the Privileges of Church-Membership, as it was at first to grant them?

If therefore there be any Blessing or Happiness in our being admitted into the Church; there must be as much Misery and Punishment in our *Exclusion* from it. For as it implies the Loss of all those Privileges and Favours we were made Partakers of by our Admission into the Church; so we must needs be punished in the same degree that we were happy.

If therefore *Baptism,* a Divine *Positive Institution* to admit us into the Privileges of Christianity, makes any Alteration in our Condition, as to the Favour of God, *i.e.,* if we are brought any nearer to God by Baptism, than we were before; then it plainly follows, *Excommunication,* a Divine *Positive Institution,* which deprives us of all these Privileges of Christianity, and, as the Bishop of *Oxford* expresses it, *reduces* Offenders *into the State of Heathens,* must needs affect our Condition with regard to the Favour of God.

For if there be anything in Baptism which is just Matter of Joy, there is something equally Terrible in Excommunication; which, when rightly executed, as effectually makes us Aliens from the Promises of God, as Baptism, when rightly administered, makes us Children of God, and Heirs of eternal Life. So that he who can ridicule and expose the *Terrors* and *Effects of* Excommunication, is acting just as Christian a part, as he who derides and despises the Benefits and Advantages of *Baptism.*

Seeing therefore the Church hath as express an Authority to turn some Men out of the Church, as it hath to admit others into it, it is as false an Account of *Excommunication,* to make it only that *common Right* which every Man has, to avoid those he dislikes; as if it should be said, that *Admission* into the Church by Baptism, implies no more, than that *common Right* which every Man has to do good Offices for those he likes. Now, my Lord, is Baptism to be administered, because Persons may do good Offices for one another? Is there a Power in the Church to increase its Members, by admitting others into Communion, for this reason, because People have a common Right to choose their Company? If not, my Lord, how comes the Exclusion of Members to be nothing but a *common Right* of avoiding those we dislike? Are not Persons excluded from all the Benefits of their Admission? So that if there was any Authority required for the Admission of Persons into the Church, if this Authority was only from God, it is certain that an Exclusion from these Church-Privileges, cannot be executed but by the same Authority, which first granted them. For no Person can be deprived of any Privileges, but by that Power which at first granted them.

When therefore your Lordship recurs to the *common Right* of Persons to avoid, if they can, those they dislike, in order to state the Nature of Excommunication; it is just as much to the Purpose, as if I should get a *Chemist* to examine the natural Qualities of Water, in order to state the true Efficacy of *Baptism*: for Men no more act by any Powers of their own when they exclude Offenders, than they baptize others into Communion by their own Authority, or than Water unites them to Christ by its natural Qualities.

Yet your Lordship sets forth the Nature of Excommunication, and the Right the Church has to it, only from that *common Right, which all Christians have of avoiding if they can those they dislike.* Thus you say, the Church may excommunicate, because *every Person has a Right to judge, nay he cannot help judging of the Behaviour of Men;** that *every Man will judge him to be a Murderer, who takes away his Neighbour's Life unjustly.*

This comes up as truly to the Nature of Excommunication, and is as just an Account of it, as if anyone should set forth the Authority of a British *Judge*, and show the Extent of his *Judicial* Power, by saying, he indeed may judge and condemn a *Murderer*, for this is the Right of every Person to judge, *and no one can help judging and condemning a Murderer.* It is as consistent with Sense, thus to set out the Power of the Judge, as it is with Reason and Scripture, to compare Excommunication to that private Power of *Judging* and *Thinking* which everyone enjoys.

For, my Lord, can it be supposed that when our Saviour tells them, that they should reject such a Person out of the Church, and look upon him as an Heathen, and that he would bind, *i.e.*, confirm their Sentence; can it be supposed, that he only meant they might *think* and *judge* a wicked Person to be a wicked Person, only in such a manner as every Man cannot help Thinking and Judging? If our blessed Lord only here intended this, what occasion was there for his Promise to ratify their Judgment? What need is there of an Assurance, that they shall privately judge, what they cannot help privately judging? Or

---

* Page 39.

indeed to what Purpose is any Promise at all made here, if nothing is to be effected? If this Sentence be only a private, unauthorised Declaration, like the Opinion or Judgment of private Men, what Room can there be for this Ratification of our Saviour? If no Effects are intended in the *Judgment* of the Church, what can be the meaning of this Promise? Or rather, since our Saviour has here instituted the Authority, and promised to ratify the Exercise of it, how dares any Christian to compare it to a private personal Power of Judging, or declare that it is without any Effect upon the Condition of Christians? For, my Lord, either something is here promised to the Sentence of the Church, or there is not; if there is something promised, then the Sentence of the Church is no more like the personal Sentence of private Men, than the Power of a Judge is like the Power of a private Man; if you will say there is nothing here promised in these Words, *whatsoever ye shall bind on Earth, shall be bound in Heaven, &c.*, then you must say that there is nothing at all meant in them; for it is impossible to shew that they can have any other Meaning, than that of a Promise; so that if no Promise is made, they are certainly so many dead Letters.

Again; That this is a *Judicial* Power, is also evident from the Case of the incestuous *Corinthian*. St. *Paul* says, *What have I to do, to judge them also which are without?* Now the Apostle could not have put this Question, if by Judging here had been meant no Authority, but a private Power of judging and thinking a Sinner to be a Sinner. For a Man can no more help judging a Murderer to be a Murderer, which is without the Church, than if he were within the Church. And it is as proper for us to judge and think aright of those who are out of the Church, as of those who are within it. So that St. *Paul* could not mean, What have I to do to think a *Murderer* to be a *Murderer* which is without the Church, it being every Man's Duty to think as truly of all Things and Persons as he can? Seeing therefore he plainly intimates that he had a Power of Judging in the Church, which did not belong to him out of the Church, it follows that this Power was *Judicial* and *Authoritative;* for a private Power of Judging and Thinking, belongs to every Man with regard to every Thing.

We shall more easily understand what is meant by the *Effects* of spiritual Punishments, if we consider them under this Division.

First, Such as are the primary and intended Effects; secondly, Such as are only the *accidental* Effects of them.

Now as to the primary and intended Effects of spiritual Punishments, they are these.

First, To preserve the Honour of God and his Church, that ill Members being cut off, it might be *presented a glorious Church, not having Spot or Wrinkle, or any such thing; but that it might be Holy, and without Blemish.**

Secondly, To reform Offenders, and reclaim them from their Vices; it is a Discipline given to the Church for the Edification, and not the Destruction of its Members. Thus St. *Paul* says, the incestuous *Corinthian* was to be *delivered over to Satan, for the Destruction of the Flesh, that his Spirit might be saved in the Day of the Lord.*†

Thirdly, To preserve the rest of the Church from the ill Influence of their Example, and that by such Punishments exercised upon others, they might fear, and learn from thence not to offend.

These are the intended Effects of the Punishments which the Church inflicts, to preserve it a Holy Society, and save the Souls of its Members.

God Almighty has instituted several Means for the Advancement of Virtue, and the Salvation of Mankind; and amongst others, he has set up this Authority of the Church to promote the same Ends. It is his *human, ordinary* Means for the Preservation of his Church; and therefore as it cannot operate infallibly, or affect People with a Divine Certainty, it is only conditional, and is to prevail towards the Salvation of Mankind, as far as human and conditional Means can prevail.

And indeed, it is an Institution which has a very natural Tendency to produce the Effects designed by it. For, considering Christianity as a Covenant with God, wherein our Title to Happiness depends upon our Use of the ordinary instituted Means of Grace, nothing can more naturally induce us to live worthy of such Means, than this Authority in the Church to withdraw them upon our Abuse, and expel us from the Terms of the Covenant. Men would not dare to transgress, when they saw they could neither break the Laws, nor corrupt the Faith of Christianity, without being turned out of the Church, by such a Power as Christ hath set up for that Purpose, and with his Promise to make good its Decrees. They must be very obstinate Sinners, who could be content to lie under a Sentence, which as effectually takes from them all Pretension to Christian Happiness, as their Baptism entitled them to those Pretensions at first.

The chief Reason why Sinners are generally so little affected with the Horror of their Condition, is because they look upon

---

* *Ephes.* iv. 25. † 1 *Cor.* v. 5.

their Punishment at the future Judgment, as a great Distance off; and since they are within the Church, and enjoy the ordinary Means of Grace, they think they can repent in time. But now Christ, by instituting this Church Authority, has suited his Discipline to the Weakness and Frailty of our Nature; and they who are only to be affected with Things present, have a present Judgment to fear; which, though it is only the Judgment of Men, yet is the Judgment of such Men as are commissioned to pronounce it in Christ's Name, and with his Promise to ratify and confirm it. So that they have as much reason to look upon themselves as effectually cast out by God in that Sentence, as they were received into Covenant with God by Baptism; for there is the same Divine Authority to support them both.

As to those other *Effects* of spiritual Punishments in the other World, they are not the intended, but *accidental* Effects of such Punishments, which are brought upon Offenders by their own wicked Behaviour under them.

Thus the Salvation of Mankind is the primary *intended Effect* of Christianity; yet it may have such Effect upon some Men by their own Impiety in it, as to make it better for them if they had never heard of the Name of Christ. For Christianity may become so much a Punishment to some Persons in the other World, that their Condition may be less tolerable than that of *Sodom* and *Gomorrah*. But then this is not the intended Effect of Christianity, but an accidental Effect which such Persons bring upon themselves; who by their own ill Conduct turn a Mercy into a Judgment, and make that which was intended to save them, the accidental Cause of their greater Ruin.

Thus it is with spiritual Punishments; they are the merciful Corrections of God intended to prevent our future Misery, but if disregarded, will certainly increase it. This will easily explain what is meant by the *Effects* of spiritual Punishments in the other World, or how *they are suspended till the Offender comes thither*. It is not the direct intended Effect of Church Punishments to increase the Misery of Sinners, or damn them in the other World; no more than it is the direct intended Effect of Christianity to increase People's Damnation: But as Christianity, if abused, will be the accidental Cause of their greater Damnation who so abuse it; so the Censures of the Church, when despised, will have this accidental Effect, as to increase the Punishment of those who so despised them. This is the Nature of those Effects, which spiritual Punishments will have upon the Impenitent in another World.

As for Instance, a Person who is turned out of the Church, may all this while be lusty and strong, and flourish in all the

Advantages of this Life; but when he comes into the other World, he may then find that the spiritual Punishment was a sore Evil, that it is ratified by Christ, has increased his Guilt, and will be Matter of Punishment hereafter.

He will then find that the Censure of the Church has increased his Guilt in these Respects.

First, As it was a *Judicial Sentence* pronounced by Christ's Authority, and therefore not to be despised or neglected without great Impiety; so that let the Sinner have been what he will before, when he continues in his Sins in Contempt of *this Tribunal* set up in Christ's Name, his Guilt is thereby exceedingly increased.

Secondly, As it is the *most powerful Means*, and the very utmost which God can do to reclaim, or even terrify Sinners from their Impiety, as it is the most awakening Call to Repentance, an Institution only less terrible than the last Judgment; those who are not affected with it, must be rendered more odious in the Sight of God, and made ripe for a severer Punishment.

These, my Lord, are the Effects of spiritual Punishments in the other World; it is thus that they alter the Condition of Offenders in the Sight of God in regard to his Favour. They are certainly under greater Displeasure, after they have despised the Censures of Church Authority, and have resisted an *Institution*, which is the last possible Means to recover them.

In former Times, God has been pleased to send his *Prophets* to forewarn Sinners of their Destruction, as *Jonah* to the Men of *Nineveh*: But in the Christian Dispensation, he governs us by his ordinary Providence; and though he does not send express Messengers to recall Sinners, yet he has instituted a *standing Authority* in his Church, to censure Offenders, and give them up to Destruction in his Name, unless they immediately repent. And what can we think more dreadful than a *Sentence* thus pronounced against us by God's Authority, and with his Promise to confirm it?

Was there anything more awakening or more dreadful in the Preaching of *Jonah*, than in this Declaration? *Jonah* could only preach and declare, he could execute nothing himself; it was his being sent in *God's Name*, which created all the Terror, and was the Motive to Repentance. Now though the Church can *only* censure and declare, yet since it is as truly commissioned to censure in *God's Name*, as *Jonah* was sent in *God's Name*, there is as much reason to dread the Consequences of neglecting the Church, as of not repenting at the Message or Preaching of any Prophet from God.

I must now beg leave here, my Lord, *to lament an Assertion from the Hands of a Christian and Protestant Bishop;* where you declare, that the *Excommunication of the incestuous* Corinthian, *neither added to God's Displeasure, nor would the want of it have at all diminished it. Neither if he had died in an impenitent Condition, would that Sentence have had any Effect in the other World.**

This, my Lord, plainly supposes that there is neither *Authority* nor *Advantage* in Excommunication; for if there were, it is certain that our *Abuse* of it as an *Advantage*, and our Contempt of it as an *Authority*, must needs increase our Guilt, and consequently God's Displeasure. Yet your Lordship here teaches the World, that if the incestuous *Corinthian, though justly censured,* and that by an Apostle directing, and the whole Congregation joining, had died impenitent, *that Sentence would have had no Effect in the other World.*

Let us therefore suppose that some great Patron of Christian Liberty had gone to the disconsolate *Corinthian,* sorrowing under the Sentence of the Church, and endeavoured to quiet him after this manner.

'Why do you disquiet yourself with vain Fears about the
' Censure of the Church, which neither hath nor can have an
' Effect upon your Condition as to the Favour of God. Let the
' Apostle and Church be as solemn as they please in the
' Denunciation; let them in the Name of Christ deliver you over
' to *Satan;* yet take Courage, and fear nothing from all this;
' for you may depend upon it, that, after all, you are but just
' where you were, before this Sentence were passed. And if you
' die impenitent, you have no Effects of this Censure to fear in
' the other World.'

Now this is the Doctrine your Lordship has taught for the Consolation of those who are, or are likely to be under the Sentence of the Church; which if it be now found Doctrine, it was as proper to be told the *Corinthian* then, as it is for your Lordship to teach it now. And if your Lordship had lived then, it would have been as proper to have told the *Corinthian*, as to tell us now; and you must have lain under the same Christian Necessity of delivering him from vain Fears, which now constrains you to set all at liberty from the like Apprehensions.

St. *Paul,* speaking of the Sentence passed upon the *Corinthian,* says, *Sufficient to such a Man was this Punishment.*† Now, my Lord, if it have nothing of the Nature of a Punishment, if it has no Effect where it is inflicted, if the Person said to be punished can feel no Effect from it, what strange Language is this? Can

---

* *Answ. to Repr.*, p. 38.   † 2 *Cor.* ii. 6.

that be called a Punishment, or a sufficient Punishment, which can in no degree be felt, which produces no Effects, or makes no Alteration in the Person where it falls?

Again St. *Paul* tells us, that he had amongst others which had corrupted the Faith, *delivered Hymeneus and Alexander to Satan, that they might learn not to blaspheme.**

Now if this Sentence can have no Effect, if it cannot signify anything to them, if they are just in the same Condition after it, which they were before, why should it teach them not to blaspheme? Why should a Sentence which they had nothing to fear from, make them any longer afraid to continue in their Errors? Here was therefore either a pious Fraud made use of by the Apostle, to fright Men from their Heresies by something which was in itself vain and insignificant, or else your Lordship has mightily mistaken the Matter, in declaring that it is vain and insignificant. The Apostle plainly inflicts these Censures, as a Terror to Offenders, and to frighten them from continuing in their evil Courses; but if, as you say, Persons be just in the same Condition after this Sentence, in which they were before, if it has no Effect upon them, though they are rightly censured, and yet die impenitent, which is what you expressly say of this *Corinthian*, then it is plain they are only pretended Terrors, and that when the Apostles use them as such, they must be charged with using them as a pious Fraud. And it must be owned that your Lordship has very frankly made the Discovery.

But whoever has Piety enough to believe those First Ambassadors of Christ, will clear them from such a Charge, and rather think it possible that you may mistake in your Plilosophy, than they in their Divinity.

To proceed; You declare that though the *incestuous* Corinthian *had died in an impenitent Condition, the Sentence of the Church would have had no Effect in the other World:* By which you must mean, that it could not affect his Condition there, so as to increase his Punishment, and that because the *Sentence did not add to God's Displeasure, which he incurs solely upon account of his own Behaviour, and not the Sentence of Men.*† As thus, I suppose, your Lordship means, that if an Adulterer is censured by the Church, he is under God's Displeasure solely on account of his Adultery, and not more so, on account of the Sentence of the Church; which cannot make him more an Adulterer, or more guilty in the Sight of God. It is for this reason that Church Censures are so insignificant, so void of all Effect in the

---

* 1 *Tim.* i. 19.   † Page 37.

other World; because it is our Sins alone, and not the Sentence of Men, which loses us the Favour of God.

Let us therefore, my Lord, suppose that God himself had delivered *this Sentence* against the *Corinthian* which the Church did, your Lordship's Doctrine would have procured him the same Ease and Quiet, and taught him to be no more concerned about it, than if it had been a *mere Church Censure*. For it is as true in your Lordship's Sense, that the *Sentence* of God did not add to his Displeasure against him, that he was not angry at him because of his *Sentence*, but upon account of the Offender's *Behaviour*. But, my Lord, will it therefore follow, that there is nothing to be dreaded in such a Sentence? Will it follow, that if the Person dies impenitent under it, that it would have no Effect in the other World? Would your Lordship go about, and preach Liberty to Persons under such a Sentence, and assure them that the Sentence itself could have no Effect, that they were but just where they were before it was pronounced? Would you think it proper to deliver Men from such Apprehensions, and persuade them that they are in no Danger from the Sentence of God? And that because it is not his own Sentence, but their Behaviour which increases his Displeasure.

This may perhaps appear a little too shocking, to set up for an *Advocate* for the *Laity* against the *Sentence* of God; but, my Lord, if you were to do so, you would have the same Argument to defend yourself against any Effect in the *Divine Sentence*, which you now have against any Effect in the Sentence of the Church. It would be then as much to the Purpose to say, that God is not displeased with them, on the account of his *own Sentence*, but purely for their own *Behaviour;* as it is to tell Offenders, that it is not the *Sentence* of the Church, but their *Behaviour* which brings them under the Divine Displeasure.

I must here therefore, my Lord, beg leave to call this a *strict Demonstration*, that if the Sentence of the Church is not to be feared; if it hath no Effect, because it is not the *Sentence*, but our own *Behaviour* which alone procures us the Divine Displeasure; if this be true, it is *Demonstration*, that if God himself was to pronounce this Church Sentence, and turn Offenders out of Communion, that there would be *nothing to be feared from it*, that it could have *no Effect* in the other World; for God's Displeasure against them, would not be occasioned by his own *Sentence*, but by their *Behaviour*. So that were the Discipline of the Church in God's own Hands, and were he with his own Voice to threaten Sinners, as the Church now doth, your Lordship would be as much obliged to comfort the *Laity* against any

Apprehension of any Effect from the *Sentence* itself, as you are now to deliver them from the *Fear of Man's Judgment.*

Again ; If the *Sentence* of the Church is not to be dreaded, if, it can have *no Effect* in the other World, because we incur the Divine Displeasure solely on account of our own Behaviour ; then it is certain, that the Sentence of Christ himself at the last Day can have no Effect in the other World.

If therefore any unwary Divine, should endeavour to alarm his Congregation with the *Effects* of Christ's Sentence at the last Day, your Lordship has taught anyone to reject the *Doctrine*, as *greatly injurious to the Honour of God ;* and that such *Doctrine was also impossible in itself to be conceived*, he might presume strictly to demonstrate.*

A *Sentence which makes not a Tittle of Alteration in the Condition of a Man, in the Eyes of God, with regard to his Favour or Displeasure, cannot be said to have any Effect in the other World.*†
But *the Sentence of Christ at the last Day is of this sort.*

Therefore the Sentence of Christ makes not a Tittle of Alteration in the Condition of a Man, in the Eyes of God, with regard to his Favour or Displeasure.

That the Sentence of Christ makes no Alteration in the Condition of a Man with regard to the Favour or Displeasure of God, is plain from hence ; that Men incur the Divine Displeasure solely on account of their own Behaviour.

Thus, my Lord, it is demonstratively certain, that as you have argued against the Effects of the Church's *Sentence* in the other World, you have taught anyone to argue against any Effect in the Sentence of Christ in the next World ; and consequently it must be as *unwary* Doctrine, to frighten People with the Effects of Christ's Sentence, as to terrify them with the Effects of the Sentence of the Church. And you have offered such an Argument for the utter Insignificancy of this Sentence, as would make it equally insignificant, and void of all Effect, though it was pronounced by God himself. So that as much as you often seem to expose it as the *Sentence* of *weak* and *fallible* Men, yet your Argument does not reject it as a *fallible* Sentence, but as it is a *Sentence* far from having any Effect. So that if it was pronounced by God himself, it must be as much without *Effect*, and every Sentence which ever can be pronounced by God, must be without any Effect as to his Favour or Displeasure, because that is solely occasioned by our own Behaviour. Therefore an *infallible* Sentence can no more have any Effect, than a *fallible* one, because it is our *Behaviour* alone which can affect us.

---

* Page 36. † Page 36.

This, my Lord, will be of great use to some People, who will be glad to find that they have no more Effects to fear from God's Sentence, either in this World or the next, than your Lordship has from the Church.

Again; if there be *no Effect* in the Sentence of the Church in the other World, because our *Behaviour* alone incurs the Divine Displeasure, then *nothing* which God inflicts upon us here, can have *any Effect* in the other World.

If therefore God's *Judgments* were visibly fallen upon some *Town* or *Country*, and an *unwary* Preacher should take occasion to excite them to a speedy Repentance, from the sad *Effects* such *Judgments* would have in the other World, if they had not their designed Effects in this, and declare that if they died impenitent under them in this World, they would feel *worse Effects* of them in the other World: A Disciple of your Lordship's might thus reprove the Falseness and Cruelty of such Doctrine. ' How can you terrify People with such vain Fears about God's ' Judgments? Is he provoked against us by his own *Thunder* ' and *Lightning?* Do his own *Judgments* add anything to his ' Displeasure against us? Can anything but our own Sins and ' Behaviour create his Displeasure? Therefore we are certainly ' in the same Condition, as to that, which we were in before his ' *Judgments* fell upon us; and if we die impenitent under them, ' they can have *no Effect* in the other World. False then and ' greatly dishonourable to God is your Doctrine, which supposes ' anything can have any Effect of that kind, but our own ' Behaviour. To alarm us therefore with the *Effects* of such ' *Judgments*, is to put false Fears into our Minds, and teach us ' to dread things which are *impossible;* for it is impossible that ' anything but our *own Behaviour* should increase our Punish-' ment.'

Now, my Lord, is it cruel and unwary Doctrine to awaken Sinners under God's *Judgments* to Repentance, from a Sense of the *worse Effects* of those Judgments in the other World, if they do not bring them to Repentance in this? If it is not, I desire to know, why it is not as Reasonable to alarm People with the *Effects* of *spiritual Punishments*, if disregarded, as with the Effects of God's Judgments, if they are neglected? What is there in the Nature of the Thing, why one Punishment may have Effect in the other World, and not the other? They are both *equally* God's *Punishments*, intended for the *same* Ends.

When Persons are rightly turned out of the Church, and denied the Ordinary Means of Grace, they are as truly under God's *special Judgment*, as a *Country* which is oppressed with

Famine or *Pestilence;* the one is his *instituted, ordinary Judgment,* to terrify Men from Iniquity; the other is his *extraordinary Judgment,* his miraculous Call to Repentance. It is therefore as sound a Christian Doctrine, to say, that if Persons die impenitent under God's extraordinary Judgment, that such Judgment will have no Effect in the other World ; as to say, that if the incestuous *Corinthian* had died impenitent under the just Sentence of the Church, *i.e.,* God's *ordinary* Judgment, that such *Sentence* or *Judgment* would have had no Effect in the other World. And consequently, to endeavour to terrify Sinners with the Effects of God's *Judgments* in the other World, if they disregard them here, is as much condemned by your Lordship, as the Dean of *Chichester's* Doctrine concerning the *Effects* of spiritual Punishments in the next World.

Lastly ; Our blessed Saviour *told* the *Jews* that if *he had not come, they had not had Sin ; but now they have no Cloak for their Sin :* Which plainly implies, that his *coming* into the World altered their *Condition* as to the *Favour* of God, because it made them more guilty in his Sight than they were before he came. Yet your Lordship's Argument against the *Effects* of Church Punishments, directly denies this Doctrine. For your Objection against any *Effects* in Church *Punishments,* is full as strong against any *Effects* in Christ's *coming* into the World. And if People may be more guilty in the Sight of God, after Christ is *come,* they may be more guilty after they have been *censured* by the Church, for the Reason is the same in both Cases. For there can be no Reason given, why Christ's coming should affect their Condition with regard to the Favour of God, but that he had a *Divine Mission,* and was an *Authoritative Call* to Repentance ; but this is equally true of *Excommunication,* that it is a *Divine Institution,* an *Authoritative Call* to Repentance ; therefore they must either both be allowed to *affect* People's *Condition* with regard to the *Favour* of God, or neither ; for the Reason is *exactly* the same in both Cases.

If therefore a learned *Pharisee,* seeing a relenting *Publican* touched with this Declaration of our Saviour's, should have reproved him after this manner :

'You need not be concerned at this Person's *coming* into the 'World, for his *coming* does not increase God's Displeasure 'against you, which can only be raised by your own *Behaviour;* 'it is solely on account of that, that you can be out of God's '*Favour.* Sinners are out of God's Favour, if this Person had 'never *come,* and his coming does not add to God's Displeasure 'against them ; neither if they die in an impenitent Condition 'after he is come, will his *coming* have any Effect in the other

'World, where their Condition will not be determined by his
'*coming*, but by their own *Behaviour*.'

I should be glad, my Lord, to know what you could have said against such a Declaration, or how a Person who would have told the *incestuous Corinthian*, that if he died impenitent under the *Censure* of the Church, that it would have no Effect in the other World, could have anything to object to the *Pharisee*, who tells the *Publican*, if he died impenitent after Christ's *coming*, that his *coming* will have *no Effect* in the other World.

The *Pharisee* has *exactly* the same Reason, to tell the *Publican*, that he was neither the more, nor the less, out of God's Favour for Christ's *coming*, that you have to tell the *Corinthian*, *that he was neither the more, nor the less, out of God's Favour for what was done by the Church*. For the Censure here was right and infallible, and passed in the Name and by the Authority of Christ; it was passed by an *Apostle*, and you affirm that *Christ was in all that the Apostles did;* therefore it may be truly said, that Christ himself *came* to the *Corinthian* in this Sentence, it was his *Authority* and *Infallibility* which censured him; and yet you say that if he had died impenitent under *this Censure*, he had been just where he was before, and it would have had *no Effect* in the other World.

Pray therefore, my Lord, let us know how anyone can be more guilty for Christ's *coming*, or why it shall have any Effect in the other World upon those who die impenitent? A few Reasons against this *Pharisee*, would be so many Reasons against your Lordship's Doctrine. For Christ as truly *comes* to Christians in his *Institutions*, as he *came* to the *Jews* in *Person;* and it is as dangerous to disregard him in the one Appearance, as in the other.

This Account of Excommunication will, I hope, be thought a sufficient Answer to your Lordship's strict Demonstration, that *it has no Effects in the other World, nor adds anything to God's Displeasure*. For from this it appears, that when you say, that *supposing no such Punishment inflicted upon a wicked Christian, he is under the Displeasure of Almighty God to an* equal Degree, *as he would be if it were inflicted:** It is as false as to say, that a *wicked Jew* was under the same Displeasure of God before Christ came, as he was afterwards; or that a Person impenitent under an *extraordinary Judgment*, is no more out of God's Favour afterwards, than he was before, or if God had never visited him. It is as false as to say, that if God himself was to pronounce the *Sentence* of the Church, that Persons under it

---

* Page 37.

would be just in the same Degree of Favour they were before, or that the Sentence of Christ at the last Day will have no Effect.

The other Part of your Demonstration proceeds thus; Excommunication has no Effect, because *supposing it wrongfully inflicted upon a Christian, he is still equally in the Favour of God.**

The whole of this Argument amounts to this, that a *right* Censure of the Church hath no Effect, because a *wrong* one hath not. I should think anyone in a mighty want of Proof, who should say that the Excommunication of the *incestuous Corinthian* could have no Effect, because the Excommunication of some virtuous Person will not have any Effect; yet this is your Lordship's Demonstration, that it can signify nothing when it is *right, because* it signifies nothing when it is *wrong*.

Is it an Argument, my Lord, that when a *Bullet* flies through a Man's Head it has *no Effect* upon him, because it will have no Effect if it *miss* him? Is it a Proof that *Motion* cannot produce *Heat*, because *Rest* cannot produce *Heat?*

If not, how comes it to be an Argument that a *right* Sentence hath no Effect, because a *wrong* one hath not the *same* Effect?

A *right* Sentence is as opposite to a *wrong* one, as *Motion* is to *Rest;* and it is as good Sense to say *Motion* has no such Effect, because *Rest* has no such Effect; as to say a *right* Sentence has no Effect, because a *wrong* one has not the same.

A *right* Sentence, is the *only* Excommunication which Christ hath instituted, and to which alone this Effect belongs; but it is strange *Logic* to infer, that this *Institution* cannot have *such* an Effect, *because* something which Christ hath *not* instituted, hath not the same Effect.

A *wrong* Sentence is as truly a *Breach* and *Transgression* of that *Excommunication* which Christ hath instituted, as Adultery is a *Breach* of the seventh Commandment; it is therefore as absurd to say, that *Chastity* hath not *such an* Effect, because *Adultery* hath not the *same* Effect, as to affirm that a *right* Sentence hath not such an Effect, because a *Violation* of that right Sentence hath not the same Effect. Your Lordship's Argument is this, that the *Sentence* hath not *such* an Effect in *some* Circumstances, because it hath not the *same* Effect in *all* Circumstances: Which resolves itself into this Proposition, *That nothing can produce any particular Effect, unless it produce the same Effect in all Circumstances.*

Your Lordship might as well have called it a *Demonstration*

---

* Page 37.

against *all Effects* in the World, as against the *Effects* of spiritual Censures: For there is nothing in the World, no Powers either *Natural, Moral,* or *Political,* which produce their Effects but in some *supposed right* Circumstances; yet this Ecclesiastical Power is *demonstrated* away by your Lordship, because it does not produce the same Effect in *all* Circumstances.

Farther; If there is no Effect in a *right Sentence* of the Church, because there is no Effect in a *wrong* one; then it will follow, that there is no Effect in either of the Sacraments when *rightly* received, because they want such Effect in Persons who do not rightly receive them. It may as often happen that the Sacraments are administered in *wrong* Circumstances, and as void of that Effect for which they were intended, as any *wrong* Sentence of the Church be pronounced; but does it therefore follow, that there is *no Effect* in the Sacraments, that they are empty and useless to those who receive them rightly, because they are so to those who receive them otherwise? Your Lordship must either affirm that the Sacraments have no Effect, or that the *Opus operatum* is always effectual; for if you say they have Effect, though not always, then it is certain that the *Sentence* of the Church may have Effect, though not *always.* Whether your Lordship will own the Popish Doctrine of the *Opus operatum,* or deny the Sacraments to be* Means of Grace, that is, to have any Effect, I cannot tell; but sure I am, if you do not hold one of these Doctrines, you must own the Sacraments to have *conditional* Effects in *supposed* Circumstances, which will sufficiently confute your own *strict Demonstration,* that Excommunication can have *no* Effect, because it has not in *all* Circumstances.

Again; I presume it may very justly be said, that the Christian Revelation hath *some Effect* towards the Salvation of Mankind; but then it hath not this Effect *always* and *in all Cases,* it is only effectual upon *certain Conditions.* Now if Excommunication can have no Effect, because it is not effectual when it is wrongfully pronounced, then the Christian Revelation can have no Effect towards saving those who embrace it as they should, because it has no such Effect on those who embrace it otherwise. The Reason of the Thing is the same in both Cases, and anyone may as justly set forth the Vanity and Insignificancy of the Christian Revelation, because it does not save all its Professors, as your Lordship exposes the Weakness and Vanity of spiritual

---

* See the Demonstration of the gross and fundamental Errors, in the Plain Account of the Sacrament, *&c.*

Censures, because they do not absolutely, and in all Cases, throw People out of God's Favour.

I hope I have here said enough, to vindicate the Authority and Effects of the spiritual Punishments of the Church, against all your Lordship has advanced against them.

I shall make an Observation or two more upon this Head, and then proceed to the other Parts of your Answer.

You say, the *incestuous* Corinthian *was never the more or the less in God's Favour for what was done in the Church.** This Doctrine I have already confuted, and shall now only set this Passage in another Light. Let us suppose that you had said, that *no Man is more in God's Favour for being rightly baptized by the Church.* Now if a Person is not more in God's Favour after he is rightly baptized by the Church, than he was before, then it is certain, that there is no need of Baptism by the Church; for anything is sufficiently proved needless or useless in Religion, if it neither procures nor loses the Favour of God. This is undeniably certain, that if we are not more in the Favour of God for being duly baptized by the Church, than if we were not baptized at all, that then that Baptism is a *useless Trifle*.

Now this is the Doctrine which your Lordship has taught; for he that says the *incestuous Corinthian*, though justly turned out of the Church, *was neither the more or the less in God's Favour for what was done by the Church;* says likewise, that he who is duly baptized into Covenant with God by the Church, is never the more or the less in God's Favour for being duly baptized by the Church. For if it be a mere Trifle, and altogether insignificant to us, as to the Favour of God, to be turned out of the Church, by such an Authority; it must be as *mere* a *Trifle* to be admitted into the Church by the same Authority. So that he who declares the one, plainly declares the other: For this is evidently plain, that if nothing be *lost* as to the Favour of God, by our being duly turned out of the Church, that then nothing is *got* as to the Favour of God, by our being duly admitted into the Church.

For if our being in the Church was any Step towards God's Favour, or rendered us more acceptable to him, those Degrees of Favour and Acceptance must be certainly lost, by our losing that which was the Cause of them.

He therefore who asserts it is a *Trifle* to be *turned* out of the Church, must also assert, that it is as fruitless and trifling a thing to be *admitted* into the Church. So that all your Lordship's Raillery and Contempt thrown upon *human Excommunications*,

---

* *Answ. to Repr.*, p. 43.

falls as directly upon *human Baptisms;* and makes them as truly fruitless Trifles without any Advantage, as it makes Excommunication a Trifle without any Punishment.

This therefore is the Sum of your new Religion, set up out of pure Tenderness to the Laity, to deliver them from the Weight and Burden of *Ordinances;* this is to be their Support against human *Excommunications,* human *Benedictions,* human *Baptisms, &c.,* that whether before or after *Baptism,* whether before or after *Excommunication,* they are still the *same Children of God.*

Again, you say, *If it be supposed (as it sometimes is upon this Subject) that a Person behaves himself under the most undeserved Censures, with any degree of Impatience, Pride, or Stubbornness, and that this displeaseth Almighty God; it is plain that he incurs no part of that Displeasure, upon account of the* Sentence *of Men, but solely upon the account of his own* Behaviour ; *it being his own Behaviour alone, and not the Sentence of Men, which has any such Effect.*

Here, my Lord, your *Philosophy* is upon the stretch, and rather than a *Christian* Institution should have any Force or Effect, you have let it run such lengths, as to make even the Ten *Commandments* as mere Trifles as the *Sentence* of Men.

As for Instance : Suppose a Person should tell a Friend that he had a great liking to some of his Neighbour's Goods, but that the eighth Commandment made him afraid to take them from him ; if his Friend were but a Master of your *Philosophy,* he might soon convince him of the Folly of such a Fear. He might tell him, that *if it be supposed (as it sometimes is supposed in this Case) that by his manner of taking Goods from his Neighbour, that he displeaseth Almighty God; it is plain that he incurs no Part of that displeasure upon Account of the Commandment, but solely upon the Account of his own Behaviour; it being his own Behaviour alone, and not the Commandment, which has any such Effect.* He might also assure him, that the *Commandment itself* cannot hurt him, that he is not more or less in God's Favour, for what that Commandment *says,* but purely for what he himself *does.*

I now, my Lord, freely submit it to the Judgment of common Sense, whether your profound *Philosophy,* does not as truly make void and set aside the Force and Effect of the Commandment, as the *Effect* of Excommunication.

For it is plainly as reasonable to tell a *Thief,* that the eighth Commandment cannot hurt him ; that if he steals, it is not the Commandment, but his own Behaviour alone, which will have any Effect ; as to declare, that an impenitent Offender is neither more or less in the Favour of God for what is done by the Church, because even supposing God to be angry at him for his Behaviour towards the Sentence of the Church, yet it is not the Sentence, but his own Behaviour, which causes the Divine Displeasure; therefore the Sentence, says your Lordship, is a Trifle without Effect. And therefore may it also be said, that the eighth Commandment is a Trifle without Effect; for it is as true of the Commandment in this Sense, and your Lordship is as much obliged to say that it is our Behaviour against the Commandment, and not the Commandment itself, which will raise God's Displeasure, as to say it is our Behaviour under the Sentence, and not the Sentence itself, which brings God's Displeasure upon us; so that it is undeniably plain, that if for this reason the Sentence of the Church be a Trifle without any Effect, that for the same reason the Commandment must be equally a Trifle, and equally without any Effect.

And now, my Lord, need we not heed the Commandments, because it is not the Commandments themselves which will have any Effect upon us? Why then are we to be exhorted, and preached up into a Contempt of the Sentence of the Church, because it is not the Sentence itself will have any Effect upon us? Is it safe to sin against the Authority of the Commandment, because it is not the Commandment itself which can punish us? If not, where is the Sense, or Reason, or Christianity of telling us, that we need not heed the Sentence of the Church, because the Sentence itself cannot punish us?

Suppose some High Churchman had writ a Treatise against Stealing, and had carried the Matter so very far, as to talk of the fatal Effect which the eighth Commandment would have upon Offenders, when it should rise up in Judgment and condemn them.

Would your Lordship think yourself obliged in regard to the *Liberty* of those who want other People's *Goods*, to tell them, that indeed they ought to take care to act with Sincerity in their acquiring the temporal Things of this Life, that they ought to consider with the utmost Impartiality the Nature of Property, and the Conditions of that *Original Contract*, which first settled the *Rights* and *Bounds* of it, and gave every Man a Right in such or such a Part of the Things of this Life; but that if they should through *Impatience* of Want, or *Pride*, or any other Passion or Prejudice, make too free with their Neighbour's Property, and so displease Almighty God; would you think yourself obliged to tell them, that *the fatal Effects of the eighth Commandment*, and its pretended rising up in Judgment hereafter, is all *Sham* and *Banter;* and that however God may be displeased with them, yet that Commandment will have no

Effect upon them? Would your Love of Liberty, your Concern for the Laity, engage you to give so much Comfort, and preach such smooth things to such a Class of People?

Thus much may be fairly affirmed, that you might as well deliver such a sort of People from their Fear of the Commandment, as to endeavour to persuade impenitent Offenders not to fear the Sentence of the Church. For as the Guilt of Stealing is aggravated by being contracted against the Authority of the eighth Commandment; so the Guilt of Impenitence is heightened, by a Continuance in it against that Authority in the Church, which is as truly founded by God to prevent the *Growth of Sin*, as the eighth Commandment was given by God to prevent *Stealing*. So that he who teaches Offenders to disregard this Sentence, which is authorised by God to awaken and terrify them into Repentance, does the same as if he should teach Thieves to disregard the eighth Commandment, which was given by God to affright People from stealing.

If it should be here objected, that there is a very great difference betwixt the Duty we owe to the eighth Commandment, and our Duty to the Sentence of the Church; because the Commandment is always right and the same, whereas the Church may err in its Sentence.

To this it may be answered, that granting all this, that the Church may sometimes err in its Sentence; yet if it is ever in the right, if it ever can be a fault, or dangerous for Sinners not to submit to, and be corrected by it, this will condemn your Doctrine, which sets it out constantly, and in all Circumstances, as a Dream and Trifle, and without any Effect.

Secondly; Here is no room left for you to plead the Uncertainty of the Church's Sentence, in regard to the Certainty of the Commandment; because you directly set forth your Doctrine in a Case (that of the incestuous *Corinthian*) where all was right and just, and yet declare that in that Case it was without any Effects; and that if the incestuous *Corinthian* had continued impenitent under it, and disregarded it as long as he had lived, it had signified no more to him than if it had never been pronounced. And in this Case, my Lord, and upon this Supposition, that the Authority judges and condemns such Sinners as it ought to do, it is as abominable to tell such that they have nothing to fear from the Judgment of the Church, as to tell a Thief that he has nothing to fear from the eighth Commandment. And I here challenge all the Reason which ever appeared against the Doctrines of Christianity, to show me, why it is not as agreeable to the Scripture to declare, that if a *Thief* lives and dies in his Sins of Stealing, that he has nothing to fear from the eighth Commandment; as to declare that an impenitent Offender, though *justly* censured by the Authority of the Church, has nothing to fear from such a Censure, though he lives and dies in the Contempt of it.

Thirdly and lastly; Though the Church may sometimes err in its Authority, and the Commandment is always right; yet your Doctrine makes it as reasonable to declare the Commandment without any Effect, as to declare the Sentence of the Church to be without any Effect. For you do not say that Excommunication is a *Trifle without any Effect*, because it is a Sentence which may sometimes be wrong; but because, though we should displease God under the Sentence of the Church, yet that Displeasure would not have been occasioned by the Sentence, but by our *Behaviour alone*. And this Doctrine plainly makes all the Commandments as mere *Trifles* and *void of all Effect*, as it makes the Sentence of the Church so. For it is as true in your Sense, and you are as much obliged to say, that if we sin against the Commandments, and incur the Displeasure of God, that it is not the Commandments, but our Behaviour alone which causes it: And so the Commandments of God have no more to do with the Favour of God, but are as mere *Dreams* without any Effect, as the human Excommunications you have so much exposed. This, my Lord, is a very compendious Confutation both of the *Law* and the *Gospel;* and is a good reason, why so many of those who have no regard for either, but think *Zeal* in Religion a Meanness of Spirit, are yet great *Zealots* for your Lordship's Opinions.

Of Church-Authority, as it relates to external Communion.

YOUR Lordship says, *I know of no Church Authority to oblige Christians to external Communion, nor anything to determine them but their own Consciences.** But to show your Desire to be informed, your Lordship frequently calls upon the Learned *Committee* to declare what the Authority of the Church is. It is something strange, that you should have been so long writing down the Authority of the Church, and yet not know what is meant by

---

* *Answ. to Repr.*, p. 112.

Church Authority; that you should take so much pains to oppose (as you say) only *absolute* Authority, and yet not know whether there be any else, or what Authority you have left in the Church, It is yet something stranger that a *Bishop* of the Church, should be frightening the *Laity* from a kind of Church Authority which is not claimed over them, and yet be at the same time pretendedly ignorant of what sort of *Church Authority* they are under. Here you have been preaching against that, which they are not concerned with; but when you should tell them *what kind* of Authority they are concerned with, you have not one word of Instruction; but call upon the *Committee* to declare, whether there be any such thing as Church Authority which is not *absolute*. My Lord, if there be not, to what purpose have you so often taken *Refuge* in the word *Absolute?* Or where is the *Honesty* or *Reason* of saying you have not denied *all* Authority, but only that which is *absolute*, if you believe there is no Authority but what is *absolute?* If therefore your Lordship has made this Distinction with *any* degree of *Sincerity*, if you intended anything more by it, than an artful playing with Words; it plainly lies at your Door to shew what Authority you have not touched; and that in supposing that which is *absolute*, you neither have, nor intended to oppose *all* Authority and Jurisdiction in Matters of Religion. But, instead of this, if the Learned *Committee* should explain to your Lordship what that Authority is, which is not *absolute;* you only venture so far as to say, that if there is any such Authority, *you are, for aught that you have said, at liberty to declare for it.** Mighty cautiously expressed, my Lord! Had a *Courtier*, who rather intends to *amuse* than *inform*, and talk *artfully* than *sincerely*, delivered himself in such inconclusive Terms, it had not been much Matter either of Wonder or Complaint. But for a *Bishop*, who makes *Sincerity* to be of more worth than all the Christian Religion; for this Bishop, in a Cause which he declares himself ready to die in; in such a Cause, as is of the last Consequence to us all, as *Men, Christians,* and *Protestants;* for this Bishop to say, *if there be such an Authority,* instead of declaring whether there is or not; and to say, *he is at liberty to declare for it,* instead of plainly saying whether he *ought or not;* however consistent it may be with Sincerity, I am sure it has too much the Appearance of the contrary.

For seeing you are charged with denying *all* Authority in the Church, if you consulted Plainness and Sincerity, if you regarded the Information of the *Vulgar,* and the Peace of the Church,

---

* *Answ. to Repr.*, p. 25.

which way could these Considerations lead you to defend yourself; but either to shew that there was a real Authority in the Church, which you had not opposed; or else plainly to own that you had denied *all Authority*, because all Authority of every kind is to be denied? But instead of declaring yourself openly and plainly for the sake of Truth, Peace, and Sincerity, you take Refuge in Words, and secure yourself behind a Cloud of *Properly's* and *Absolutely's*, to the Disturbance of honest Minds, and to the Satisfaction of the Profane.

Since your Lordship calls out so often to be told *what* that Authority is which obliges us to *external Communion*, I shall beg leave to offer these following Considerations upon this Head, and hope they will sufficiently both assert and explain that Church Authority or Obligation, which we are all under to join in external Communion.

Your Lordship says; *I know of no Church Authority to oblige any Christians to external Communion; nor anything to determine them, but their own Consciences.** I shall therefore beg leave to observe to your Lordship, what *Authority* there is to oblige *All* Christians to *external Communion;* and to show, that they are no more left at liberty in this Matter, than they are at liberty to *steal* or *murder*.

I suppose it is not proper or true, to say, that you know of no Authority to oblige any Christians, or anything to keep them from the Practice of Stealing, but their own Consciences; because there is the express Authority of God against this Practice. Now if it would be improper and false to say this, because the Authority of God has so plainly appeared in it; I shall easily prove, that it is as false and improper to say, that we have *nothing but our Consciences to determine us* in the Case of *external* Communion, since the Authority of God is as express in obliging us to this *external Communion*, as in requiring us to be just and honest in all our Dealings.

I desire no more to be granted me here, than that it is necessary to be a Christian, and that we are called upon by the *Authority* of God to embrace this Religion as necessary to Salvation. This, my Lord, is the express Doctrine of the Scriptures; so that I hope I may presume upon it, as granted by your Lordship, that there is an Authority to oblige People to be Christians, and that this Authority makes it as necessary, that they should be Christians, as it is necessary to obey God, and conform to his Will.

First; If Christianity be a Method of Life necessary to Sal-

---

* Page 112.

vation, then we are necessarily obliged to external Communion; for we can no other way appear to be Christians, either to ourselves or others, but by this external Communion. A Person who lives in a *Cloister*, may as well be taken for a *Field General*, as he who is not in *external* Communion, for a Christian. For the Christian Religion is a Method of Worship distinct from all others, in those Offices and Duties which constitute external Communion; so that if you are so far obliged to be a Christian, as to serve God differently from other People, you are obliged to *external Communion*, because that Service which distinguishes the Christian Worshipper from all other People, is such a Service as cannot be performed but in an external Communion in such and such Offices, *viz.*, *Professions of Faith, joint Prayers*, and the Observance of the *Sacraments*. *External* Communion is only another Word for the Profession of Christianity, because the several Duties and Obligations which concern anyone as a Christian, and distinguish him from other People, are Duties which as necessarily imply *external Communion*, as walking implies Motion. Therefore to ask whether a Christian be obliged to *external Communion*, is to ask whether a Person who is obliged to walk, be obliged to move. The short is this; No Man can be a Christian, but by taking upon him the Profession of Christianity; the Profession of Christianity is nothing else but *external* Communion with Christians; therefore it is as necessary to be in external Communion, as to be a Christian.

I hope I need not prove to your Lordship, that there is an *Authority* to oblige People to the Profession of Christianity; intending here only to prove, that the same Authority obliges us to external Communion.

Had your Lordship therefore declared to the World, that you know of no Authority to oblige People to be Christians, it had been as *innocent* and *true* a Declaration, as this you have made concerning *external Communion*; there being plainly the same Authority obliging us to the one, as to the other. For, my Lord, what is implied in external Communion, but our communicating with our Fellow Christians in those Acts of Worship and Divine Service which Christianity requires of us? And what Marks or Tokens can we shew of our Christianity, but that we are of the Number of those who are baptized into Christ's Church, for the joint Worship of God in that particular Service which the Christian Religion has taught us? So that if we prove ourselves Christians, we must prove ourselves in this external Communion, because to be a Christian implies no more, than the being of the Number of those who visibly unite and join in such Acts and Offices of Divine Worship, as are proper to Christians. If therefore there be *no Authority* to oblige us to external Communion, then no one is obliged to be a Christian.

Secondly ; If there be *no Authority* to oblige, or *anything* to determine Christians to *external Communion* but their own Consciences, then it is plain, it is as lawful for all Christians to be their own *Priests*, and confine themselves to a private Worship separate from every Christian in the World, as to join in external Communion. For where there is no Authority or Obligation to determine our Practice, there the thing must needs be indifferent ; and to do it or let it alone, must be *equally* lawful. If there was no Authority which obliged us to be baptized, it would not only be *lawful* to let it alone, but *idle* to trouble our Heads about it. The same is true of this external Communion ; if we are under no *Law* concerning it, it is no part of our *Duty* either to do it, or let it alone.

It cannot here be said, that though we are not obliged to external Communion with this or that Church, yet we ought to join with some particular Persons, and not worship God constantly by ourselves, and perform no Offices with other People. For if we are obliged to communicate with any one Person in the World, we are to hold Communion with the whole Church of Christ. For we are not obliged to communicate with this or that particular Person on account of any *Civil* or *Natural* Relation, but as we are *Christians*, and from the *Common Nature* of our Christianity. Since therefore our Obligation to communicate with any particular Persons, does not arise from any private *particular* Relation, but from the *common Nature* of our Religion ; this does equally oblige us to hold Communion with *all* Christians, as with any *particular* Christians, they being all equally related to us as Christians ; and consequently it is as necessary to hold Communion with the external visible Church, as with any particular Christian. From this also it is plain, that it is as lawful to avoid Communion with every particular Christian in the World, as to refuse Communion with any sound Part of the Church on Earth.

I beg of your Lordship to produce but one Argument, why any *two or three* should meet together for the Service of God, which will not equally prove it necessary that Christians should join in external Communion. May it all be laid aside, my Lord ? Need there be any more of this *assembling* ourselves together for performing of Duties, which we thought we could not perform separately ?

I have shown in my second Letter, that your Lordship cannot consistently with your Principles, urge any Reasons to any *Dissenters* to come over to the Church of *England ;* and here, my

Lord, it will appear, that you have not one Argument against the *Absenters* from *all Public Worship*. For it would be as odd and unreasonable in your Lordship to offer any Argument to such an *Absenter*, why he should join in some Public Worship, after you have denied an Authority which obliges us to external Communion, as it would be for an *Atheist* who had denied the Necessity of *any* Religion, to persuade a Man to be a *sincere Mahometan*.

If your Lordship should tell this *Absenter* from all Communions, that he ought to join with some Communion or other in the Worship of God; might he not fairly ask your Lordship, how you came to tell the World that *you know of no Authority to oblige any Christians,* or *anything* to determine them to external Communion? Can anyone be obliged to join in Divine Service, who is not obliged to *external Communion?* Could anyone imagine that if he was not obliged to join in external Communion, that it was not lawful to stay at home? Could he think that when your Lordship was declaring against any Obligation to Church Communion, that you meant he ought to join himself with some of the Dissenters? Had your Lordship plainly declared, that no Christian need read *any Book* in the World, could you consistently with yourself offer any Arguments why he should read the *Bible?* Yet this is as consistent, as to desire any Person to communicate with any Body of Christians, after you have plainly disowned any Obligation to external Communion.

For whatever Arguments your Lordship can offer to an *Absenter* from all Public Worship, may be answered in this manner. 'Either your Arguments for my joining with any 'Christians are invented by yourself, and of your own making, 'or they are not; if they are Fictions of your Lordship's, and 'destitute of any Foundation in the Will or Authority of God, 'then they are vain and to no Purpose; but that all such Argu-'ments are mere Fictions and Inventions of your own, is plain 'from your Lordship's express Declaration, that *you knew* of no '*Authority, or anything* to oblige or determine Christians to 'external Communion; so that all the Arguments you can offer 'for my external Communion, are declared by yourself to be 'such as are of *no Authority,* or have *anything* in them to *deter-*'*mine* me to external Communion.'

And indeed, had your Lordship first declared that there was no such thing as *Figure* in *Bodies,* and then pretended to prove that the World is *round,* it would be no more miraculous, than first to give out, that no Christians are obliged to external Communion, and afterwards take upon you to persuade anyone to join himself to some *Body* of Christians. Here therefore your Lordship has so preached up and advanced this Kingdom of Christ, that consistently with yourself, you cannot so much as require anyone to be a visible Member of it, or offer the least Shadow of an Argument, why an Absenter should rather go to some Church, than trust to his own Religion at home. Your Lordship wrote a *Treatise* some Years ago on the *Reasonableness of Conformity to the Church of* England. But pray, my Lord, where is the *Reasonableness* of conforming, if we are under no *Obligation* to conform? Where is the Reasonableness of doing that, which is not our *Duty* to do? Where can be the *Reasonableness* of going two or three *Miles* to Church for the sake of external Communion, if there be *no Authority, or anything to determine us to external Communion?* Can it be *reasonable* to spend our Time and some Part of our Wealth in making up such Meetings, as God has not required at our Hands?

Your Lordship must either therefore retract what you have said, and allow that there is *an Authority* to oblige us to external Communion, or acknowledge that no Christians are under any *Obligations* to serve God in any Communion, but may confine themselves to a private Religion, separate from every other Christian in the World. That is, that no one is *obliged* to worship God in the public Assembly, or join with anyone else in the Service of God.

Thirdly; If there be no Authority to oblige us to *external Communion*, then it may well be questioned, how your Lordship can answer for your joining in external Communion in the Church of *England*. Your Lordship knows that the Communion of the Church of *England*, gives great Offence to the *Papist* and *Protestant* Dissenters of all kinds; how then can your Lordship justify your doing that, which you need not do, which gives so much Scandal to so many *tender* Consciences?

Will your Lordship be of a Church, though it is this very Church Communion that is so very offensive? Your Lordship knows that the Animosities and Church Divisions amongst Christians is one of the most sore Evils under the Sun; that all the Party Heats and Controversies are concerning whom we are to communicate with, and in Defence of particular external Communions. Now, my Lord, what should that Christian do, who is all *Sincerity*, who believes there is no *Obligation* to external Communion, and who sees that the *pretended Necessity* of it, causes all the Difference and Division amongst Christians? Can that *sincere* Person who believes and knows all this, keep at the *Head* of a particular Communion? Can he support so *unnecessary*, so *needless* an Evil? Can that *sincere* Person be a

Bishop in that Communion, which stands distinguished from other external Communions, chiefly as it is *episcopal Communion*, when he allows there is no Necessity of being in Communion either with *Bishops* or *anybody* else? Could that *Pope* be reckoned *sincere*, who should declare that he knew of no Authority, or anything to determine him to exercise the *papal* Powers, could he be a sincere Christian, if he yet continued to exercise them to the *Scandal* and *Offence* of so many Christian Countries? If he could, so might your Lordship for continuing at the Head of an external Communion, which divides and disturbs Christians, though you know of *no Authority to oblige, or anything to determine you* to this external Communion.

Surely your Lordship will have more Compassion at last for your *dissenting Brethren*, more Concern for the Peace of Christ's Kingdom, than to keep up such unnecessary Communions, and disturb so many weak Consciences, by joining externally in the Church of *England*, when you *know of no Authority, or anything to oblige you* to join with any Body.

Suppose the Peace of *Great Britain* was miserably destroyed by *Party* Rage and Dispute about the *Stars*. Would your Lordship head one Party of *Star-gazers* against another? Would you join yourself to such a vain and useless Cause at the Expense of the public Peace? Now, my Lord, if there be *nothing* to *oblige* us to *external Communion*, it is all a *Trifle*, and mere *Star-gazing;* and a Person who appears in the Cause, and at the Head of this external Communion, can be no more a Friend to Christianity, by keeping up such an unnecessary Cause of Division, than he could be a good Subject, who should join in the needless idle Quarrels of *Star-gazing Party-men*. In a Word, if your Lordship knows of anything that obliges you to continue in the Church of *England*, you ought not to have said that *you know of no Authority to oblige, or anything to determine any Christian to external Communion:* But if you know of nothing that obliges you to continue in the Church of *England*, then you ought rather to leave it, than to bear a part in so needless a Community, and which gives so much Offence to all those who dislike the Terms of it.

Fourthly; If there be no Authority to oblige us to external Communion, how comes there to be such a Sin as *Schism?* How comes the *Schismatic*, or Divider of Communions, to be so frequently in the Scriptures ranked amongst the most guilty Offenders?

Can it be a Sin to be divided, unless we are under some Obligation to be united?

It has been always granted that *Schism* is the Separation of ourselves from such a Communion of Christians, as we *ought* to have held Communion with. Now if separate Worship from any Christians in the World be the Sin of *Schism*, then there must be some Law that obliges those *Schismatics* to join with those Christians, from whom they separate, and consequently there is an Authority which obliges Christians to external Communion.

Your Lordship must either shew that *Schism* does not consist in refusing to communicate with some Christians, or that though it be the damnable Sin of Schism to refuse Communion with some Christians, yet there is no Authority to oblige us to external Communion with any Christians, *i.e.*, that though Schism be a Sin, yet it is the Transgression of no Law.

The Apostle says, *Mark those who cause Divisions contrary to the Traditions which ye have learned of me, and avoid them.* My Lord, what strange Language is this, if there is nothing to oblige us to external Communion? If there is no Obligation to be united, why must they be marked who cause Divisions? If there be no Authority that requires external Communion at our Hands, why must those Persons be avoided who prevent external Communion?

Either the Apostle, or your Lordship must be mightily mistaken; the Apostle tells us that *Divisions* in the Church are contrary to the Doctrine which he had taught, and therefore there is the express Authority of the Apostle to oblige us to external Communion. But your Lordship says there is no Authority to oblige us to this Duty, therefore you must either maintain that the Apostle taught no such Doctrine, though he said he had, or that there is no Authority in his Doctrine to oblige us.

I suppose, my Lord, that the Apostle by Divisions here means *external visible Divisions,* because he bids them *mark* those who cause them, and *avoid* them; for *invisible* internal Divisions can no more be *marked*, or invisible Schismatics *avoided*, than we can mark People's Thoughts, or lock out a *Spirit*. If therefore the Division here spoken of be external Division, then the Sin here condemned is a Breach of external Communion, and consequently we are here required by the Apostle to join in external Communion; unless we can suppose, that the Apostle could condemn those who were *externally divided*, without meaning that they ought to be *externally united.*

Fifthly; If there be no Authority to oblige us to external Communion, then there is no *Authority* to oblige us to be baptized. For Baptism is an external visible Ordinance of God, which as plainly implies external Communion with others, as any Contract in the World implies Correspondence with others. And any Person might as well be obliged to bargain and merchandise with others, without being obliged to be concerned with others, as be obliged to be baptized, without being obliged to external Communion.

For as we cannot baptize ourselves, this shows that the Christian Religion is not suited to the State of single independent Persons, but requires our external Communion to the Performance of its Obligations. And as we cannot be baptized by others, but by resigning up ourselves to the Observance of new Laws, this plainly proves that the Person is baptized into a State of *Society* and external Communion. That Baptism does not leave the baptized Person to a separate independent Worship, is very plain from the following Instances.

The Church of *England*, in the Office for Baptism, thus expresses herself: *We receive this Person into the Congregation of Christ's Flock, &c.* Again, *Seeing now——This Person is regenerated and grafted into the Body of Christ's Church, &c.* I should think it very plain, my Lord, to every Reader, that these Passages show that Baptism necessarily implies external Communion, and puts it out of the Power of every baptized Person to refuse external Communion, unless he will break through the Conditions of his Baptism. For can we be *received into the Congregation of Christ's Flock,* without being obliged to keep up this Congregation, or to perform any Duties or Offices considered as a Congregation or Flock? Can we in any Sense be considered as a Congregation or a Flock, but in our Communion in those Offices which shew us to be Christ's Flock? Can we be said to be grafted into the Body of Christ's Church, if we are at liberty never to meet as a Church, or act as a Church?

The Apostle says, For *by one Spirit we are all baptized into one Body.** What can more manifestly denote external Communion, than this Account of Baptism? Can we be baptized into one Body, and not be obliged to act as a Body? Can we act as a Body, by running away from one another, and refusing to unite in that Service, into which we are baptized? I suppose we are here to be considered as a *Christian Body;* but how a Number of People can be a Christian Body, who are not united in Christian Worship, is hard to conceive.

When therefore you declare that you know of *no Authority* to oblige Christians to external Communion, you desert the Doctrines of Christ, as plainly as if you said, that you know of no Authority which obliges People to be baptized.

Sixthly; If there be no Authority to *oblige*, nor anything to

---

* 1 Cor. xii. 13.

determine us to external Communion, then there is no Authority to oblige, nor anything to determine us to communicate in the blessed *Sacrament* of the Body and Blood of Christ. For if there is any Law which obliges us to join externally in the Observance of this *Institution*, then it is out of all doubt, that we are obliged to external Communion. Now if you will say that there is no Law of God as to this Matter, then the thing itself must needs be indifferent, and *private Mass* must be allowed to be as right and lawful, as a joint Communion in the Holy Sacrament. Either therefore you must defend *private Mass*, or show some Authority against it; if you can produce any Authority against it, then you produce an Authority for external Communion, and contradict your other Declaration, where you give out, that you do not know of *anything* to determine us to external Communion.

From all this it plainly appears, what *kind* of Authority that is, which obliges us to external Communion; it is that *same* Authority which obliges us to be *baptized*, to receive the *Communion*, to profess the *same* Faith, to worship God in the public Assemblies, and to avoid the Sin of *Schism;* or, in a word, that same Authority which obliges us to be *Christians*.

For all the Offices of Christian Worship and Devotion which *constitute* external Communion, are everyone *expressly* required by God; and therefore *external Communion*, which consists only of these Offices, is *equally* required by God.

And this Authority may be very justly called *Church Authority*, because it arises from the very Nature of the *Church*, because it is the *Institution* of the Church, from whence this Obligation to Communion ariseth. For Christ has instituted this Church, in order to oblige Mankind to enter into it for the Salvation of their Souls: As the Church therefore is instituted for this End, the *Existence* of the Church lays an Obligation upon all, who have any Opportunity, of entering into it; and this Obligation will last as long as the Church of Christ shall last. The short is this; God has instituted an *Order* or *Society* of People, for the *particular* manner of serving and worshipping him; this Society is not a *voluntary* one, which we may be Members of, or not, as we please; but it carries, in its very *Nature* and *Institution*, an Authority obliging us all, as we hope for Happiness, to be Members of it; we are obliged to be of the Church, because Christ has *instituted* the Church; therefore it is the *Institution* of the Church, which lays us under an Obligation of entering into it; and this, and no other, is that *Church Authority* which obliges all People to *external Communion*.

Farther; This may be very properly called Church Authority,

because it was in the *Church*, or that *Order* of Men, which Christ had instituted, before the Scriptures were written.

When there was only this Order of Men, before the Writings of the *New Testament* were in being, there was then this Authority arising from that *instituted* Order of Men, which obliged others to enter into Communion with them; therefore this Authority which began with the Existence of the Church, and flowed from the very *Nature* of the Church, may very justly be called *Church Authority*.

If it should be asked, whether this Authority be *absolute*? I answer, it is just as *absolute*, as that Authority which obliges us to be baptized. Our Saviour has told us, that *if we are not baptized, we shall be damned*: Here therefore is an *Authority* for Baptism; the Scripture has not said whether this be so *absolutely* obliging, that there is no room in any Case for a Dispensation; therefore it is no Case which concerns us. Now the *Authority* which obliges us to *external Communion*, is just upon the *same Terms*; the thing is as plainly required as *Baptism*; but whether in *any Cases* it will be dispensed with, is what we have nothing to do with. If there be any *Sincerity*, any *Weakness*, any *Ignorance*, or the *Want* of anything which will excuse those who refuse to be *baptized*, those *same* Considerations may excuse the Refusal of *external Communion* with the Church.

This, my Lord, is the *Nature* of that *Church Authority*, which obliges to *external Communion;* it is that very *same* Authority which obliges us to the Profession of *Christianity*, or to enter into Covenant with God. For he who is in external Communion with the Church of Christ, is of the Church of Christ, or in Covenant with God; and he who is not in external Communion, is not of the Church of Christ, nor in Covenant with God; and consequently it is that *same* Authority which obliges us to be Christians, or in Covenant with God, which obliges us to external Communion.

So that when you say, you *know of no Church Authority to oblige, or anything to determine People to external Communion*, it is directly saying, that you know of no Church Authority to oblige, or anything to determine them to the *Profession* of Christianity, or to enter into *Covenant* with God.

If your Lordship should here say, that you only meant, you know of no *human* Authority to oblige People to external Communion, *&c.*

To this it may be answered, that you might as well have meant nothing at all by it, as have meant this. For,

First; Suppose the Question had been, whether there be any Authority, or what Authority it is, which obliges People to be *baptized?* and that in order to settle this Point, you had here declared, that *you know of no Church Authority to oblige, or anything to determine them to be baptized, but their own Consciences.*

Could it be thought, my Lord, after this, that you had not denied *all Authority* for Baptism? Could it be supposed, that by this Declaration, you only meant to deny, that the Authority which obliges us to be baptized, is *Human* or *Civil* Authority? Could anyone who only meant thus much, express himself in this manner?

Yet thus it is, that you have expressed yourself in the Dispute concerning our Obligations to external Communion, you *know of no Church Authority to oblige, or anything to determine People to it;* which makes it equally absurd to suppose, that you only deny that our Obligation to *external* Communion arises from *any human* or *civil* Authority.

Secondly; If you only meant to deny an *human* or *civil* Authority in this Matter, how came you not to say so? How came you not to tell us what *Divine* or *Scripture* Authority there is to oblige us? Is it not as proper and as necessary in a Dispute about *this* Authority, to declare the true and right Authority, as to protest against the wrong Authority? But indeed nothing can be more trifling than to say, that you have only denied any *human* or *civil* Authority in this Matter.

For, my Lord, whoever imagined that our Obligations to profess Christianity, that is, to be Members of Christ's Church, could proceed from any human Authority? Human Authority may and ought to encourage us in the Practice of our Christian Duties; but that our Obligation to serve God as Christians, that is, in the external Communion of the Church, should arise from any human Authority, can be supposed by none, but those who imagine Christianity to be a Creature of the *State.*

Thirdly; You not only say that you know of no *Church Authority* to oblige, but also add these Words, *nor anything to determine People to external Communion, but their own Consciences.*

Now, my Lord, if you only meant to deny a *human* Authority in this Matter; if you intended to own a *Divine* Authority to oblige us to external Communion; how come you to express yourself thus contrary to your Meaning? For if you believe there is a *Scripture* or *Divine* Authority which obliges us to external Communion, surely this *Authority* is *something,* and has *some* Right to *determine* us to external Communion; yet you expressly say that you do not know of *anything* to determine Christians to external Communion.

If it was asked, whether Christians are obliged to *pray* for their *Enemies*, and you should answer, I do not know *any* thing to determine them to pray for their Enemies; would it not be *Nonsense*, and *Contradiction* after this Declaration, to suppose, that you acknowledge that the Scriptures require Christians to pray for their Enemies?

But to suppose, that you acknowledge a *Divine* or *Scripture* Authority which obliges to external Communion, after you have expressly declared that you do not know of *anything* to determine us to external Communion, is *equally* contradictory.

Lastly; You say you do not know *of anything to determine Christians to external Communion, but their own Consciences.*

Now this farther shews, that you deny all *Divine* as well as *Human* Authority to determine us to external Communion. For if there was a Divine Law which required this Practice, we are no more left solely to our own Consciences in this Practice, than if it was determined by an express human Law.

For can it be said that the *Jews* had nothing but their own Consciences to determine them to *abstain* from *Blood?* Can it be said that *Christians* have nothing but their own Consciences to determine them to receive the *Holy Sacrament?* If this cannot be said, because there is a Divine Law in both these Cases; then it is as false and absurd to say, that there is nothing but our own Consciences to determine us to external Communion, if there be a *Divine* Authority which requires this Practice. And consequently, you have plainly denied all *Divine* or *Scripture* Authority for external Communion, when you say that you do not know of *anything to determine People to external Communion, but their own Consciences.* The short is this; if you will say, that you own a *Divine* and *Scripture* Authority which obliges us to external Communion; and if you will allow this Authority to be *something*, then your Contradiction in this Matter, is as palpable and gross as ever appeared in any Writings; for you have expressly said, that you do not know of *anything* to determine us to external Communion: But if you own a Scripture Authority that obliges us to external Communion, then your Contradiction proceeds thus, that you do know of *something*, but you do not know of *anything* to determine us to external Communion. If you will not assert both Parts of this Contradiction, then you must stand to that which you have asserted, *viz.*, that you do not know of *anything* to determine us to external Communion, which I have already shown, is the same thing as declaring, you know of no Authority, or *anything* to determine People to profess Christianity, or enter into Covenant with God. But to proceed,

If you should say that you do not deny an *Authority* that

obliges us to external Communion in *General*, but only an *Authority* that can *oblige* us to any *particular* external Communion.

To this I answer, that this is a groundless, false Distinction; for our *Obligation* to external Communion with the Church of Christ in *general*, and our *Obligation* to external Communion with this or that *particular* Church, is exactly *one* and the *same* Obligation.

For we are not obliged to join with this or that *particular* Church, for any *private, particular* Reasons, but because we are obliged to be Christians, or of the Church of Christ. And as no sound Part of Christ's Church, is more his Church than another sound part, so if we separate from any sound part, we are as truly out of Christ's Church, as if we had separated from every part. And we can give no Reasons for separating from such a part, but such as will equally justify our separating from every part of Christ's Church; and consequently there can be no Reasons offered why we should be Christians, or of the Church of Christ, but will equally oblige us to enter into that particular part of Christ's Church which offers itself to us. For the whole Intent of entering into this or that *particular* Church, is only to be a Christian, or of the Church of Christ, and therefore it must be one and the same Authority which obliges us to be Christians, that obliges us also to be of any *particular* Church.

There is a *Scripture Authority* which obliges us to forgive our *Enemies:* Now it would be as *proper* to say, that though there is an Authority which obliges us to *forgive* our Enemies in *general*, yet that Authority does not oblige us to forgive our *particular* Enemies, as to say, that though we are obliged to be of the Church of Christ in *general*, yet we are not obliged to be of this or that particular part of Christ's Church.

For the Church of Christ in *general*, as truly consists of these *particular Parts*, as our Enemies in *general*, consist of our *particular* Enemies.

So that, as it is *one* and the *same* Authority which obliges us to forgive our *Enemies*, that obliges us to forgive our *particular* Enemies, for it is *one* and the *same* Authority that obliges us to be *Christians*, that obliges us also to communicate with that *particular* sound part of Christ's Church where we live.

There is therefore no room for this Distinction, to suppose, that though we may be obliged to be of Christ's Church, yet we are not obliged to be of this or that *particular* sound part of Christ's Church; it being fully as absurd, as to suppose that we may be obliged to be Christians, and yet not be obliged to be Christians.

When therefore you declare, that you know of no *Church Authority* to oblige, *or anything* to determine us to *external Communion*, it will be to no purpose to say, that you do not mean *Communion* with the Church of Christ in *general*, but only with any *particular* part of Christ's Church; for I have shown that this Distinction is *false*, and fully as *absurd*, as to imagine, that we may be obliged to obey Christ's Commands in *general*, but not be obliged to obey his *particular* Commands.

From what has been said upon this Subject, these following Propositions are plainly true:

First; That as our entering into any particular part of the Church, implies our entering into the Church of Christ, or in other Words, our embracing Christianity; it evidently follows, that the *same* Authority which requires us to embrace *Christianity*, requires us also to enter into that sound *part* of Christ's Church where we live.

Secondly; That this Authority does not arise from any *human* Laws, or the Power which any Men in what Station soever have over others, but is the Authority of God, who has instituted this Church, in order to oblige all Mankind to enter into it.

Thirdly; That this Authority from God, may be very properly called *Church Authority*, because God manifested this Authority to the World by the *Institution* of the Church, because it began with the Church, and flowed from its very Nature; Mankind being therefore obliged to enter into this Church, because there was such a Church instituted by God.

Fourthly; That this Account does not in the least make it either *unjust* or *improper*, in our *spiritual* or *temporal* Governors, to make Laws for our Conformity to this or that part of Christ's Church; for though the Authority which makes it necessary that we should enter into such a *part* of Christ's Church, is from God, yet this no more excludes our Governors from requiring the *same thing* by their *Laws*, than they are excluded from requiring us to observe any *moral Duties*, because the *same moral Duties* are made necessary by the Authority of God. And as our Violation of any *moral Duties* that are commanded, both by Divine and Human Laws, receives an higher Aggravation, so the Guilt of opposing any sound part of Christ's Church is enhanced, by our breaking through the Laws both of God and Man.

Fifthly; From this Account of the Authority which obliges us to external Communion, it will be very easy to discover the *Weakness* and *Fallacy* of several of your Lordship's Arguments upon this Matter.

Thus when you say, *It is evident that there is no Choice of Judgment left to Christians, where there is a superior Authority to oblige them;——that in* Italy, *or* Spain, *or* France, *they are as much obliged by the Church Authority in* Italy, Spain, *or* France, *as Christians in* England *are obliged to a particular external Communion in* England, *by any human Authority, as such, in* England.*

Now, my Lord, what could you have thought of less to the Purpose, than these Words thus put together? For does anyone say, that our Obligation to be of the Church of *England*, arises from any *human* Authority, as *such*, in *England*? No, my Lord, if *human* Authority should not only desert the Church, but make the severest Laws against it, yet we should be still under the same Necessity of communicating with it; because that Necessity is independent of *human* Laws, is founded upon the Authority of God, and constantly obliges in the *same Degree*, let the Laws of the *State* be what they will.

Granting therefore, my Lord, that the *human* Authority, *as such*, in *France* or *Spain*, obliges the People of those Kingdoms to conform to those Churches, as truly as the Laws of *England* oblige the People of *England* to conform to the Church of *England*. What follows? Does it follow that therefore the People of *France* or *Spain* are as truly obliged to Communion with the Church in those Kingdoms, as the People of *England* are obliged to Communion with the Church in *England*? No, this will by no means follow; for since we should hold the same Necessity of joining with the *Episcopal* Church in *England*, though all the human Laws in *England* should forbid us; since we allow only an *accidental* and *conditional* Authority in *human* Laws as they establish any particular Religion, it follows, that in *France* and *Spain*, &c., they ought to pay the *same* regard to *human* Laws, and no more continue in their Church because it is *established*, than we ought to leave our Church though it was *persecuted*. The short is this:

The *Church Authority* which obliges us to external Communion with any *particular* part of Christ's Church, is that *same divine* Authority which calls upon us to be *baptized*, and enter into *Covenant* with God.

Now if *human* Laws, whether of *Church* or *State*, strike in with this Authority, then they oblige us, as they do in other Cases, where they require us to do that, which the *Laws* of God required before; but if *human* Laws, whether of *Church* or *State*, require us to enter into *such* a Communion, as hath not

---

* *Answ. to Repr.*, p. 115.

the *Authority* of Christ for it, or forbid our joining with *such* a Communion as is a *true part* of Christ's Church, such Laws are no more to be observed, than if they had established *Idolatry*, or forbid the Worship of the *true* God. For *human* Laws are not supposed to make it our *Duty* to enter into such a Communion, but are applied as proper *means* to induce us to do that, which the *Laws* of God had made it our *Duty* to do before. And it is undeniably true, that though there should be ever so many *human* Laws to command us to enter into any particular Communion, that we must not comply with such Laws, unless it be in regard to *such* a Communion, as it was our *Duty* to enter into, though no such *human* Laws were in being.

So that *human* Laws create no *Necessity* of external Communion, any more than they create the *Necessity* of *praying* to God; but they may be applied as very *proper means* to induce People to perform the *Duty* of *external* Communion, and to perform the Duty of *Prayer* to God.

The Question therefore in any *Country* is not this, whether the Laws either of their *Church* or *State* require us to enter into *such* a Communion, but whether it be *such* a Communion, as it would be our *Duty* to enter into, were there no *human* Laws to enjoin it, whether it be a *part* of Christ's Church, which we are obliged to enter into on Pain of everlasting Damnation.

When therefore you say, if the People of *England* are obliged by an *human* Authority, *as such*, to enter into the Church of *England*, then the People of *France*, *Spain* and *Italy*, are as truly obliged by the human Authority there to enter into those particular Communions; you say exceedingly true, but to no more purpose, than if you had made the following Declaration.

If the People of *England* are obliged to enter into Communion with the Church of *England* by any *Military* Authority, *as such;* then the People of *France*, *Spain*, and *Italy*, are obliged to Communion with the Churches in *Spain*, *France*, and *Italy*, by the *Military* Authority, *as such*, in *Spain*, *France*, and *Italy*.

This, my Lord, is as much to the Purpose as what you have said; for our *Obligation* to enter into a particular Part of Christ's Church, is no more founded in any *human* Laws, *as such*, than in any *Military* Authority, *as such;* but is founded in the Will of God, who has instituted the Church on Earth, and made our Salvation depend upon our Entrance into it. This is the *Authority* which obliges, this is the *Necessity* which lies upon us, to enter into any Part of Christ's Church.

If therefore you would show, that in *Spain*, or *France*, &c., they are under the *same Necessity* of being of the Church in those Kingdoms, which the People of *England* are of being Members of the *Episcopal* Church in *England;* you ought to show that the *Established* Church in *Spain,* or in *France,* is as truly a *sound* Part of the Church of Christ, as the *Established* Church in *England* is a sound Part of the Church of Christ; and that the way of Worship *there,* is as certainly that *necessary Method* of Salvation which Christ has *instituted,* as the way of Worship in the Church of *England,* is that *necessary Method* of Salvation which Christ has instituted.

For this is the only *Authority* or *Necessity,* which obliges us to enter into any *Church* in any Part of the World; namely, a *Necessity* of being Christians, by entering into that Church which Christ has instituted; so that if this same Church be in *Spain,* and *France,* and *England,* then there is an *equal* Necessity of being of the Church in each Kingdom; but if the Church in *Spain* be not the Church which Christ has *instituted,* and the Church in *England* be that Church which Christ has *instituted,* then there is as great a *Necessity* of *refusing* to communicate with the Church in *Spain,* as of joining in Communion with the Church of *England.*

This therefore being the Nature of the *Authority* or *Necessity* which obliges to external Communion, nothing can be more trifling, than to argue from the *Necessity* of complying with the Church in *one* Kingdom, to a *Necessity* of complying with the Church in *all other* Kingdoms; unless you could *demonstrate,* that because the *Established* Church in one Kingdom is the true Church of Christ, therefore the *Established* Church in *every other* Kingdom is the true Church of Christ.

Yet your Lordship has spent a great many Pages, in declaiming against any *Authority* or *Necessity* which can oblige People to communicate with the Church of *England;* because then there would be the *same Necessity* that the People of *Spain,* and *France,* and *Italy,* should communicate with the Church in those Kingdoms. But I hope the most ordinary Reader will be able to tell your Lordship, that there is no more *good Sense,* much less *Divinity,* in this way of instructing the World, than if you had said, there is no *Necessity* that the People of *England* should believe things which are *true,* because then the People of *Spain* will be under the *same Necessity* of believing things which are *false;* and again, that there is no *Necessity* that in *this* Kingdom we should comply with *good Laws,* because in *other* Kingdoms People will be under the *same Necessity* of complying with *wicked Laws.*

But to conclude this Point; I have here stated the Nature of that *Authority* or *Necessity* which obliges us to external Communion, that it does not arise from the *Laws* of any Men, whether in *Church* or *State*, but from the Will and Authority of Christ, who has instituted such external Communion, as a *necessary Method* of Salvation.

I have shown also, that *human* Laws, though they, *as such*, do not create a Necessity of external Communion, yet they have a very proper *Significancy*, and are as useful in this Matter, as in any other Parts of our Duty.

Of Sincerity and Private Judgment.

IF you should here say, that by denying the Necessity of external Communion to arise from *human* Laws, *as such*, I have resolved the Choice of a particular Communion into *private Judgment*.

To this I answer;

First; That by entering into any *particular Communion*, we are to understand the *same thing* as entering into the *Church of Christ*, or embracing the Religion which Christ has *instituted*.

Secondly; That when Christ came into the World, People were left to their choice, whether they would embrace Christianity.

Thirdly; That Christianity is still upon the *same Terms* with Mankind, and it is still left to everyone's private Judgment, whether he will comply with the Terms of Salvation.

Fourthly; That this does not destroy the *Force* and *Obligations* of Authority, or make it without any Effect upon the Condition of Men. For it does by no means follow, that there is *no Authority*, or that there are *no Effects* to be feared from such Authority, because Men may disown it if they please. For to say there is *nothing* in Authority, that it is insignificant and without *any Effect* upon the Condition of Men, if they may use their *private Judgments*, is as *ridiculous* as to say, there is *nothing* in the Happiness of *Heaven*, or Torments of *Hell*, that they can have *no Effect* upon the Condition of Men, because Men may *judge* of these things as they please.

Fifthly; There is a Choice of Judgment left to us in every Part of our Duty;

Whether we will believe a God,
Whether we will worship him,
Whether we will believe in *Jesus Christ*,
Whether we will acknowledge a World to come,
Whether we will believe there is such a Place as Hell.

And now, my Lord, is there *no Authority* for these things, because we are not forced to believe them against our *Judgments*? Have those who refused to believe in Christ, nothing to fear from his *Authority*, because he appealed to their *Reason*, and left them to *determine* for themselves? Is there no *Authority* for the Torments of *Hell*, or nothing to be feared from that *Authority*, by those who deny there is any such Place.

Now if there can be an *Authority* in these Matters, though the Use of *private Judgment* is allowed in these *same* Matters, if this Authority will condemn those who acted contrary to it; then it is certain, that there may be an *Authority* or *Necessity* which obliges us to be of such a *particular* Religion, though the Exercise of our private Judgment is allowed in the Choice of our Religion; and that we may have as much to fear from acting contrary to such *Authority*, though by following our own Opinions, as they have who act contrary to the Will of God in any other Respect, though by following their own Opinions.

So that an *Authority* or *Necessity* which obliges us to be of this or that *particular Communion*, that is, particular Religion, is as consistent with the Exercise of *private Judgment*, as the Necessity of believing a God, and worshipping him, is consistent with the Exercise of our *private Judgment*.

And if you will say, there is an end of all Authority, if Men may choose one Communion before another; you must also say, that if Men might consider whether they should follow Christ, then there was an end of all Authority in Christ over them.

And again; If Men may reason and consider whether there be a God, or Providence, then there is an end of all Necessity of believing either a God, or Providence.

If they may *consider* whether the Scriptures are the *Word* of God, or any *particular* Doctrines be contained in Scripture, then there is an end of *all Necessity* of believing the Scriptures to be the *Word* of God, or of believing any *particular* Doctrines to be contained in Scripture.

If they may consider and examine whether any *particular* Religion comes from God, then there is an end of *all Necessity* of receiving any particular Religion from God.

All this Reasoning is full as just, as to conclude that there is an *end of all Authority* to *oblige People to any* particular Communion, if they may consider the Excellency of one Communion above another, which is what you over and over declare.

Now, my Lord, let us suppose that the Question was, Whether it be *necessary* to believe the *Scriptures* to be the *Word* of God? Would it not become every honest Man, not only to assert this

Necessity, but to show wherein it is founded, and explain to every one that *Authority*, which calls upon us to receive the Scriptures as the Word of God, and which will rise up in *Judgment* against us, if neglected.

And what might we not justly think of him, who, instead of showing the *Authority* or Necessity which obliges us to receive the Scriptures as the Word of God, should deliver himself in this manner.

'You are reasoning whether there be any *Authority* or *Necessity* 'which obliges you to receive the *Scriptures* as the *Word* of God. 'Whereas your very Reasoning upon this Matter, shows there is 'no Necessity or *Authority* to which you are obliged to submit. 'For since you are allowed to reason and enquire whether this 'be necessary, it is certain, there is an end of all Authority or 'Necessity, to oblige you to receive the *Scriptures as the Word* 'of God; and if you do but sincerely follow your own private 'Persuasions, you are entitled to the same Degrees of God's 'Favour, whether you receive the Scriptures as his Word or 'not.'

Now, my Lord, thus it is that you have instructed the World, in relation to the Authority which obliges us to *external Communion*.

The Question is, Whether there be any Authority which obliges us to any *particular external Communion?*

Now, my Lord, what has anyone to do in this Dispute, but to show whether Christ has *instituted* external Communion, or not? For on this alone must the Necessity of it depend. And if it appears that external Communion be instituted by our Saviour as a Method of Salvation, then it will follow, that we are under a *Necessity*, as we hope for Salvation, of being in that particular Method or Manner of external Communion, which Christ has instituted; so that unless it can be shown, that all *pretended* Christian Communions, are as truly that *Method*, or particular Communion which Christ has instituted, as any other Communion is; it must be as necessary to be in some *one particular* Communion, as it is necessary to obey Christ; and as dangerous to join in some other Communions, as it is dangerous to despise his Authority.

But now your Lordship, instead of considering what external Communion is *instituted*, and what *Necessity* arises from such *Institution*, or where we may find such external Communion, amongst the many *pretended* Christian Communions, has wholly passed over this Point, and determined the Question, by telling us, that since we are allowed the Use of our Reason in the Choice of Religion, it matters not what *Authority* we oppose, either of God or Man, and that there can be no *Necessity* of our being of any *particular* Communion, but where our private Judgment *sincerely* directs us.

Thus you say; *If the Excellency of one Communion above another may be regarded, then there is an End of all human Authority to oblige us to one particular external Communion.** And to show that you can as easily destroy all *Divine* Authority or Necessity of any *particular Communion,* or Religion, you tell us, that *our Title to God's Favour cannot depend upon our actual being or continuing in any* particular Method, *but upon our real Sincerity.*† So that here the *Sincerity* of *private Judgment* as effectually destroys all *divine Authority* and *Necessity* of any particular Communion or Religion, as it destroys that which is *human;* and we are rendered as *happy* and as *high* in the *Favour* of God, for *breaking* his Laws, as if we had *observed* them.

For here it is proved, that there is no *Necessity* of any particular Communion or Religion, not because there is none *instituted* by God, but because, whether instituted or not, our *sincere Persuasion* will equally justify us, whether it complies with or opposes such Institution.

But to proceed.

I shall now show, how this Doctrine of yours of *Sincerity* exposes all the *Terms* of Salvation as delivered in Scripture.

In the Scripture we find that *Baptism* is made a *Term* of Salvation; but if *Sincerity without* Baptism be as *certain* a *Title* to the Favour of God, as *Sincerity* with Baptism, then it is plain, that *not to be baptized,* is as much a *Condition* or *Term* of Salvation, as *Baptism* is a *Term* of Salvation. For, if Baptism *with* Sincerity was *more* a Term or Condition of God's Favour, than *no Baptism* with Sincerity, then it is certain that it is not *Sincerity alone* that procures the Favour of God : And it is as certain, that if Sincerity alone procures us the Favour of God, then *Baptism* is no *more* a *Term* of Salvation, than the *Refusal of Baptism* is a *Term* of Salvation. So that this Doctrine makes *Baptism,* and the *Refusal* of Baptism, either equally *Terms,* or equally *no Terms* of Salvation; equally *advantageous,* or equally *insignificant.*

When therefore our Blessed Saviour says, that except we are *baptized* we cannot enter into the Kingdom of God,‡ and he that is not *baptized* shall be *damned;* according to this Doctrine of yours, we may also say just the contrary, that except we *refuse* Baptism we cannot enter into the Kingdom of God; and he that is *baptized* shall be *damned.*

---

* *Answ. to Repr.,* p. 115. † *Preserv.,* p. 90. ‡ *Job* iii. 3.

This, my Lord, is very shocking; but I shall easily show that these Assertions are as *proper* and as *just*, as the contrary Assertions, if your Doctrine of Sincerity be right.

For, since your Doctrine puts the sincere *Acceptance*, and the sincere *Refusal* of Baptism, upon the same Foot as to the *Favour* of God, there can be no more Danger in sincerely *refusing* Baptism, than in sincerely *accepting* of Baptism. Now if there is no more Danger in the *one* Practice than in the *other*, it must be plain to the most ordinary Understanding, that it is as *just* and *proper* to declare *one* Practice dangerous as the *other;* that is, it must be as proper to say, he that *is* baptized shall be *damned*, as to say, he that is *not* baptized shall be *damned*.

Now I know your Lordship cannot, upon these Principles, show, that it is more dangerous to *refuse* Baptism sincerely, than to *receive* Baptism sincerely; and so long as this is granted, you must allow that it is as just to fix danger upon *Baptism itself*, as upon the want of Baptism. And consequently, all your Reasonings upon this Subject are one continued Censure upon our Blessed Saviour's Doctrine in relation to Baptism, which according to your Notions, is only as *just* and *proper*, as the quite contrary would have been.

Again, our Saviour tells us, that *except we eat the Flesh of the Son of Man, and drink his Blood, we have no Life in us.**

Here we see, the *eating* the Flesh and *drinking* the Blood of the Son of Man is an *instituted Term* of Salvation, and insisted upon by our Saviour; but if your Doctrine be true, we may as well declare the *contrary* to be a *Term* of Salvation, and say, *except we sincerely refuse to eat the Flesh and drink the Blood of the Son of Man, we have no Life in us.*

For, my Lord, if Sincerity in *refusing* to eat this Flesh, be the *same Title* to God's Favour that the *eating* of it with Sincerity is, it is plain, there is no more Advantage *in eating*, than in *not eating;* and consequently it is as well to say, that except we *forbear* eating the Flesh of the Son of Man we have no Life in us, as to say, that except we *eat* the Flesh of the Son of Man we have no Life in us; there being plainly from this Doctrine, no more Danger in *forbearing* to eat, than in *eating;* nor any more Necessity of eating, than of forbearing to eat, since both these Practices are *equally good* and *advantageous* with *Sincerity*, and *equally* bad and insignificant without it.

And now, my Lord, let the World judge, whether you could have thought of a Doctrine more *contradictory* to the express Words of our Saviour, and all the *instituted Terms* of Salvation,

---

* *John* vi.

than this of yours about Sincerity, which makes it no more *necessary* to *observe* the *instituted Terms* of Salvation, than to *break* them; and which also makes it as proper, to declare it as *dangerous* to *observe* such Institutions, as to *reject* them. This I have shown particularly in Baptism, where your Doctrine makes it as proper to say, he that *is baptized* shall be *damned*, as to say, that he who is *not* baptized shall be *damned;* and in the same manner does it contradict and confound the Scriptures, and make the *contrary* to every *Institution* as *much* a Means of Salvation, as the *Institution* itself.

Your Lordship has given us a *Demonstration*, as you call it, that your Doctrine of *Sincerity* and private *Persuasion* is right.

Thus you ask: *What is it that justified the Protestants —— in setting up their own Bishops? Was it, that the Popish Doctrines were actually corrupt, or that the Protestants were persuaded in their own Consciences, that they were so? The latter without doubt.* And then comes your *Demonstration*, in this manner; *take away from them this Persuasion, and they are so far from being justified, that they are condemned for their Departure; give them this Persuasion again, they are condemned if they do not separate.**

You want to be shown the Fallacy in this Demonstration, which I hope I shall show to your Satisfaction.

It is granted, that Corruption in Religion is no *Justification* of those who leave it, unless they are persuaded of that Corruption.

It is also granted, that they who are fully persuaded that a Religion is *sinful*, are obliged to separate from it, though it should not be *sinful*. But then it does by no means follow, that they who leave a *true* Religion, and they who leave a *false* Religion, through their particular Persuasions, are *equally justified*, or have an equal Title to the *same Degree* of God's Favour.

Here lies the *great Fallacy* in this Argument, that you use the same Word (*viz., justified*) in relation to both these People in the very *same Sense;* whereas if they are *justified* (if this Word must be used) it is in a very different *Sense* and different *Measure*, and they are not entitled to the *same Degree* of God's Favour. Now, a Fallacy in this Point destroys the whole Demonstration, for the Question wholly turns upon *this Point*, Whether they who are sincere in a *true* Religion, and they who are sincere in a *false* Religion, are *equally* justified and entitled to the *same Degrees* of God's Favour?

This very Thing was objected to you by the learned *Committee*,

---

* *Prefer.*, p. 85.   *Answ. to Repr.*, p. 103.

who said, *that an erroneous Conscience was never, till now, allowed wholly to justify Men in their Errors.**

To which you have no better Answer to make than this, *That it must either justify them, or not justify them. It must either wholly justify them, or not justify them* at all.†

My Lord, I suppose a Man is justified by his living *soberly, righteously,* and *godlily* in this present World. I ask therefore, Does his living *soberly* justify him wholly, or does it not justify him *at all?* If it justifies him *wholly,* then there is no occasion of his living *righteously* and *godlily;* if it does not justify him *at all,* then there is no need of his living *soberly.*

Your Answer to the *Committee* has just as much *Sense* or *Divinity* in it, as there is in this Argument.

Here I must desire, that it may be observed, that the Question is not, Whether *Sincerity* in *any* Religion, does not recommend us to the Favour of God? But whether we are entitled to the *same Degrees* of God's Favour, whether we are sincere in a *true* or *false* way of Worship?

I shall therefore farther consider this Point.

First; If *true* and *right* Religion hath anything in its own Nature to recommend us to God, then Sincerity in this *true* and *right* Religion must recommend us *more* to God, than Sincerity in a *false* and *wrong* Religion; because we have a Recommendation from our *Religion,* as well as from our *Sincerity* in it. For instance, if it be in *any Degree* in the World more acceptable to God, that we should follow *Christ,* than *Mahomet,* our Sincerity in following *Christ,* must recommend us to just *so much* more of God's Favour, than our Sincerity in following *Mahomet;* as it is more acceptable to him that we should follow one than the other. Now to say that *true* and *right* Religion, has nothing in its own Nature to recommend us to God, is saying, that things *true* and *right* are no more acceptable to God, than things *false* and *wrong;* but as it would be Blasphemy to say this, so it is very little less, to say, that Sincerity in a *false* and *wrong* Religion, is just the same *Justification* or *Recommendation* to the Favour of God, that Sincerity in the *true* and *right* Religion is.

Farther; The whole *End* and *Design* of Religion, is to *recommend* us to the Favour of God. If therefore we can suppose a Religion *instituted* by God, which does no more, as such, recommend us to the Favour of God, than a Religion *invented* by *Men* or *Devils,* as *such,* recommends us to the Favour of God; then we must also suppose, that God has instituted a Religion, which

---

* *Repr.,* p. 7.   † *Answr. to Repr.,* p. 95.

does not *at all* answer the general *End* and *Design* of Religion, *viz.*, the *recommending* us to the Favour of God.

Unless therefore we will profanely declare, that God has instituted a Religion, which, *as such*, does us no Service, nor any better promotes the general *End* of Religion, than any corrupt *Inventions* of Men, we must affirm, that Sincerity in his Religion will entitle us to greater Degrees of his Favour, than Sincerity in a Religion not from Him.

Secondly; If there be any *real Excellency* or *Goodness* in one Religion, which is not in another, then it is certain, that *Sincerity* does not *equally* justify us in any Religion; and on the contrary, it is as certain, that if Sincerity in *any* Religion does entitle us to the *same Degrees* of God's Favour, then there is no such thing as any real *Excellency* or *Goodness* in one Religion, which is not in another.

When you are charged with destroying all Difference between Religions, by this Account of Sincerity, you retreat to an Answer as weak as could possibly have been thought of. Thus you say; *What I said about* private Persuasion, *relates to the* Justification *of the Man before God, and not to the* Excellency *of one Communion above another, which it leaves just as it found it.**

Here, my Lord, you suppose that one Religion may very much exceed another Religion in *Goodness* and *Excellency*, and yet that this *Goodness* and *Excellency* has nothing to do with the *Justification* of Persons; for you say, you were not speaking of the *Excellency* of one Communion above another, but of what relates to the *Justification* of a Man, *&c.*, which plainly shows, that you do not allow the *Excellency* of Religion to have anything to do with the Justification of Men; for if you did, it must have been necessary to speak of the *Excellency* of one Religion above another, when you were speaking of what it is which *justifies* a Man before God.

Now, my Lord, to grant that there is an *Excellency* and *Goodness* in some Religion, and yet exclude this *excellent* and *good* Religion, from having any more in it to *justify* and *recommend* us to the Favour of God, than what is to be found in any other Religion less excellent; is just as *good Sense*, as to allow, that some Food is *much more* excellent and proper than other Food; and yet exclude this *most excellent proper* Food, from having anything in it to preserve *Health* and *Strength*, more than in *any other* Food.

For the *Goodness* and *Excellency* of Religion, is as *truly* a *relative* Goodness and Excellency, as the Goodness and Excel-

---

* *Answ. to Repr.*, p. 113.

lency of Food is a *relative* Goodness and Excellency. And as that Food can only be said to be *better* than another Food, because it has a *better* Effect upon the Body than any other Food; so that Religion can only be said to be *better* than another, because it raises us higher in the Favour of God than any other Religion.

It is therefore most certain, that if any one Religion can be said to be *better* than another, it must be, because one Religion may be of more Advantage to us than another.

For as Religion in general is *good*, because it does us *good*, and brings us into Favour with God; so the *particular Excellency* and *Goodness* of any Religion, must consist in this, that it does us a *more particular Good*, and raises us to *higher* Degrees of God's Favour, than a *less excellent* Religion would have done.

So that when your Lordship talks of the *Excellency* of one Religion above another, as having nothing in it, *as such*, to recommend us to higher Degrees of God's Favour, or effect our *Justification;* it is full as absurd, as to say, that though one kind of *Learning* may be more *excellent* than another kind of *Learning*, yet no Men are more *excellent* or *valuable*, for having one kind of *Learning* rather than another.

For as no kind of Learning can be said to be *peculiarly* excellent, but because it gives some *peculiar Excellency* to those who are Masters of it; so no kind of Religion can be said to be *more excellent* than another, unless those who profess it, reap some *Advantage* from it, which is not to be had from a Religion *less excellent*.

From all this it appears, first, that there can be no such thing as any *Goodness* or *Excellency* in one Religion above another, but as it procures a *peculiar Good* and *Advantage* to those who profess it.

Secondly; That your Lordship can allow no other *Goodness* or *Excellency* in Religion, even from your own express Words, but what implies as great an Absurdity, as to allow of good *Food*, good *Learning*, or good *Advice*, which can do nobody any good *at all*.

For since you expressly exclude the *Goodness* or *Excellency* of any Religion, from having any part in recommending us to the Favour of God, and will only allow it to carry us so far, as Sincerity in a *worse* Religion will carry us; it is certain, that this *good* and *excellent* Religion, is just as good as *that*, which does us no good *at all.*

So that whether you will yet own that you have destroyed all the difference betwixt Religions, or not, I cannot tell; yet I imagine, everyone will see that you have only left such a *Good-*

ness in one Religion above another, as can do nobody any good *at all*.

The short is this; If you will own there is no *Excellency* in one Religion above another, then you are guilty of making *Christianity* no better than *Mahometanism;* but if you will acknowledge a *Goodness* and *Excellency* in one Religion above another, and yet contend that it is *Sincerity alone*, which does us *any Good*, or recommends us to the Favour of God, in all Religions alike, this is as absurd, as to say, such a thing is *much better* for us than any other thing, and yet assert, that *any other* thing will do us *as much good* as that.

I have, I hope, sufficiently confuted *your* Doctrine of Sincerity, from the Nature of Religion. I shall now, in a word or two, examine it farther, by considering the Nature of *Private Persuasion*, which can do all these mighty things.

And, first, I deny that *Persuasion* was the *only* thing which justified the Protestants, or which recommends People to the Favour of God in the Choice of a Religion; and that, because if their *private Persuasion* was founded in *Pride, Prejudice, worldly Interest*, or *anything*, but the *real Truth*, and the *Justice* of the Cause, that their *private Persuasion* did not *justify* them before God; nor had they, upon this Supposition, so good a Title to his Favour, as those who did not reform.

If you say, that Persons cannot be *sincere* in their Persuasions, who are influenced by *Pride*, or *Prejudice*, or any *false* Motive: To this I answer;

First; That according to your *own Principles*, that Man is to be esteemed *sincere*, who *thinks* himself to be *sincere*. For, as it is a first *Principle* with you, that a Man is *justified* in point of Religion, not because he observes what in its own Nature is *true* and *right* Religion, but because he observes that which he *thinks* to be *true* and *right* Religion; so according to *this Principle*, a Man is to be accounted *sincere*, not because he acts up to *true* and *just* Principles of *Sincerity*, but because he *thinks* in his own Mind, that he does act up to such *just* and *true* Principles of Sincerity. So that, my Lord, Sincerity it seems is as truly a *private Persuasion*, as Religion is a *private* Persuasion; and therefore anyone may as easily think himself *truly* sincere, and yet not have true Sincerity, as he may think himself in the *true* Religion, and yet not be in the true Religion.

Unless therefore you will maintain, that a Person who is mistaken in his *Sincerity*, and mistaken in his *Religion* too, who hath neither *true* Religion, or true *Sincerity*, hath as good a Title to the Favour of God as he who is *truly* sincere, and in a *true* Religion, you must give up this *Cause* of Sincerity. For it is *demonstrable* from your *own Principles*, that anyone may as often happen to be mistaken in his Sincerity, and take that for *Sincerity* which is not Sincerity, as he may be mistaken in his *Religion*, and take that for *Religion* which is not *Religion*.

And consequently it is as reasonable to talk of *sincere* Persons who are influenced by *wrong Motives*, as to talk of Persons being *justified* in Religion, who live in a *false* Religion.

So that, my Lord, this is the Result of your Doctrine, that Persons neither *truly* sincere, nor in the *true* Religion, are yet entitled to the *same Degrees* of God's Favour, with those who are *truly* sincere in the *true* Religion.

The short is this, according to a Maxim of your own, you are obliged to acknowledge that Man to be *sincere*, who *thinks* himself to be *sincere;* because you say a Man is to be esteemed Religious, not because he practices *true* Religion, but because he *thinks* he practices *true* Religion ; therefore you must say, that a Man is sincere, not because he is *truly* sincere, but because he *thinks* himself to be *sincere*.

It is also as *possible* and as *likely* for a Man to be mistaken in those things which constitute *true* Sincerity, as in those things which constitute *true* Religion.

And therefore if *this* Sincerity be the *only* and the *same* Title to God's Favour in any Religion, it follows, that Sincerity, though influenced by *false* Motives, and in a false way of Worship, is as acceptable to God, as a *sincere* Persuasion governed by *right* Motives, in a *true* and *instituted* way of Worship.

So that all the fine things which you have said of Sincerity, as implying in it all which is *rational* and *excellent*, are come to nothing ; and you are as strictly obliged to allow that Man to be *sincere*, who mistakes the *Grounds* and *Principles* of *true* Sincerity, because he *thinks* himself to be sincere, as to allow that Person to be justified in his Religion, who mistakes the true Religion, because he thinks himself in the true Religion.

So that it is not *Sincerity*, as it contains all that is *rational* and *excellent* which alone justifies, but as it may be an *idle, vain, whimsical* Persuasion, in which People think themselves in the right. This Persuasion, though founded in the Follies, Passions, and Prejudices of human Nature, consecrates every Way of Worship, and makes the Man thus persuaded as acceptable to God, as he who through a right use of his Reason, serves God in that Method which he has instituted.

I shall end this Point with only this Observation, that however hearty a Friend you may be to the Christian Religion yourself, this I dare say, that the heartiest *Enemy* it has, will thank you for thus *defending* it. And they who with all the Distinctions betwixt Religions confounded, and maintain that we have nothing to hope or fear but from our *own Persuasions*, are the only Persons who can call you their *proper Defender*.

Of the Reformation.

I PROCEED now, in a Word or two, to show, that the *Necessity* of Communion with any *particular* Church, and the *Effects* of Excommunication, are perfectly consistent with the Principles of the *Reformation*.

You say, *If there be a Church Authority to oblige People to external Communion,——I beg to know, How* can the *Reformation itself be justified?——For there was then an Order of Churchmen, vested with all spiritual Authority;——there was therefore a Church Authority to oblige Christians, a Power of some over others. What was it therefore to which we owe this very Church of England?**

To this it may be answered,

First; That this Argument proceeds upon a false Supposition, namely, that it is the *Laws* of *any Men*, which obliges us to *external Communion*. Which I have already shown to be as false, as to suppose that it is the *Laws* of *any* Men which obliges us to be *Christians*.

Secondly; That there may be a *real* and a *great* Authority which obliges us to *external Communion*, though this Authority be not founded in any *human Laws;* for there is as real and apparent an Authority for *Baptism* and the *Supper* of the Lord, and other Parts of external Communion, as if they were the express Matter of any human Laws.

Thirdly; That the Laws of Men in this Affair of Religion, are of the same Obligation and Force that they are in other Matters. If they command Things indifferent, they are to be obeyed for the Authority of the Command; if they enjoin Things in their own Nature good, the Necessity of Obedience is greater; but if they command Things unlawful, we are not to comply, but obey God rather than Man.

Fourthly; The Question therefore at the *Reformation* was not, Whether the *Laws* of the *Pope* or the *Prince* were on the side of the Church of *Rome?* But whether that *Faith* and those *Institutions* which constitute the Christian Religion, were with

---

* *Answ. to Repr.*, p. 118.

the *Reformers*, or with the *Papists*. For the Church Authority which obliged *them then*, and which obliges now to external Communion, was not an Authority which obliged them to comply with any *number* of Bishops, or any *State Laws*, but to enter into Communion with that Bishop or Bishops, who observed that way of Worship which Christ had instituted. The Necessity of being in external Communion, does not oblige us to be in Communion with the *Pope* or any *Number* of Bishops *as such*, whose Authority we may happen to be born under; but it obliges us to be in that Communion, which is that *Way* or *Method* of Salvation which Christ has *instituted*.

So that though we should grant, that at the *Reformation* we broke through the *human* Laws of the *Church*, which required us to continue in Communion with the Church of *Rome*, it will by no means follow, that we broke through *that Authority* which obliges us to external Communion, because *that Authority* is not founded in any *human Laws*, but is the Authority of Christ, requiring us to observe all those things which constitute *external Communion*. For as it is the Authority of Christ which obliges us to be *Christians*, so that same Authority obliges us to enter into that Communion, where the *Institutions* and Faith of Christ are preserved.

When therefore you say, *if Church* Authority (meaning human Laws) *be a sufficient Obligation upon them* to determine them, then *our Forefathers ought not in Conscience to have separated from the Church of* Rome :*

This, my Lord, is no more to the Purpose, than if you had said, if the King of *France* has a Right to be obeyed all over *Europe*, then all over *Europe* they ought in Conscience to obey him.

For since it is neither pretended, nor allowed, that *human Laws* are a *sufficient Obligation* to external Communion, to argue from this Supposition is as foreign to the Purpose, as to suppose that the King of *France* was Governor of all *Europe*.

The next Step you take is also very extraordinary, where having rejected *human* Authority from being a *sufficient Obligation* to external Communion, you thus proceed, *But if Men are their own Judges by the Laws of God and of Christ in this Matter; if they have a Right to use their Judgment, and be determined by it;*——then here is a *Justification* of the *Reformation, and particularly of the Protestant Church of* England.†

The most *complaisant* Justification, my Lord, that could possibly have been thought of, because it as *peculiarly* justifies

---

* Page 118. † Page 181.

all the Enemies of the Church of *England*, of what kind soever, as it justifies the Protestant Church of *England*.

For your Argument proceeds thus ; if there be no *human Authority* to which we are absolutely obliged to submit, but have a Right to use our own Judgments, then the *Reformation* is justified. Here we see the Doctrines of the reformed Church are not taken into the Question ; she is not said to be justified, as being a *true* Church, or as preserving those *Orders* and *Institutions*, which constitute the true Church ; but is justified, because Men may use their Reason, and not enter into any Communion which *human Laws* have happened to establish. Now if we of the Church of *England* are justified in the Choice of our Religion, because no *human Laws* have an absolute Power to oblige us to be of any particular Religion, then all People, whether *Papists* or *Protestants*, whether *Quakers, Ranters, Jews, Turks*, and *Infidels*, are *equally* justified in the Choice of their *particular Ways* of Worship, because *human Laws* have not an absolute Power to oblige them to be of any particular Religion. So that though you call this a *Justification* of the Protestant Church of *England*, you might as justly have called it a *Justification* of *Quakers, Jews, Turks*, and *Infidels:* For it is as truly a Justification of *every one* of them, as it is a Justification of the Church of *England*.

But to proceed.

How comes it, my Lord, that the *Reformation* is *justified*, because People may use their Reason, and are not under a Necessity from human Laws of being of this or that Church? Why must the *Reformation* be *right and just*, because *human Laws* are not sufficient to hinder a *Reformation*. Is there no *other Authority* that can make any particular Religion necessary, because *human* Authority cannot ? May it not be our *Duty* to be of *this* Communion, and a *Sin* to enter into *another* Communion, though *human* Laws as such cannot make the one a *Duty*, or the other a *Sin ?* Does *Baptism*, the *Supper* of the Lord, and a *Belief* in *Jesus Christ*, cease to be necessary, because that necessity does not arise from *human Laws ?*

Now if Things may be *necessary* to Salvation, though they are not made so by *human* Authority, then it is no Justification of the *Reformation* to say, that the *Reformers* might use their Reason, and not choose that Religion which *human* Laws commanded them to choose ; this will be no Justification, till it appears, that they chose that Religion which the *Authority* of God required them to choose.

For it would be Nonsense to say, People are justified for having such a sort of *Baptism*, because the *Necessity* of Baptism does not arise from *human Laws*. Yet this is as *good Sense*, as to say, such a People are justified in their Religion, because no Religion is made necessary by *human* Laws. For as they are only justified in Point of *Baptism*, who observe such Baptism, as the *Authority* of God has *appointed*, so are they only justified in their *Religion*, who enter into that *Religion* which the *Authority* of God has *instituted*.

But your Lordship has no sooner shown that *human* Authority, *as such*, cannot oblige us to be of any *particular Religion*, but you presently congratulate your Readers upon an entire Freedom from all Authority in Religion, and without once mentioning that the Reformation is right and just, because of the *Orders, Doctrines* or *Institutions*, which it maintains; you say it is justified for *such a Reason*, as justifies in an *equal* Degree every Religion, and every Change of Religion in the World. You have so far justified it, as to show that it is as well to be of it, as of any other Church, and as well to be of any other Church as of it.

Who would not think, my Lord, that the *instituted Terms* of Salvation had something to do with the Justification of Christians? Yet you can justify People without any regard to them. Who would not think that a Religion is unjustifiable, if it is contrary to the Religion *instituted* by Christ? Yet your Lordship has justified *all Changes* in Religion, without any regard to the *Institutions* of Christ solely for this Reason, because Men may use their own Judgment, and not submit to the Laws of Men, *as such*, in the Choice of Religion. As if, because they are not to be altogether governed by the Commands of *Men* in the Choice of a Religion, neither are they to be determined by the Authority of God, or any more tied down to *his Institutions*, than to *human* Laws. Who would think that no *Change* in Religion is *dangerous*, because Religion is only instituted by God, and has his Authority to make it necessary? Yet your Lordship banishes all Danger from *every Change* of Religion, and pronounces the *same Safety* in every Opinion, because People are under no absolute human Authority.

It is very surprising, after all this, to see your Lordship breaking out into *passionate* Expressions for the *Cause* of the *Reformation*, and so often *declaring*, that it is for the sake of the Reformation that you have taken so much Pains, and with so much Pleasure, in your *late Writings*.

Now it seems, your Adversaries have undermined the very Foundations of the reformed Church of *England*; and that in this Manner.

First; They justify the Church of *England*, by showing that it maintains all those *Orders, Institutions,* and *Doctrines,* which Christ has made necessary to Salvation; that it is a *true* Church, because it consists of all those Things, which by the *Institution* of Christ constitute a *true* Church.

For this, your Lordship rebukes them as Enemies to the *Reformation,* as Friends to *Popery;* and declares that the Protestants are not justified because they have chosen a *true* and *right* Religion, but because they *think* they have chosen a true and right Religion.

Again, your Adversaries insist upon the *Necessity* of entering into Communion with the Church of *England,* because it is a true Church of Christ; and declare those guilty of the heinous Sin of *Schism,* who separate from her Communion.

Here again you condemn them, as conspiring the Ruin of the *Reformation,* because if the *Dissenters* are not justified in their Separation from the Church of *England* by their *private Persuasion,* neither is the Church of *England* to be justified for its Separation from *Rome.* So that the Difference between your Lordship and your Adversaries, in relation to the Reformed Church of *England* is this.

They support and recommend this Church, because it contains all the *necessary* Doctrines and Institutions of Christ, and consequently give it an Advantage over every other *way* of *Worship,* which is either *corrupted* or *defective,* in these Doctrines and Institutions of Christ.

But you *support* and *recommend* it (pardon the Expressions) not from anything which relates to it at all, but from *private Persuasion;* and consequently allow every Religion in the World to be as *just,* and *good,* and *safe,* if Men are but *so persuaded.*

They defend the Church of *England,* by showing what it is, and by asserting the Truth of its Doctrines.

You have no Title to be mentioned amongst its *Defenders,* but as you may be called a *Defender* of *Quakers* and *Fanatics, Jews* and *Turks,* and every Religion in the World, which anyone *thinks* to be *right.*

To proceed; As a farther *Defence* of the Reformation, you ask, *How did the first Reformers behave themselves? Did they not think and speak of them (viz.,* Absolution and Excommunication) *as having nothing to do with the Favour of God, as human Engines, and mere Outcries of human* Terror? *And did they mean by this to claim to themselves the Right of Absolution, which they had denied to others, because they were fallible and weak Men;* or to assert a *Power of Excommunication, so as to affect Men's eternal Salvation, to themselves in one Church, which they had disregarded and trampled upon in another?* No: They treated all Excommunications as alike, and upon an equal foot; *and could upon no other Account neglect and disregard them as they did, but because God had not given to any Man the Disposal of his Mercy or Anger.**

The Argument, my Lord, here proceeds thus: First; That all Absolutions and Excommunications must have been esteemed alike, and equally *insignificant* by our Reformers, because they were not terrified at the Excommunications of the Church of *Rome*, nor thought an Absolution from that Church necessary.

Secondly; That the Reformers having thus disregarded *these Powers* in that Church, ought not to pretend, that the same Powers have any more Effect when they exercise them in this Church.

To this it may be answered, that if we ought not to pretend to *any Effects* in *Absolution* or *Excommunication*, because we disregarded *those Powers* as exercised by the Church of *Rome;* that then we ought not to pretend the Necessity of *any Faith*, because we disregarded the Faith of the *Romish* Church; nor the Necessity of any *Sacraments*, nor the Necessity of the *Canonical Writings*, because we disregarded the Canonical Books of the Church of *Rome*. And it is as good Sense to cry out here, ' Did they not treat their *Sacraments* as mere *Inventions* ' of Men? Did they mean by this to claim to themselves a ' Power to make Sacraments *necessary* in *one Church*, which ' Power they had trampled upon in *another?* Did they deny ' the Necessity of *seven* Sacraments *there*, in order to assert the ' Necessity of *two* Sacraments *here?* No: They treated *all* ' Sacraments as *alike*, and upon an *equal foot* with respect to ' God's Favour, and could upon no other Account neglect and ' disregard them as they did, but because God's Favour or ' Displeasure was no ways affected *by any Sacraments.*'

Here let common Sense judge, whether this Argument of yours, showing the Unreasonableness of pretending to any Significancy in *Excommunication*, because we disregarded the Excommunication of the Church of *Rome*, does not prove it as unreasonable to insist upon the *Necessity* of *any Faith*, or any *Sacraments*, or any *Canonical Books*, because we denied the Romish *Creed*, the Romish *Sacraments*, and *Canon* of Scripture?

For our Reformers no more intended to show that Excommunication was a *Dream* and *Trifle*, because they disregarded the Excommunication of the Church of *Rome*, than they intended to show that all *Sacraments*, all *Faith*, and all *Scripture*,

---

* *Answ. to Repr.*, pp. 121, 122.

were *Dreams* and *Trifles*, by their not owning either the *Sacraments*, or the *Creed*, or the *Canon* of the Church of *Rome*. And, my Lord, what a worthy Defender of *Christianity* and the *Reformation* would he be, who should ask us what we mean by the Necessity of *Sacraments*, or *Faith*, or *Scripture*, since we have not allowed the Necessity either of the Romish *Sacraments*, *Faith*, or *Scripture*? Yet such a *Defender* is your Lordship, who contends that we ought to reject Excommunication as a *Trifle* and *Dream*, because we disregarded the Excommunication of the Church of *Rome*.

I have now gone as far in the Examination of your *Doctrines*, as my present Design will allow me, and am apt to think that in this and my *former Letters*, I have gone so far, as to show, that a few more *such Defences* of *Christianity* and the *Reformation*, as you have given us, would complete their Ruin, as far as *human Writings* can complete it.

And had you meant ever so much harm to *Christianity* and the *Reformation*, I believe no one who wishes their Confusion, would have thought you could have taken a better way to obtain that End, than by writing as you have lately written.

For he must be a very Bitter *Enemy* to them both, who would not think it sufficient to set *Christianity* and *Mahometanism*, the *Reformation* and *Quakerism*, upon the *same* foot.

And he must be very slow of Apprehension, who does not see that to be plainly done, by resolving all into *private Persuasion*, and making *Sincerity* in *every* Religion, whether *true* or *false*, the *same Title* to the *same Degrees* of God's Favour.

I shall not with your Lordship make any Declarations about *my own Sincerity*; I am content to leave that to God, and to let all the World pass what Judgment they please about it.

I am, Your Lordship's

Most Humble Servant,

William Law.

Postscript.

THE Learned *Committee* observed to your Lordship, that *an erroneous Conscience was never, till now, allowed wholly to justify Men in their Errors.*

This Observation I have shown to be *true* and *just*, as it implies, that though Sincerity in an *erroneous way* of Worship should in *some degree* or other recommend Men to the Favour or Mercy of God, yet it is not that *entire Recommendation* to his Favour, which is effected by our sincere Obedience in the *true way* of Salvation: That is, though it should justify them in *some degree*, yet it cannot justify them in *that degree*, in which they are justified, who sincerely serve God, in that true Religion which he himself has instituted.

Now our Justification, as it is effected by the Merits of Christ, is in *one and the same degree;* but as our Justification is effected by our own Behaviour, it is as capable of *different degrees*, as our Virtue and Holiness is capable of *different* degrees; and it is also necessary that our Justification be *more* or *less*, according as our Holiness is *more* or *less*.

Yet in answer to this Observation of the Learned *Committee*, you say, *it must either* justify *them, or* not justify *them; it must either justify them* wholly, *or not justify them* at all. This, my Lord, is as contrary to the Scripture, as it is to the Observation of the *Committee*. For our blessed Saviour, speaking of the *Publican*, says, *I tell you, this Man went down to his House* justified, rather *than the other.**

Here, my Lord, is as plain a Declaration of *Degrees* in Justification, as can well be made, so far as Justification can be effected by our own Behaviour.

For, it is plain, the *Publican* was not *wholly* justified, because then there would be no need of his embracing Christianity; it is also plain, that he was justified *in part,* or else he could not be said to be justified *rather* than the *Pharisee*.

If therefore your Answer confutes the Observation of the Learned *Committee,* it must also confute this Passage of *Scripture*.

I shall only add one word in relation to another Point.

I have already shown the Falseness and evil Tendency of your Argument against *Excommunication*, which you asserted to be a *Dream* and *Trifle* without *any Effect*, because it is our

---

* *Luke* xviii. 10, &c.

own *Behaviour alone* which can signify anything to us with regard to the Favour of God. Now, my Lord, this *Philosophy* strikes at the very Vitals of the Christian Religion: For, if this Sentence can have no Effect, if it is a *Dream* and *Trifle*, because it is *our Behaviour alone* on which the Favour of God depends; then how shall we account for these Passages of Scripture, which attribute our *Justification* to the *Merits* and *Death* of Christ. As thus;
*Jesus Christ, who gave himself for our sins;**
In whom we have Redemption through his Blood;†
Being justified by his Blood, we shall be saved from wrath.‡

It is the constant, uniform Doctrine of Scripture, that our Reconciliation and Peace with God, our Justification and Sanctification before God, is owing to the *Merits and Death of Christ*. But if what you have said be true, that it is our *Behaviour alone*, which procures the Favour of God, then the *Blood* of Christ must be as truly without any Effect, as Excommunication is without any Effect.

For if the Favour of God depends entirely upon our *Behaviour alone*, then it can depend upon nothing else; and if it depend upon nothing else, then everything else is equally trifling and without any Effect as to that Purpose; and consequently every Passage in Scripture which ascribes our *Acceptance with God* to the *Merits and Blood of Christ*, is as much condemned by your Doctrine, as the *Effects* of Excommunication are condemned by it.

Whether your Lordship did not perceive the *Inconsistency* of this Doctrine, with that *Satisfaction* and *Redemption* which the Scriptures teach; or whether you *knowingly* intended to oppose this Doctrine, is, what I shall leave to everyone's own Judgment. Thus much I shall only say, that as you have here directly contradicted this first Principle of the Christian Religion, if it is not what you intended, I hope you will, for the sake of Christianity, venture to declare, that though you have asserted, that it is our *Behaviour alone*, yet it is not *our Behaviour alone*, but more particularly the *Merits* and *Death* of Christ, which recommends us to the Favour of God.

FINIS.

---

* *Gal.* i. 3.   † *Ephes.* i. 7.   ‡ *Rom.* v. 9.

www.ingramcontent.com/pod-product-compliance
Lightning Source LLC
Chambersburg PA
CBHW070740160426
43192CB00009B/1517